Engaging Equity

New Perspectives on Anti-Racist Education

Leeno Karumanchery, Ph.D.

Editor

DETSELIG
ENTERPRISES LTD

Engaging Equity: New Perspectives on Anti-Racist Education
© 2005 Leeno Karumanchery, Editor

Library and Archives Canada Cataloguing in Publication

Engaging equity: new perspectives on anti-racist education / edited by Leeno Luke Karumanchery.

Includes bibliographical references.
ISBN 1-55059-286-6

1. Discrimination in education. 2. Racism. I. Karumanchery, Leeno Luke, 1969-

HT1521.E64 2005   306.43   C2005-905213-9

Detselig Enterprises Ltd.
210, 1220 Kensington Road NW
Calgary, Alberta
T2N 3P5

www.temerondetselig.com
Email: temeron@telusplanet.net
Phone: (403) 283-0900
Fax: (403) 283-6947

We acknowledge the support of the Government of Canada through the Book Publishing Industry Development Program (BPIDP) for our publishing program.

We also acknowledge the support of the Alberta Foundation for the Arts for our publishing program.

SAN 113-0234
ISBN 1-55059-286-6
Printed in Canada

Cover Design by Alvin Choong

Table of Contents

Preface

The philosophers have only interpreted the world in various ways; the point is, to change it.

-Marx, *Thesis on Feuerbach* [1]

. . . the people—as long as they are crushed and oppressed, internalizing the image of the oppressor—construct by themselves the theory of their liberating action. Only in the encounter of the people with the revolutionary leaders-in their communion, in their praxis—can this theory be built.

-Freire, *Pedagogy of the Oppressed* [2]

In the summer of 2002, when I began thinking about putting this anthology together, I was unsure as to the purpose of the work and the audience to whom it would speak. I found myself reflecting on Freire's understanding that if the oppressed were to ever taste freedom, they would have to first develop a theory of action that was respective of, and responsive to, their specific social contexts. Simply put, social change does not occur in a vacuum, and must by design, work to effect change within a system that resists that change. Keeping Freire's recommendation alive, I began searching for articles that would address both the issue of resistance, and the issue of strategic reform. However, in the course of that literature review, while I found valuable sociological works that dealt with revolutionary critical theory, some addressing the sociological and political implications of racism for the identity formation of oppressed and others looked specifically at the practical realities of strategic resistance. I was surprised to find that few articles, if any, could speak to the holistic realities of anti-racist praxis as such. It was with this realization that I found myself asking "what sort of moment is this, in which to explore new possibilities for resistance and oppositional theory?"

Much like Stuart Hall's use of the "the moment" as a starting-point from which to rethink essentialist analyses of race and ethnicity, I see this moment, and this work as an opportunity to revisit and revise existing anti-racist educational praxis. By focusing on the tensions that run between the political call for a "strategic essentialism" in anti-racism and those forms of analyses that have developed respective of the transitory relationship between racism and power in Western contexts, I am looking to help develop a space where we might all critically reevaluate our politics and methodology. After all, while "knowledge" is always mediated by our positions in the moment, I would argue that there is a reality to racism and oppression that must be addressed. It is a reality that cannot, and must not, be lost in poststructural challenges to what can be known as truth. In asserting the existence of an "oppressive reality," I mean to suggest that in this time, space and place, the social, political and historical fabric of existence has constituted a relationship between oppressor and oppressed. This is a relationship constructed through discourse, and through the institutional structures that work to subjugate the margins. However, that reality must also be understood to be in flux – it is not fixed. To suggest that there will always be an oppressor/oppressed relationship between the centre and the margins would be to ignore the agency of the subject, and negate the possibility of social change and resistance. But with that said, how can we work to affect change in our lives? How do those that resist their oppression, frame and manage that resistance? These questions are the points of central focus for this anthology.

As suggested by Marx above, I wanted this text to be more than a simple philosophical exercise engaging theory for theory's sake. I wanted this work to mean something. I wanted to create an anti-racist reader that would benefit from the strength of insurgent voices working in solidarity towards social change. My hope is that at the level of individual consciousness and agency, we might generate change in a manner that is not possible at the structural level; that anti-racist strategies engaging the development of a greater critical consciousness might offer the oppressed and our allies a new perspective on power and resistance. As my point of departure from other similar projects, I have set out to use this book as a guidebook of sorts: a starting-point from which to critically address the theoretical foundations and machinery for racism as it exists in Western educational systems today. Understanding that it is impossible to move beyond theoretical narration without first establishing a firm ground in theory, I am using this space to develop a praxical framework through which we might approach the problematics of agency and resistance in educational contexts. To this end, the papers included in this reader were chosen not only for their critical scholarship, but also because they help to tell a story. Working together, these pieces help to connect theoretical and practical ties in a manner that makes anti-racist praxis more than just imaginable – they make it both understandable and actionable.

In Section One, the first four articles explore the history and theoretical salience of the race concept with a specific eye towards Whiteness, Colonialism and Imperialism as the fundamental sociohistorical contexts in and through which racism is activated in society. The essays in this section interrogate the processes and dynamics of racial categorizations/differentiation and their implications for understanding and interpreting human relations and conflict. Of particular importance is the interrogation of the sociohistorical specificities that engender the reproduction of oppression in socially and racially structured spaces. These works help to establish a firm sociohistorical account through which we might better engage the contemporary ideological, material and social effects of racism in education. In *The Dialectics of Power*, Shirley Steinberg explores how "reason" in historical configurations of knowledge, intelligence and civility, became "Whitened," and how in turn, human nature itself became grounded in a racial essentialism that resonates even today. In *Racism "Renewed,"* Kayleen Oka explores how the events and the aftermath of September 11, 2001, worked to reinvent the notion of "national fantasy" in the minds of citizens and non-citizens alike. Pulling strands from academic discourses and from popular U.S. media discourse and imagery, she interrogates how nationalist practices have been employed in the post-9/11 era to construct and defend "new" notions of citizenship that are generally exclusionary and specifically racist. Carl James, in his article *The Ties that Bind*, begins the work of piecing together how these historically structured sociopolitical and cultural relations of power are activated in today's social schema, leaving little or no space to expand educational contexts beyond a Eurocentric, middle-class mono-culturalism. Then, adding to the tensions discussed in James' article, in *Spectacles of Race and Pedagogies of Denial*, Henry Giroux explores how quality public education has been compromised via public discourses that reinstitute racism on a daily basis. Focusing especially on the discourse of color-blindness relative to today's neoliberal racism, Giroux addresses how the banality of oppression is subtly, and yet powerfully, at work within our educational systems.

Having explored the theoretical frameworks as taken up in the aforementioned papers, Section Two engages how the reality and impact of oppression is often minimized and/or muted in the mainstream generally, and in educational contexts specifically. Moreover, in this section, we explore how the social schema is inundated by oppressive discourses in every moment, in every space, and in turn, how we formulate our understandings of self and *other* when daily experiences are framed by isolation and marginalization. The papers in this section take up the materiality of oppression in relation to how these relations of power manifest themselves in both systemic and everyday experiential ways. In *Empire Building for a New Millennium*, Christine Sleeter unveils what might be a more pointed agenda framing the future of public education in North America. She engages in a careful examination of how elite State-sponsored discourses effectively drive history and social studies teaching in California's public schools, functionally producing a body politic that is in line with, and supportive of, U.S. imperial interests. Expanding on the international scope of these educational dilemmas, David Gillborn considers a range of research evidence that suggests racism is a complex, sometimes subtle, but always powerful presence at the heart of contemporary educational systems. With this key consideration in mind, his paper, *Racism in Educational Sites*, explores how the notion of "ability" is employed to measure student potential and shape students' chances of educational success in Britain. Again, building on Sleeter's policy analysis and on Gillborn's examination of oppressive practice in schooling, Fine and Burns' article helps us to flesh out a more comprehensive understanding of the experiential nature of oppression in educational systems. In *Lessons in Civic Alienation*, the authors draw from research conducted with poor and working class youth to detail the penetrating psychological, social and academic ramifications of substandard school environments on youth in California public schooling. Arguing that "schooling for alienation" systematically under-educates poor and working class youth, and youth of color, Fine and Burns interrogate the potential consequences for schools, communities and the democratic fabric of the nation itself.

In Section Three, we build on the preceding theoretical and material engagements with everyday oppression to explore some of the hopeful work being done within today's educational spheres. Recognizing that we are trudging uphill in this work, I firmly believe that we must steel ourselves within a philosophy of hope – a belief that the development of a greater critical consciousness carries the potential to nurture communities of resistance and to bring about social change. Believing that multiple voices, knowledges and approaches must be heard and involved in the process of social change, I framed this Section of the reader to speak both to the power of community in resistant politics, and to the insurgent possibility for social change through anti-racist praxis. In the first paper, *Unmasking Racism: A Challenge for Anti-Racist Educators in the 21st Century*, George Dei engages this philosophy of hope with a cautionary analysis of the dilemmas facing models of anti-racism that speak to the demands of solidarity in resistant politics. Focusing specifically on the need to manage competing marginalities, Dei frames the challenges facing solidarity and resistance in the general area of schooling in Canada and more specifically in the context of the education "crisis" in Ontario. Building on this recognition of the importance of solidarity in social reform efforts, Joe Kincheloe guides us through the evolving sub-discipline of Whiteness Studies. In his paper, *Reinventing and Redefining Whiteness: A Critical Pedagogy for Insurgent Times*, Kincheloe explores the possibilities for a critical pedagogy of Whiteness that might facilitate and support White students' examinations of the ideological, social, political and psychological dimensions/dynamics of White supremacy. Continuing the theme of social change through solidarity, the next paper, co-authored by French-Canadian community developer/educator Ginette Lafrenière, African pedagogue Papa Lamine Diallo and Aboriginal social justice advocate Donna Dubie, illustrates the determining factors which have shaped their experiences as collaborators and in turn, a critical understanding of the benefits of transformative social change through alliance-building. In their article, *Dancing With Turtles: Building Alliances Between the Community and the Academy*, the authors share a very personal exploration of how their individual experiences of oppression contributed to the conceptualization, implementation and nurturing of an Aboriginal specific project aimed at survivors of the residential school system. Finally, in an effort to try and pull together some of the strings of theory and practice as discussed in the previous articles, I end the text with some new perspectives on critical pedagogy as a starting-point to discussions of social change. In my article, *Implications for Anti-Racist Education: A Pedagogical Needs Assessment*, I focus on how shifts in critical pedagogy might greatly improve the delivery of education for oppressed children in the mainstream and offer in conclusion, an alternative to conventionally accepted models of schooling.

We can no longer afford to focus our efforts on proving the existence and scope of racism to the eyes and ears of privilege because such strategies implicitly assert that our work and pain can only be valid if accepted as "real" by those with power. In much current sociological work, there still seems to be an overriding need to "prove the knowable." However, as Brunner (1994) asserts, "Complex problems do not have simple solutions, and all research is not meant to provide answers." I did not develop this anthology to provide concrete answers to the problem of racism and social oppression in educational spheres. Rather, my intent was to introduce new perspectives on how the oppressed might view, review, write and [re]write their constitution as subjects within the moment, and in turn, rewrite their activity as agents for change. I believe this project to be, not only important, but imperative as a decided move away from the often hopeless and stereotypical study of failures and hardship that so often frame oppositional work. The key for me, as a writer, researcher and pedagogue, is to be productive in our efforts towards change. After all, the old cliché is right: it is easier to tear things down than it is to build them up. I think it is vital that we continue the work of Dei, Giroux, Kincheloe and the other scholars in this reader, towards uplifting explorations of how we can work to create new possibilities for ourselves, as well as new strategies for social change and equity. I have compiled this reader towards these ends, for the oppressed and our allies who are in need of a more critical understanding of the challenges of oppression and the possibilities of anti-oppressive reform in educational contexts. I hope this helps us along our journey towards a greater critical consciousness and towards a greater solidarity.

Acknowledgements

When I first began putting this reader together, I could not have imagined the amount of work that would be required to bring it to fruition nor the generous support, goodwill and solidarity that would be shown by so many of my colleagues as they helped push this work through to the presses. In the truest sense of the word, this was a "collaborative" effort.

I would like to extend a heartfelt thanks to all those scholars who contributed to this anthology. The enthusiasm and dedication you each showed for this project was/is deeply appreciated. I believe we have done something special here and I am honored to have had this opportunity to work with you.

Section One

Theoretical Underpinnings

Chapter 1

The Dialectics of Power

Understanding the Functionality of White Supremacy

Shirley Steinberg, Ph.D.
Department of Graduate Literacy
Brooklyn College, CUNY

Introduction

> Because he lives in a racist society, social relations have been structured by him so that the black is not present for him. Negritude, black history, black social existence, are made not to matter. The man in control is technically insulated from the racial reality and influenced only by the capital whose fortunes he must superintend. . . . Later, he will salve his racial conscience by contributing to the black college of his choice. He might even scold the White bigots and feel genuinely outraged at them.
>
> -Kovel, *White Racism: A Psychohistory*[1]

Contrary to mainstream assumptions that frame the oppressor as generally ignorant of his role in the maintenance of the status quo, I contend that those with power and privilege "know"[2] they have it – and whether that knowledge is accessed consciously, subconsciously or other-wise, he bears responsibility for his participation in the system.[3] That being said, I recognize there is a challenge to difficult knowledge and that as a defence mechanism, it becomes necessary to not only deny the reality of oppression, but to see and frame that reality in ways which are less personally harmful. This ability to sanitize and camouflage oppression is, in fact, one of the most powerful and important tools at the oppressor's disposal in that it allows him to minimize his relationship to the mechanisms of power, even while actively employing those mechanisms to nurture and solidify his position along the top rungs of the social hierarchy.

Again, the *problematic* is far more complex than simple denial because the reality of oppression remains obscured to the common sense gaze. As Kovel (1988) clarifies, oppression is infused into the everyday in such a way as to make it a difficult aspect of experience to separate and recognize, let alone implicate. In fact, these invisible privileges are perpetuated, regenerated and recreated within a system that normalizes oppression by vesting the oppressor with power and social advantages that he himself need not consider.[4] So while the privileged may participate in the banality of everyday oppression, they tend to be unable to perceive the relational tissue that binds their freedoms to the marginalization of others.[5] The systemic functionality of power works in concert with its invisibility to strengthen the privileges it creates and maintains. As evidenced in the White proclivity to rationalize racism by pathologizing people and communities of color as solely responsible for their own misfortunes,[6] those with skin color privilege have the luxury of interpreting race as something that other people have – they do not have to see it unless forced to do so in moments of "racial collision." As Grillo and Wildman (1999) clarify, even though their White skin is infused with meanings and markers, the privilege that frames their Whiteness also ensures that they do not have to think about race or how it positions them in society.[7]

This type of ongoing self-reflection is not a part of the everyday White experience. It is for this reason that we must undertake an extensive analysis and deconstruction of how power and privilege function before we seek to critically engage how those relations then shape the social sphere with deleterious effects for some, and beneficial effects for others. We must engage a critical interrogation of how Whiteness is interconnected with and within the larger social relations of power as a basic step towards exposing the functionality of White supremacy. With that imperative in mind, my purpose here is to establish a firm sociohistorical account that will explore the practical applications of power and privilege that fuel and maintain contemporary forms of racism relative to the functionality of Whiteness and White power in Western contexts.

The White Archetype: Colonial Constructions

Understanding "Whiteness" in contemporary contexts is a difficult and challenging proposition. As put forth by Kincheloe and Steinberg (1998), even today's critical theorists continue to struggle when seeking a functional definition of Whiteness because it continues to shift relative to new circumstances and changing interactions with various manifestations of power.[8] I am convinced that any meaningful interrogation of Whiteness, and its role as the material/non-material lynchpin of contemporary White supremacy, must be preceded by a basic understanding of its sociohistorical nature and an interrogation of its origins in European space.

The emergence of Whiteness as a cohesive notion can be traced back to how the European Enlightenment's transcendental vision of the rational, White, male subject was naturalized as a universal entity. This "White Archetype" operated as more than a mere ethnic positionality; it functionally represented an authoritative, delimited and hierarchical mode of thought.

In fact, as historical configurations and understandings of human nature became grounded in the White capacity for reason, the notion of "reason" itself became linked to Whiteness, and in this way, rationality emerged as the conceptual base around which civilization and savagery were delineated.[9] In order for Whiteness to place itself in the privileged seat of rationality and superiority, it would have to construct pervasive portraits of non-Whites, Africans in particular, as irrational, disorderly and prone to uncivilized behavior.[10] In contrast, Whiteness presented itself as a non-colored, non-blemished pure category – so pure in fact that even a mere drop of non-White blood was enough, historically, to relegate a person to the category of "colored."[11] Any such "contamination" would leave the individual susceptible to the inherent frailties of his/her undesirable gene-pool. Held up against these standards, science and social theory became the primary discursive fields in/through which race was reified, catalogued and disciplined. So much so in fact, that in the decades and centuries that followed the Enlightenment, White and non-White races became dichotomized along a racial continuum where non-Whites were consistently framed in terms that placed them at the tail-end of the racial continuum while Whiteness was made to represent orderliness, rationality and self-control. Importantly, as noted above in relation to the "one drop rule," this modernist conception of the rational White subject was not only shaped through social convention, it was also framed and confirmed by its close association with the science/pseudo-science of the times.

In this privileging of mind over body, intellect over experience, and mental abstractions over passion and tactile understanding, Whiteness has been naturalized and universalized to assume an invisible power unlike all previous forms of domination in human history.[12] We see this invisible power deployed by those who are best able to identify themselves within the boundaries of "White reason" while notions/assumptions of irrationality, sensuality and spontaneity are projected onto the *other*.[13] For example, European ethnic groups, such as the Irish in nineteenth-century industrializing America, were differentiated from other ethnic groups who were framed as "passionate," "hot-blooded" and unable to regulate their emotional predispositions. The discourse surrounding this "innate" irrationality worked to construct them as inferior beings that had no claim to the same rights as "rational" Europeans. It was through this conflation of Whiteness and reason that European colonizers were empowered with the moral justification to exploit, enslave and eradicate entire peoples during the Enlightenment and post-Enlightenment eras.

As Foucault often argued, reason is a form of disciplinary power; employing this axiom, critical multiculturalists argue that discourses surrounding the notion of reason must always be understood to function in, and through, applications of disciplinary power. Those without reason (as defined in Western scientific frameworks) are excluded from power and are relegated to subordinate positions in the social hierarchy – positions that reflect their supposed savagery and their uncivilized nature. In contrast, Whites in their racial purity, understood the dictates of the "White Man's Burden" and became the benevolent teachers of the barbarians. Essentially, the West became the subject of the political discourse of "savior," roughly from the eighteenth century onward.[14] To Western eyes the contrast between White and non-White culture was (and in many respects continues to be) stark: reason as opposed to ignorance; scientific knowledge instead of indigenous knowledge; philosophies of mind versus folk psychologies; religious truth in lieu of primitive superstition; and professional history as opposed to oral mythologies. Thus, rationality was inscribed in a variety of hierarchical relations between European colonizers and their colonies early on, and between Western multinationals and their "underdeveloped" markets in more recent times. The underlying power relations were effectively obfuscated by the White claim of cultural neutrality relative to the trans-historical norm of reason. Again, in this construction, rationality was not assumed to be the intellectual commodity of any specific culture. Rather, colonial hierarchies immersed in exploitation were justified through the interplay of pure Whiteness, impure non-Whiteness, and the neutral/objective measuring stick of "reason." Traditional colonialism was grounded on the fundamental belief that colonialized peoples deviated from the norm of rationality, and therefore, colonization could be interpreted and understood as a rational and measured response to racial inequality.

In the twentieth century, "rationality" continued to be used as the lynchpin in the ongoing maintenance of White supremacy, as its use was extended into the economic sphere where the philosophy of a free-market and a commodity-culture were universalized into signifiers of civilization. The effects of the "evolved colonialism" were, and continue to be, mammoth in their implications for Whites and their consequences for non-Whites. As transnational flows of culture, politics and discourse continue to breakdown national boundaries, we see the "White reason" of marketization being infused in and through the world's ever-globalizing contexts: human worth has become a calculable, knowable thing; the values of abstract individualism and financial success have been embraced by communities across the globe; and educational systems are bending to the needs of a market economy that sees the cultivation of human capital as being the first order of business in schooling. Not to draw too fine a point on the present situation, but the commodification and regulation of people in general, and *other* peoples specifically, has reached unprecedented levels, as information systems are increasingly used to record and mark credit histories, institutional affiliations, psychological health, academic credentials, work experiences and family backgrounds. Ultimately, I would argue that the accomplishment of this prodigious global colonial task will mark the end of White history in the familiar end-of-history parlance. That is not to say that we would see the end of White supremacy as such, but that it has produced a hegemony so seamless that the need for further structural or ideological change may become unnecessary.[15]

Whatever the complexity of the concept, Whiteness cannot escape the materiality of its history or its effects on the everyday lives of the marginalized; and if we are to see the development of real and meaningful oppositional movement against this seemingly inevitable trend towards an all-encompassing globalized Whiteness, critical scholarship on Whiteness should focus its attention on the documentation of such effects. The study of Whiteness in a critical multiculturalist context needs to begin delineating the various ways in which these material effects work to shape cultural and institutional pedagogies, as well as how they effectively position and frame individuals relative to the power of White reason. Understanding these dynamics is central to the curriculums of Black studies, Chicano studies, postcolonialism and indigenous studies, not to mention educational reform movements in elementary, secondary and higher education.

Because the history of the world, and its diverse peoples specifically, has, for the most part, been recorded and told from a White historiographical vantage point, most such historical accounts have functionally erased the values, epistemologies, and belief systems that grounded the experiences and cultural practices of non-White peoples. Without such cultural grounding, students, and particularly students of color, are being systematically "disciplined" to overlook, ignore and/or devalue the ongoing and immeasurable social/scientific and cultural contributions to the world made by members of non-White groups. Caught in the White interpretive filter, they find themselves unable to make sense of diverse historical and contemporary cultural productions as anything other than proof of White success and superiority.[16] Such harsh realities push us to engage the unpleasant truth that White power is alive, well and present in all aspects of contemporary life in the West.

I began this paper with a quotation from Joel Kovel's (1988) work *White Racism: A Psychohistory,* because in it, he talks about two kinds of White racists: the hate-filled, rock-throwing, name-calling lower-class racial bigot and the silent, sophisticated, powerful patriarch – the man in control. According to Kovel, it is this "unseen" patriarch who institutionalizes racism and supports/bolsters the hate-filled rock-throwing bigot.[17] While Kovel makes an important point about systemic racism, I think it crucial that we go further in such analyses and recognize that both of these racists exercise power, and avail themselves of the mechanisms of that power, in every aspect of their lives simply by virtue of engaging their Whiteness. It is in/through this daily, banal and "invisible" access to White power and privilege that the ongoing colonial agenda is advanced most effectively. As discussed above, over the last three centuries the concept and framework of Western reason was a crucial element in the invention of Whiteness, but we must recognize that there are many other social forces that work to construct and sustain the meaning of Whiteness. Simply put, Whiteness is not an unchanging, fixed, biological category impervious to its cultural, economic, political and psychological context. Rather, there are many ways to be White, and it is important that we begin to unravel the means and manner through which Whiteness has been, and continues to be constructed.

Whiteness as Social Construction

So what is Whiteness? What does it mean to be White? Is there an all-consuming "truth" to what Whiteness entails or does it evolve and change relative to its interactions with other social positions and other race-related cultural dynamics as Dei, Apple, Kincheloe and other prominent critical scholars would assert? Whiteness, like any other racial category, is a social construction in that it can be invented, lived, analyzed, modified and discarded, but its ephemeral nature is shrouded in the everyday experience and generally appears as a static racial category. As noted above, in order to peel back this shroud, we have to engage how Whiteness has shifted relative to the sociohistorical contexts of time and space. Case in point, Irish, Italians and Jews have all been viewed as non-White in particular places at specific moments in history.

Prior to the late 1600s, Europeans did not use the label "Black" to refer to any race of people, Africans included. It was only after the racialization of slavery in and around 1680 that Whiteness and Blackness were framed as racial categories. It was at this historical juncture that the concept of a discrete White race began to take shape relative to its differences from these other groups. However, it is of some importance to note that a distinction must be drawn between notions of difference and superiority. Whiteness did not come to signify an elite racial group until it became conflated with notions of rationality, orderliness and civility throughout the eighteenth and nineteenth centuries. In time, Whiteness was not only viewed as a position of power, it (White identity) was often sought by those who did not possess it (i.e., immigrant workers from southern and eastern Europe aspired to procure Whiteness in the new American industrial workplaces of the mid-nineteenth century – and eventually attained it). These types of evolutionary shifts in the nature and boundaries of Whiteness continued into the twentieth century, and profound shifts in the construction of Whiteness, Blackness and other racial identities are taking place even today.

With all this talk of shifting meanings and contextual boundaries, how are we to make sense of the assertion that Whiteness is a social construction? In order to answer this question in a manner that is helpful to Whites and other racial groups, it is important to focus our attention on the nature of the social construction process itself. To this end, Fiske's (1994) notion of an ever-shifting and realigning power bloc is very helpful.[19] Important at the onset of this discussion, I would assert that if we are looking for logical consistency in the social construction of Whiteness, we are not going to find it because the discourses that shape Whiteness are not unified and singular, but diverse and contradictory. Similar to Miliband (1969), Karumanchery and Portelli (2005) and other critical theorists in their engagements with "class consciousness," I do not subscribe to contentions that frame the social construction of Whiteness and White power as contingent effects of some "conspiracy of the powerful."[20] Like these theorists, I engage the pluralist stance that cross-cutting cleavages engender competition between various elites and their ideological conceptions, thereby ensuring that notions of a "singular racial bloc consciousness" is likely theoretical at best. However, with that said, I feel it reasonable to contend that dominant powers (e.g., racial, economic elites) will possess a high degree of cohesion because their common purposes will often supersede their individual differences. As asserted by Karumanchery and Portelli (2005), this speaks less to conspiracies of the powerful, and more to the nature of social formations as subjective and contextual conditions relative to political moments of class unity.[21] The functionality of any power bloc arises in the ability to align its various resources around the discursive construction of very specific issues – issues in the case of Whiteness, that alignment centres on issues of race. For example, as noted by Kincheloe (1999), the discourse of White victimization that emerged over the last two decades appeared in direct response to social justice movements like affirmative action and employment equity (movements that were looking to ameliorate systemic oppression by addressing issues such as preferential hiring and inequitable admissions policies). Clearly, the notion of White victimization evolved as a very space and time specific phenomenon. Because they fashion and refashion hierarchic power relations between differing social groups, such oppressive discourses hold profound material consequences for the marginalized in Western contexts.

Haymes (1996) argues that to understand racial identity formation, we need to appreciate the way White is discursively represented as the polar opposite of Black – as a reflection of the Western tendency to privilege one concept in binary opposition to another.[22] The darkness-light, angel-devil discursive binarism, like other such constructions, has reproduced itself in the establishment of racial and ethnic categories. Through its relationship with Blackness, Whiteness configured itself as more than simply different, but rather as evolved, powerful, and as aligned with destiny. In this almost parasitic relationship, Blackness, or Africanness, served to empower Whiteness through the ongoing violation and degradation of non-White peoples. Through this relationship with Africanism, Whites learned to see themselves as the racial barometer by which other groups were measured. In short, this discourse of Whiteness served to construct not only the ways in which *other* peoples were known, but also the ways in which they were made knowable.

As asserted by Homi Bhabha (1994), the ideological construction of the *other*, as fixed and knowable, is a major feature of colonial discourse.[23] Interestingly though, while such discursive formations work to ensure that the marginalized peoples remain intrinsically knowable within the social consciousness, the "truth" of these racial realities needs to be constantly repeated, regenerated, reintegrated and reinvented in the public psyche in order to retain its currency.[24] Dei, Karumanchery and Karumanchery-Luik (2004) note that it is exactly this nature that allows racist discourses to engage and function within changing social contexts and shifting historical specificities and conjunctures. It is through this ambivalent interplay between sign, symbol and meaning that both Whiteness and the *other* have been, and continue to be, constructed as effects of discourse.[25]

As the bodies, cultures and histories of *other* peoples became charged and embedded with meaning, every support structure for the race concept developed alongside new methods through which these communities and cultures could be seen, understood, represented and managed. As noted by Dei, Karumanchery and Karumanchery-Luik (2004), it was within the context of empire building that the race concept truly began to take form as each insurgent discourse framed new "truths" about the other. European discursive fields did more than create these bodies:

> . . . they effectively formulated a manageable and violable classification of people: a stylized sub-species both inherently inferior and intrinsically in need of administration. These 'others' in all their biological inferiority, moral depravity and mental deficiency, became the perfect foil for the Western archetype and as the *other* became objectified, so too did his/her existence become manufactured as a product of classification and stereotype.[26]

The White world view became conflated with notions of objective knowledge – beyond dispute and above the need for validation. For example, see Balfour's 1910 House of Commons speech about managing Egypt:

I take up no attitude of superiority. But I ask [Robertson and anyone else] . . . who has even the most superficial knowledge of history, if they will look in the face of the facts with which a British statesman has to deal when he is put in a position of supremacy over great races like the inhabitants of Egypt and countries in the East. We know the civilization of Egypt better than we know the civilization of any other country. We know it further back; we know it more intimately; we know more about it. It goes far beyond the petty span of the history of our race, which is lost in the prehistoric period a time when the Egyptian civilization had already passed its prime. Look at all the oriental countries. Do not talk about superiority or inferiority.[27]

As Said (1979) notes, two crucial themes emerge in Balfour's validation of the British occupation of Egypt – *power* and *knowledge*. Functioning as a tool for the management of colonized spaces, Orientalism (as coined by Said), in effect, was the lynchpin in the machinery of colonial domination and pivotal in the subjugation and oppression of *other* peoples. It was through this discourse that the West gained the ability to settle, describe, marginalize, rule and denigrate all things *other* – in effect, all things non-White.[28] Said's work helps to emphasize how European culture and ontology have managed to control and constitute every social aspect and meaning attributed to the concept of the racialized *other*. As this socially constructed dichotomy between the West and the East was drawn, and as meanings were established, all racialized concepts of Whiteness became known and understood in their relation to other repressed or negated notions.[29]

Avoiding Essentialism: The Instability of Whiteness

In order to critically interrogate how the Western world constructs and disciplines White and non-White peoples within a global hierarchy, it is important to examine the discursive machinery through which such systemic order is made possible. As noted by Said, with respect to the social construction of the Orient and the Oriental, the "machinery of colonialism" took such a position of authority over the non-Western world, that no one writing, thinking or acting on the *other*, could do so without taking account of the limitations imposed on such labor by colonial discourse.[30] Importantly, these racist discourses became, and continue to be solidified within "regimes of truth" that are continuously bolstered by the strength of their legal, political, institutional and cultural support structures. Simply put, we "know" these racial categorizations to be real. With respect to Whiteness, like other racial categories, it has always operated under the assumption that it was in some way permanent, fixed and knowable in its most essential manifestations. A critical pedagogy of Whiteness understands the contingent connections that link a rationalistic modernist Whiteness, and the actions of people with light-colored skin. However, in attempts to frame race in concrete terms, those doing race work (e.g., academics, politicians, pseudo-scientists) have functionally re-inscribed and re-cemented the foundations of racial difference throughout history.[31]

Before the advent of large-scale non-White immigration in the 1970s, U.S. governmental agencies routinely employed only three racial categories (i.e., White, Negro and Indian) to classify, sort and label its citizens.[32] This begs critical questions of fit and belonging. After all, how were we to "organize" and "administer" Latino/as, Asians and every other group that did not fit into these pigeon-holed classifications? Such biological criteria simply cannot work in any logically consistent manner, and have always served to frustrate regulatory efforts to impose a rationalistic racial order for administrative purposes.[33] Case in point, originally, in the state of California, Mexicans were classified as White, while Chinese and other Asian groups were catalogued as Indian. Clearly, there is a dissonance in these arbitrary designations, and any basic analysis of such configurations inevitably reveals the ambiguity of racial groupings framed by similarities in skin tone, hair texture and eye shape. Just as these larger racial categorizations stand fraught with dilemmas, so too, do individual racial categories themselves when collapsed. That being said, in looking to interrogate the nature of Whiteness supremacy in this paper, we must be careful to attend to the subtle but crucial distinction between Whiteness (i.e., with its power to signify) and White people themselves.

As noted by Kincheloe (1999), the diversity that exists within the category of Whiteness makes generalizations about the activation and application of White privilege dangerous and highly counterproductive.[34] In this sense, while Whiteness must be understood to be a marker of power and privilege, the intersections of other social positions (e.g., gender, sexuality, class, ability) within the White body, will mediate engagements with that privilege. Again, as Kincheloe clearly illustrates, "it is difficult to convince a working class White student of the ubiquity of White privilege when he or she is going to school, accumulating school debts, working at McDonalds for minimum wage, unable to get married because of financial stress, and holds little hope of upward socioeconomic mobility."[35] As a further cautionary note, I would add that critical analysts often look pointedly towards the social, historical, rhetorical and discursive contexts of Whiteness when mapping its role in the shaping of larger sociopolitical structures. But in relation to the micro-dynamics of everyday life, the lived experiences and anxieties of White peoples cannot be dismissed on the whole, and must be incorporated into any such explorations. Understanding the social/discursive construction of Whiteness necessitates that we search for its essential nature or its authentic core, and that requires us to speak of the saliency of race, even as we recognize the intersections of race with other forms of difference. Recognizing that there are contextually bound variations in the intensity of oppression for different bodies, understanding Whiteness and White supremacy requires us to acknowledge the influence and effect of these intersections and interlocks. As there is no fixed essence to Whiteness, we can debate both its meaning in general, and its meaning in the lived experience of White people, but ultimately, a recognition of this basic ambiguity is central to the project of understanding the social and psychosocial implications of Whiteness, and in turn, White supremacy.

Whiteness scholarship to this point has frequently failed to recognize that its greatest problem is the lapse into essentialism. I refuse to use *race* as an essentialist grounding of identity, and so engage race as an unnatural classification whose cultural boundaries are constantly negotiated and transgressed. As researchers and educators, our attention should always be focused on a continuous re-imagining and re-invention of racial identity, such that we might point out and address the inaccuracies and inequities embedded in contemporary racial configurations. I make this pointed assertion because in our engagements with oppression, we consistently risk reifying the perceived differences between groups without tackling the hybridity that binds and connects us. We need to interrogate these false dichotomies because they effectively encourage the development of an isolationist identity politics that troubles the possibility for solidarity between oppressed groups. Within this perspective, it is inappropriate for a White man to ever criticize a Black man, or for a straight man to speak as an ally or partner to a lesbian. Such politics serve to sabotage the possibilities for solidarity between individuals from a variety of groups who want to pursue collective forms of resistance. It is crucial that we begin sidestepping the essentialist dogma framing race-talk and Whiteness studies.

We cannot ameliorate essentialism's hold on the world's psyche by embracing notions of racial erasure. We need to adopt a middle-ground stance that explores the socially constructed, ephemeral nature of racial identities while carefully tracing the manifest material effects of racism.[36] As Kincheloe (1999) put it, we must "walk a Wallinda tightrope between racial essentialism on one side and a liberal color-blindness on the other." This approach separates Whiteness from White people, and "understands" how some Whites might view themselves as racial victims who feel the need to build an emotional community around their Whiteness.[37] Ever aware of the ambiguities at play, we must be able to simultaneously appreciate the plight and pain of those Whites whose lives are experienced at the intersections of power and oppression (e.g., the White lesbian, the working class White woman), while exposing the ways in which Whiteness works to conceal normalized forms of sociopolitical and economic privilege. In the postmodern world, individuals engage their identities as they travel in and out of ever-changing sociocultural locales. The notion of "genuine culture" is fast becoming a thing of the past as in-group mores and folkways shift and change with each successive generation. Once we have removed the crutch and safety of essentialism, we must engage the imperative to refigure and rewrite racial analyses around an understanding of the evolving complexity of identity formation.[38]

Racial Mutations at the Turn of the Century: Whiteness Made Visible

Engagements with the complexity of identity politics has exploded over the last thirty years, and in generating a widespread angst about the meaning of Whiteness, this "new reality" has moved many Whites to confront their own ethnicity for the first time. However, when we link contradictory articulations of what it means to "feel White" with the myriad socio-economic and political forces that continually undermine stable notions of White identity, we may begin to understand the drive to deny or sidestep one's own implication in the relations of power. As noted by Kincheloe (1999), White people around the world are facing an unprecedented crisis of Whiteness in that they are realizing they may not constitute a majority of the population for long, recognizing challenges to White supremacy and watching themselves being labelled as oppressors in the eyes of the world.[39] In attempting to understand the barriers to partnership and support from White sites, we must try and understand the nuances of how this sociocultural phenomenon has affected White people in the post-civil-rights era. We cannot, and must not, simply dismiss or mute the paradoxical concerns that many White people express when they speak about having pride in White culture when "everyone else" is talking about pride in their ethnicity, race and culture. The fact that White culture, ethnicity and race are naturalized and normalized into the fabric of Western society is not the point here, but rather that most White people do not see it. Again, the invisibility of that privilege is the point, and their ability to ignore its implications arises as a direct effect of their power. That being said, make no mistake about it, the great crisis of Whiteness today is framed around the increasing visibility of that previously unseen power and privilege. Simply put, there is a new consciousness about Whiteness in contemporary Western societies – a new vantage point that is forcing Whites to explore who they are and how they fit into the larger puzzle of social oppression.[40]

When bell hooks (1992) argued that Whites could assume their racial invisibility, I don't know that even she realized just how quickly that racial camouflage would be exposed.[41] This crisis of Whiteness has effectively troubled the traditional notion of White racial invisibility and left in its place, an increasingly complex question about how to reframe and construct a new White identity in the context of an ever-diversifying and diasporic world. Whites gaining consciousness of the racialization of their identity have found themselves in an almost untenable situation where implication and active participation are framed as coterminous, and little or no distinction is made between personal responsibility and group complicity. For White people coming to a greater critical consciousness of their power and privilege, the guilt and shame generated in these articulations of Whiteness can be immobilizing. In fact, as noted by Kincheloe (1999) quite often, Whites in the midst of such an identity crisis (generally young adults), will engage in a form of racial self-denigration that expresses itself in the belief that non-White cultures are superior to White culture (i.e., more authentic, natural and sacred).[42]

On the other hand, confronting the racialization of Whiteness will often engender quite aggressive movement in the opposite direction. Given the way in which conservative discourses have shaped cultural expression in recent years, Whites in crisis will often find greater cultural solidarity with right-wing racial codes that respond to, and articulate, their own personal racial anxieties in the moment. Under the clarion call of the extreme right, organizations like the KKK in the United States and the Heritage Front in Canada, are indoctrinating young Whites into dangerous belief systems that fan the flames of White anger against non-Whites and effectively up the ante of racial hostility within a framework of White supremacy.[43] As Kincheloe explains:

> This reactionary form of the new White identity appropriates Whiteness as the defiant signifier of the new self. After all the talk, argument, and litigation about race starting with the Civil Rights movement in the 1950s and 1960s, right-wing analysts discovered that they could engage in identity politics as well. As it latched on to the Whiteness signifier, right-wing identity politics touted values such as the Eurocentric cultural canon, English language-only legislation, the symbol of family values, and the work ethic.[44]

As Gresson (1995) asserts, right-wing leaders effectively intertwine and blend these "virtues" with understandings of Whiteness in such a way as to deploy a new brand of ethnopolitics whose purpose is simply the recovery of White supremacy.[45] That being said, we must be careful not to discount this "White recovery" movement as the terrain of ignorant militant extremists – to do so would be both dangerous and simplistic. In point of fact, this movement has developed, and continues to develop, from within various social sites, education included. Case in point, after *The Chronicle of Higher Education*[46] ran an article describing the proliferation of Whiteness studies, Eisenman (1995) wrote a reaction paper to the editor that reflected many of the same themes that bolster and sustain the recovery rhetoric.[47] Entitled "Take Pride in Being White," Eisenman argued:

> [I]t is bad enough that Whites are victims of a quota system called affirmative action which causes them (especially White males) to be discriminated against, to work (as I have in the past) for an incompetent supervisor . . .

In this homage to White virtue and competence, his rhetorical explorations of Whiteness did more than simply extol the intellectual contributions made by the White world. Rather, like all dichotomies, (or false dichotomies as is the case here), by linking Whiteness and White spaces with "the social good" (i.e., low crime rates and declining AIDS infection rates), he effectively frames Blackness and all things *other* as directly related to, and responsible for, social declines in America. Warning that lax immigration laws will minoritize America's White population early in this new century (an absolute demographic absurdity given present immigration trends), Eisenman employs various powerful and frightening techniques to bolster this "spirit of White recovery." Concluding that someone must defend White people and in effect, the White way of life, he cements this rhetoric within a clear and unmistakable message of fear that carries dangerous connections to the type of hate-mongering framed in the mainstream as only existing in the far, far, far-right.[48]

Exploring Victimhood in White America

For anyone who read John McWhorter's problematic and violating text, *Losing the Race: Self-Sabotage in Black America*, the anger of Eisenman and the millions of other White males he represents should come as no surprise.[49] After all, if an educated Black man like McWhorter could so miss the mark when it comes to understanding the implications of race and the intersectionality of class, gender and sexuality in oppressive relations of power, why are we surprised to find White scholars with similar praxical "blind spots?" Indeed, while we can understand the internalized racism that problematize works framing oppression as self-victimization, and while we can understand the irony of Eisenman's simpleminded argument-that someone needs to defend White males (the world's most powerful group by far in contemporary times) – we must not make the mistake of assuming ignorance is the key. To follow that path is to assume that only ignorant or dimwitted White men are the problem, and clearly, both McWhorter's and Eisenman's arguments prove quite the contrary.

White privilege and the rhetoric which bolsters it, does not rest on the rational and intellectual exploration of power relations. Rather, the social importance of these discourses revolves around their emotionality as the driving force behind the perceptions that Whiteness is under siege and that people of color are their own worst enemies. This White identity crisis is very real and must not be simply dismissed as so much privileged angst. It is important to clarify this point because we cannot ignore the fact that gender, ethnicity, sexuality and class all infiltrate and implicate the experience of Whiteness such that it is clearly problematic to generalize when we speak of White privilege. But that being said, this work necessitates that I engage the relations of power and difference when I speak of the saliency of race, even while recognizing how race intersects with other forms of difference. Of course there are relative saliencies for different identities as well as contextual variations in the intensity of oppression for such bodies. After all, theoretical terms often offer us a certain degree of distance from the real, lived experience and we must remember not to develop needless tensions between the theoretical and the practical. Simply put, it is difficult to see the privilege of a homeless White man. My use of critical anti-racist theory in this context reflects a clear acknowledgement of the severity of these intersections and interlocks for certain bodies. However, in employing a politics that moves beyond reactive responses in the moment, and towards an agenda that is framed in/through the power of self definition, I would ask the reader: how would the intersection of race and class shift the experience of a Black or Aboriginal homeless man from that of a homeless White man? We cannot sidestep how oppressions intersect and interlock to generate a complex of disabilities for certain bodies. Of course, like everyone, White people have problems of their own. But in attempts to claim the currency of marginality, we neglect to ask how those same problems might intensify or shift if they were further complicated by issues of race, gender, class, sexuality, et cetera.

The color-blind worldview framing discourses of White victimization function through this privileged ability to deny difference. For instance, disregarding the sociopolitical, historical and economic contexts that mediate how we experience the world, we, as a society, work with the assumption that being White is no different than being any other race or ethnicity. Erasure is the name of the game as White privilege is denied and historical facts are severed – rewritten to "whitewash" any and all connection between historical patterns of injustice and today's current social hierarchies. By eliminating these connections, we effectively limit our ability to interpret the relationship between White wealth and racial exploitation. By ensuring that the ethical, moral and political dynamics of such a relationship never enter White consciousness, such sociohistorical amnesia allows McWhorter, Eisenman and others of their ilk to imagine that "real" racism at the beginning of the twenty first century is rare; a thing to be found among only a few White supremist organizations and a minority of "backward" individuals.[50] In discussing today's self-portrayals of White victimhood and the resulting reclamation/continuation of White dominance, Gresson (1995) is earnest in his challenge of how non-Whites are being framed as the new oppressors. In these contexts, Whiteness is being increasingly constructed as a signifier of material deprivation and repression while non-Whites are seen as actively undermining White progress and exploiting White guilt about racism's past and false legacy.[51] Signaling a shift in organized racial thought, mainstream

White reflections on racism and oppression are no longer simply defined through privileged denial, but through a clear articulation of White victimization.[52]

Throughout this work, I have tried to explore how contemporary White supremacy is a relational phenomenon that functions through the interplay of complex social, cultural, political and historical forces and contexts. However, returning to Kovel's (1988) astute observations, as noted in the opening quotation, the oppressor is privileged in his ability to disregard, obfuscate and downplay the realities of oppression that circumscribe the lives of those he oppresses. As Dei, Karumanchery and Karumanchery-Luik (2004) explain:

> . . . the abstract nature of privilege and the almost metaphysical character of social control as applied within oppressive relations of power, carries the potential to 'scar without marking', to 'push without shoving'. In fact, one of the peculiar endowments of White privilege arises in its ability to obfuscate its relationship to the mechanisms of power, while at the same time, employing those mechanisms in language, discourse and every other aspect of our lived reality.[53]

The viability and functionality of power relations are intrinsically tied to disciplinary power and the regulation, or self-regulation, of the oppressed. Simply put, the insidious nature of oppression manifests itself in the ability to implicate the oppressed in the maintenance of their own oppression. Similarly, because these discursive disciplinary systems also "automize" and "disindividualize" our perceptions of the process, those of us in positions of power and privilege need never connect the dots that link "their oppression" with "our privilege." For this reason, I am earnest in my contention that any interrogation of contemporary White supremacy necessitates a counter-hegemonic politics capable of challenging the normality of Whiteness itself. Like Frankenberg (1993), I call for an unmasking of Whiteness.[54] Centering our analyses around interrogations of racism that do not shift attention away from the concerns of the oppressed, a rupturing of the "White recovery movement" is crucial to any further subversion of contemporary White supremacy. It is still possible to work towards a critical deconstruction of White supremacy, but in order to do so, White people must first refuse to retreat from our personal and group responsibility in the maintenance of the status quo. Secondly, these same White allies must be willing to actively explore new possibilities to rupture Whiteness' status as the overriding paradigmatic archetype of the Western world.[55] No easy task this, but certainly, a clear starting-point for change.

Chapter 2

Racism "Renewed"

Nationalist Practices, Citizenship and Fantasy Post-9/11

Kayleen U. Oka
The Ontario Institute for Studies in Education
University of Toronto

Introduction

> [T]he state of emergency in which we live is not the exception, but the rule. We must attain to a conception of history that is in keeping with this insight.
>
> Walter Benjamin[1]

The events of September 11, 2001, not only exemplified a state of emergency for the United States, but they also acted as a catalyst for the incorporation of crisis and security measures worldwide. This sudden disruption of "normality" worked to reinvent the notion of *national fantasy* in the minds of citizens and non-citizens alike. Through their contribution to a larger narrative about belonging, citizenship, security, borders and intruders, national fantasies work to tell us who *we* are in relation to who *they* are and most importantly, they establish the laws required to protect us from the difference.[2] These emerging conceptions of nation and nationhood arose as exceptionally urgent post-9/11, and the effect of that emergence[3] continues to be felt today.

The spectacle of September 11 was especially compelling both at home and abroad because for the first time in history "everyday Americans"[4] (working people, travellers, flight attendants, fire fighters) living their everyday lives were attacked[5] and killed on national soil.[6] The use of American instruments and means (e.g., commercial airplanes, letters of correspondence), ensured that the extreme nature of the event was juxtaposed against the ordinary backdrop of the American everyday in a way that fueled the fires of the national panic to otherwise unattainable levels. The resulting fanaticism that gripped the public psyche was largely engineered by the mainstream media, as was the sometimes subtle, often overt, racism employed to describe the spectacle of 9/11 to both the national citizenry and the world.

As asserted by Herman and Chomsky (1988), the Western mainstream media has always contributed to the "manufacturing of consent" as part of the "government-media propaganda model."[7] In fact, Chomsky (2003) contends that this propaganda model was visibly functioning throughout the events of September 11, in its immediate aftermath and particularly in relation to the acts of American retaliatory aggression in Iraq after the fact.[8] As we examine the media's power and influence over the production and regulation of such a national fantasy, it is also imperative to further explore the elements surrounding its construction, how certain figures are drawn in while others are excluded and the larger narrative to which it speaks. To these ends, I examine how the events and subsequent public discourse surrounding 9/11 have contributed to the production and "renewal" of a fundamentally racist national fantasy.

In this article, I pull strands from academic discourses and rely on popular U.S. media discourse and imagery to interrogate how nationalist practices have been employed in the post-9/11 era to construct and defend "new" notions of citizenship that are generally exclusionary and specifically racist. How is this done? How is this all part of an ongoing story about myth making, racism and the continuation of dominance? What conditions enable this to occur and what are the implications for researchers, educators and consumers of First World media information? I argue that this "revitalized" national fantasy has everything to do with race and racism, often without even employing these terms. They are firmly entrenched in the language, images and nuances that mediate the constructed knowledge of who we are and who we ought to be. While this paper focuses on the U.S. context, it looks at our[9] complicity as a whole and asks questions of how hegemony impacts and affects us all locally and globally, regardless of geographic location.

Media Matters, Manipulations and Fantasy

In her exploration of popular media discourse, Berlant (1997) focuses on the media's aura of "ordinariness" wherein its disciplinary power can be applied. Similarly, I assert that the seductive banality of mainstream media discourse is positioned in ways that functionally obscures its manipulation of the public consciousness. This seduction takes us unaware and unprepared precisely because it occurs in spaces that are framed as "objective" and "neutral." Along these lines, Berlant examines:

> the moments of oppressive optimism in normal national culture: to see what kinds of domination are being imagined as forms of social good; what kinds of utopian desires are being tapped and translated into conservative worldviews; what means are being used to suppress the negative fallout of affirmative culture; what [might it] take to make linked kinds of knowledge, power, and experience no longer seem separate.[10]

The "normality" and truthfulness with which these imaginations, desires and tendencies are manifested in the media belies the reality of control, regulation and suppression that lay at their heart – that is the danger of it. During the coverage of 9/11, the U.S. media demonstrated how relations of power (e.g., elite discourses) could suddenly reshape our knowledge about *others* and our notions of citizenship in public and private spheres in a manner new, yet somehow familiar.

This ability to reinforce old or hidden suspicions has a profound effect on society's consciousness and conceptions of "normality." In fact, when I speak of the media's power and the relations of power, I do not necessarily assume it to be a totalizing coercive force from above that oppresses all below it. Unlike traditional juridic-discursive readings that tend to view power as a possession flowing downward from a centralized point, I prefer to follow Foucault's (1977) reading of power as functioning beyond simple dichotomous top-down relations.[11] I read power as *productive* – it functions through various techniques and methods of application (present in many forms – government, education, the military) to produce reality. Through this perspective we may begin to perceive how the media acts in cooperation and collaboration with other social organizations to produce a regulated citizenry as an effect of discourse. It is through these systemic relations of power that notions such as normalcy/deviance, law-abiding/criminal and citizen/non-citizen are dichotomized and produced as discursive effects.

Reflecting on Benedict Anderson's study of nationalism and imagined communities,[12] Loomba (1998) emphasizes the significance of the media and other forms of communication in forging shared national interests and other forms of communal solidarity.[13] With that in mind, this analysis of media representations and discourse is primarily focused on the Cable News Network (CNN) online coverage of September 11 and its aftermath, because CNN and its corporate relatives have been working for the past 80+ years on forging such interests and bonding national and international communities.[14] Moreover, CNN's Western origins, dominance in the marketplace, vast corporate affiliations and substantial audience reach make it a prime example of how such media machines function to produce reality.[15] While CNN clearly has an American agenda and American interests at heart, it is also important to recognize that its influence is not limited to the United States alone. Rather, its broadcast ability, technology and vast affiliations make it a world media power and as such, its ability to regulate and inform the world's social and political landscape must not be overlooked or underestimated. What grand narratives does it contribute to telling, and how are those narratives conveyed through the positioning as "everyday news"? Moreover, how do its political and economic agendas influence, maintain and inform our conceptions of truth, rightness, and normality? Like other media machines, CNN is positioned to obscure the manipulations of interest, desire and fear through which our lives are subtly circumscribed. Consequently, it becomes increasingly important to critically investigate this version of "reality." To do this, I begin with the premise that the notion of *national fantasy* pervades this interrogation, often in ways unrealized.

When we think about the notion of "fantasy," we think about visions, whimsical images and Disney-like daydreams where imaginings and longings culminate in a kind of hopeful utopia. The other side of fantasy that is often ignored is that it is also an invention, a way in which images are constructed and organized to help shape our experience of the world. In other words, fantasy is an invention of reality supported and sustained by imagery, narratives and discourses that infiltrate and filter the public consciousness. In these increasingly complex and hurried times, we yearn for fantasies because they satisfy our longing for the surreal, but in ways that can also be controlled and manipulated.

One of the world's prevalent fantasies is that of the American Dream: the notion that anyone can go to the United States and have the life they dream of, if only they work hard to overcome the obstacles set before them. The salience of this national fantasy is continually reinforced as immigrants from around the world travel to the United States in search of this dream. However, while the narrative of American immigration is framed by this fantasy, it is also framed by the fantasy of meritocracy as a corollary to explain away stories of hardship, failure and oppression. The connective tissue that binds the two together is the notion of "worthiness." That is, the worthy succeed in spite of the obstacles they encounter, the worthy both deserve and earn their place in American society, and although immigration gives one the opportunity, only the worthy succeed. This notion of "worthiness" has become entrenched into the psyche of America's citizenry and it extends itself to the notion that that which is worthy needs to be protected. However, not all are privileged to imagine this sense of security. As Berlant states, "the fantasy of a private, protected national space is a fantasy only a non-stigmatized person, a privileged person, can realistically imagine living."[16] *Other* bodies, marked bodies, become representative of that which "non-stigmatized" bodies need protection from. After all, the nature of this national fantasy establishes that those who do not succeed in their pursuit of the American dream do so, not because the obstacles were too large to overcome, but because they themselves were unable/unwilling to work hard enough to overcome them. Simply put, the fantasy of the American Dream functionally marks certain bodies for deviance and as solely responsible for their "failures" – the American Dream serves to pathologize some while glorifying others.

Fantasies constantly circulate and reinvent themselves, and although they are illusions that are almost always unattainable (which is precisely their allure), they nonetheless give meaning and purpose to the subject's life, and the meaning and purpose which makes life worth living is itself part of the fantasy. People don't *have* fantasies. They *inhabit* fantasy spaces of which they are a part.[17] However, it is important to understand that these fantasy spaces are always produced and managed through mainstream sites of power and privilege to obfuscate the subtle, more disguised forms and effects of everyday racism and oppression. The end result is the marking and positioning of certain bodies as *other*, as deviant and as deserving of their experiences of pain, marginality and frustration. So while the North American landscape is slowly evolving into a physical reflection of the world community, the lived reality of these spaces continues to be cemented in forms and functions that produce, and reproduce, power and privilege as set within White Eurocentric frameworks. Racial meanings are deeply embedded into the sociohistorical contexts of Western society and they function to normalize Whiteness and the hegemonic social/spatial order in spite of the fantasies of freedom, equity and meritocracy that complicate and disguise that "reality." While these national fantasies claim freedom and opportunity as the "truth" of the American landscape, systemic relations of power and oppression continue to frame who is and who is not a citizen, who does and who does not belong, who is and who is not safe. In fact, the particular fantasy space of *nation* in the U.S. has taken on "renewed" and powerful meanings in the post-9/11 era.

Nationalism and Nationalist Practices

In his discussions of nationalism and nationalist practices, Hage (2000); asserts that such practices assume "first an image of national space; secondly, an image of the nationalist himself or herself as master of this national space and, thirdly, an image of the "ethnic/racial other" as a mere object within this space."[18] These articulations of spatial power, while always at work, became particularly pronounced and evident under the unstable and unpredictable sociopolitical conditions that arose in post-9/11 times. The media's management of the public consciousness throughout and following the event resulted in the production of an American national fantasy that was infused with an increasingly exclusionary and oppressive mandate. While mainstream discourses were encouraging traditional values and patriotism alongside images of an America united,[19] the longing for a particular kind/"color" of nation was also being progressively reinforced and ingrained into the American consciousness. As suggested by O'Leary and Platt (2001), these measures were intentional:

> In the aftermath of September 11, people are hungry for social rituals and eager to communicate a deeper sense of national belonging. Yet this new wave of orchestrated patriotism is aimed at closing down debate and dissent through the imposition of a prescribed allegiance.[20]

When Renan stated that "a nation is a soul, a spiritual principle,"[21] could he have imagined the collective national sentiment and "orchestrated patriotism" that arose in the wake of September 11? We have all seen the familiar flag-raising photo of firefighters amongst the rubble in New York[22] or the shadowy image of the Statue of Liberty standing strong in the New York City skyline.[23] Such images worked to fuel the nationalistic furor of the moment while framing patriotism and patriots in and through very specific forms, shapes and hues. I argue though that it is a certain brand of patriotism and a certain kind of citizen that is able to celebrate and fully participate in these nationalistic rituals.

Post-9/11 discourse is steeped with the symbols and language of patriotism, but it is framed in such a way as to manufacture that patriotism in almost dichotomous terms. As evidenced in President Bush's numerous public statements in the aftermath of the event: *If you were not* "with us" *then you were most certainly* "against us" – *If you did not act as* "our friend" *then we would have to consider you* "our enemy."[24] Bush's ongoing *crusade* against evil painted a very stark and very clear picture as to who was evil and who was good (i.e., in the direct aftermath of the events of 9/11, President Bush referred to his campaign to "find and punish" the responsible parties as a "crusade," until advised to change his terminology). Moreover, the fantasy that grew parallel to these dichotomous relations also clearly established the criteria for a certain brand of patriotism: blind allegiance, unwavering, unquestioning support and most notably, mute dissent. To voice your dissent out loud in public was unanimously un-American. Ensuing sanctions were vividly illustrated in the cases of the U.S. country music band the Dixie Chicks[25] and of Sunera Thobani, the Canadian scholar who spoke out against U.S. foreign policy and subsequently suffered immediate and vehement public retaliation.[26] Thobani's case spoke even more to the story of the *other* by the fact that she is a South Asian woman of color. Her critique went beyond the simplified "for" or "against" stances and looked at the realities of U.S. foreign policy. The result of this stance found form in massive public/personal attacks. She was not only attacked for her political and academic agendas, she was also personally attacked and labelled a "hate-monger."[27] Her public dissent apparently stepped beyond the accepted confines of public comment and discussion. In the national space, post-9/11 established no middle ground for dissent and only very limited room for debate. This, as Chomsky says, is a purposeful practice of Western media:

> What the media do[es], in effect, is to take a set of assumptions which express the basic ideas of the propaganda system, whether about the Cold War or the economic system or the "national interest" and so on, and then present a range of debate *within* that framework—so the debate only enhances the strength of the assumptions, ingraining them in people's minds as the entire possible spectrum of opinion there is.[28]

Alongside the growing sanctions to any and all forms of dissent and opposition to this patriotic fantasy, consumerism was encouraged, not only because the economy was going into ruin, but also because shopping was considered patriotic, an investment in your country. Prevalent in overt messages in the news, in subway stations and on car bumper stickers, as well as subliminal messages in the kinds of stories covered, movies made, music played etc., these messages combined to add to our sense of what being American entailed – *or what we were to believe it entailed.* Suddenly, the major broadcasting networks displayed a collective conscience by "toning down the violence" and carefully choosing programming that would bolster public solidarity. Even Hollywood delayed the launch of certain movies deemed in bad taste at the time. What better medicine for America's wounds than the reaffirmation that things were still *good* in the United States? But again, it is important to recognize that public notions of "the good" were/are being scrupulously policed and framed in this version of America's national fantasy.

Nationalistic practices became prevalent and increasingly commonplace in this fantasy. As noted by Hage (2000), nationalists believe they have "managerial capacity over this nationalist space" and this imagined privilege translates into exclusionary practices that further solidify and bolster their self-perceptions as "enactors of the national will within the nation."[29] While the ending to this particular drama was unknown when it began, it was nonetheless unfolding along familiar lines and with a very familiar cast of characters – the perpetrators, the saviors and of course, the victims needing to be saved. All the major American players, framed as the enactors of the will of the American people and of citizens around the globe, sought to preserve the peace of national and international spaces. Bush was portrayed as "standing firm" against terrorism after the attacks. In his avowal that he wanted the terrorists "dead or alive"[30] he invoked imagery of the Old West and the fight for justice with himself as the Old West's sheriff. Good *must* prevail over evil. But importantly, these feelings of entitlement to defend and protect were not the purview of the elite alone. As we have seen, this sense of personal investment extended itself to everyday citizens feeling sanctioned, empowered and justified in protecting their national space. How do these fantasies filter in and through the sociopolitical landscape?

Elite discourses are, as van Dijk contends, "a top-down phenomenon where elites prefigure the narratives that later find popular expression."[31] Just as governments deemed it necessary to tighten borders, travel documentation and airport security, ordinary people acted on the perceived need to protect themselves-sometimes violently (i.e., the number of hate crimes in the United States almost quadrupled in the three months after September 11).[32] Almost justifiably, private spaces, personal freedoms, and individual rights became matters of public concern and interest while at the same time, issues once considered to be public domain became regulated by individual acts. As Berlant states,

> the dominant idea marketed by patriotic traditionalists is of a core nation whose survival depends on personal acts and identities performed in the intimate domains of the quotidian. It is in this sense that the political public sphere has become an intimate public sphere.[33]

This private/public performance of identities was also demonstrated in a seemingly unified notion of what constituted justice. As such, justice and the means to achieve it were presented in very specific ideological forms. Balibar suggests:

> the process of unification (the effectiveness of which can be measured, for example, in collective mobilization in wartime, that is, in the capacity to confront death collectively) presupposes the constitution of a specific ideological form. It must at one and the same time be a mass phenomenon and a phenomenon of individuation.[34]

As the world "united against terrorism" and the American President vowed to rid the world of "evil-doers,"[35] we watched as nations became collectively mobilized under the utilitarian principle of "the greatest good for the greatest number." The development of this conceptual solidarity effectively rekindled the world fantasy that the U.S. was "a country worthy of being loved" and it bolstered the self-reassuring national sentiment that Americans generously care about those outside their borders. The propagation of these collective sentiments and unified actions accomplished two ends: first, it legitimated a mass phenomenon that framed nationalists as justified in defending their public and private spaces against those *others* who were constructed as obstacles, menaces and threats within those spaces. Secondly, it created the illusion that American nationalists in post-9/11 times were also cosmopolitans in that they were acting on behalf of the greater good and thus illustrating their "fairness, kindness and generosity"[37] as world citizens. This reactionary surge in pro-American rhetoric around the globe paralleled a similar reformation back "home" in the Western psyche. Much of the public discourse of the times framed the backdrop and aftermath of 9/11 by asking questions such as: "How could this have happened?" and "Why is hatred of the US so deep?"[38] The underlying principle behind this outcry was the belief that the United States was a virtuous/untouchable nation where contemplation of such acts of war and violence were unfathomable.

Building on the global outpouring of sympathy and support that was directed towards the U.S. after 9/11, the mythos of "hero now victim" became reinforced in both the national and world imaginations. Over and over again in/through the subtle language of the 9/11 coverage, the American responses to the attacks were framed in heroic terms such as *defiant, brave, determined* and *steadfast* while the "perpetrators" were clearly constructed as *cowardly, crazy, fanatical* and *evil*. America was almost universally painted as the hero in these events while those responsible others were, by default, painted as the villains of the piece. These shifts saw Americans no longer viewing themselves solely as world leaders leading the way to a better future. Instead, the notion of "savior" was becoming firmly planted into the nationalist fantasy and Americans were learning to see themselves as "crusaders" in search of justice and truth around the globe. This illusion however, conveniently ignored decades of self-serving U.S. foreign policy that resulted in equally abhorrent acts of violence, exploitation and oppression in other "non-White" countries.

This maintenance of an innocent "why me?" attitude allowed everyday Americans to silence, ignore and absolve U.S. actions and culpability overseas while solidifying their role as heroic victim at home. As the image of the "good White American" became increasingly framed against the image of the "evil Brown Arab/Foreigner," a sense of safety was being constructed through the renewal of racial dichotomies. These "us" and "them" frameworks clearly established who could and who couldn't be trusted – who was and who wasn't dangerous – who is and who isn't American. Nationalism and nationalist practices then, worked in private and public spheres to restore the fantasy disrupted by the events of 9/11. Re-establishing the social order of things (what makes us feel safe, who we know to be dangerous) and restoring our faith in those institutions that maintain it (government, the military, schools) becomes an imperative project for the nation state and its citizens.

Which Citizens?

As discussed above, the gradual restoration and rebuilding of this American fantasy came at a cost; I argue however, that it was at a cost for only some Americans. In exploring the terrain of nationalism and national fantasy it becomes important to ask "who is considered a citizen?" The notions of "citizen" and "citizenship" are not without complication. In fact, while the legal definition and condition of citizenry may be quite transparent, the lived reality of "being" in these contexts is anything but clear or simple. Glenn (2000), for instance, contends that citizenship is legally and socially defined and constructed through the membership, rights, duties and conditions necessary for practice – the result being that throughout history, certain groups have always been marked for unequal participation in and exclusion from the category of "citizen."[39] Similarly, Labelle and Midy (1999) suggest that "citizenship refers to the prerogatives and privileges of citizens vis-à-vis non-citizens, to the power they can legitimately exercise within a given political community arising from their incorporation and their participation in this community."[40] However, in Berlant's (1997) treatment of citizenship, there is no truly public sphere, "no context of communication and debate that makes ordinary citizens feel that they have a common public culture, or influence on a state that holds itself accountable to their opinions, critical or otherwise."[41] The project of conservative political forces then, has been to "[reroute] the critical energies of the emerging political sphere into the sentimental spaces of an amorphous opinion culture, characterized by strong patriotic identification mixed with feelings of practical political powerlessness."[42] The post-9/11 period provided the perfect conditions in/through which this rerouting of national energies might take place. The very powerful feelings of patriotism and solidarity that developed after the attacks, while contrived, allowed vulnerable "citizens" to create some measure of comfort and security at a time when security and comfort were anything *but* real in the everyday American experience. In this moment, these "real" Americans (i.e., those privileged to feel this national connection), became enactors of the national will – choosing how citizenship, belonging and patriotism were to be framed – and ensured that they were/are not constructed in transposable terms. For while Arab and Arab-looking Americans may be citizens in the legal sense of the word, that citizenship is carefully policed and confined to spaces that are not necessarily accessible in relation to what Hage (2000) terms, a "practical nationality."[43] This practical nationality is activated as a form of *cultural capital*[44] where characteristics such as family background, social class, language and skin color all work to limit or expand one's place within the citizenry.

> Elements such as language, looks, cultural practices, a class-derived capacity to intermix with others from different cultures (cosmopolitanism), all of these give the person either some already contextually validated national symbolic capital or the advantages of proximity with the dominant national culture which can quicken the process of cultivating and accumulating national capital.[45]

People of color do not have these forms of cultural capital. In fact, skin color, and *other* cultural markers (e.g., turbans, veils and "foreign"/undesirable accents) are all used to frame certain bodies as less/un-American. Hage (2000) asserts that "no matter how much national capital a "Third World-looking" migrant accumulates, the fact that he or she has acquired it, rather than being born with it, devalues what he or she possesses compared to the "essence" possessed by the national aristocracy."[46] By contrast, nationalists need not acquire this capital because they already possess it. They "only have to be what they are, because all their practices derive from their value from their authors, being the affirmation and the perpetuation of the essence by virtue of which they are performed."[47] Thus, the logic works in reverse for Whites who, through their cultural capital and its *associations*, don't need to be monitored as closely.

Before September 11, there was little widespread public awareness of what it meant to be Muslim, where Afghanistan was or what a burka symbolized. However, after September 11, we know that certain countries of origin are suspect, we know which bodies are to be searched more frequently at airports and other points of entry to the United States and we know who we need to fear. Values and meanings have been deeply inscribed into these perceptions, entrenched by the media and ingrained within our consciousness in a way that supports and bolsters the assumptions we already had of the *other*. Edward Said contends that, "the history of other cultures is non-existent until it erupts in confrontation with the United States"[48] and when such confrontations occur, citizenship is always carefully framed along racial and cultural lines. Wise (2002) notes, for instance, that while White supremacist and militia groups were both watched more closely after the Oklahoma City bombings, it was still only *those specific types* of White people who were then framed as possibly dangerous. In the wake of September 11, however, there was "a general response of fear towards all persons fitting the physical, ethnic, and religious description of the terrorists."[49] Even though these descriptions were interpreted broadly and often mistakenly, they were always made at grave cost to those other peoples now mis-marked and framed as "terrorists." Thus, the insurgent discourse around safety and security worked to reframe and spell out the *legal* definition of citizen while the *social* definition of citizenship in these spaces became increasingly problematic.

In the aftermath of 9/11, border crossings in the form of immigration restrictions and illegal immigration arose as two important and incendiary governance "hotspots."[50] The furor surrounding these issues found voice in the nationalist discourse of "homeland security" and was manifested in tighter restrictions on immigration, more stringent airport checkpoints, a closer scrutiny on the granting of work permits and a drastic increase in racial profiling. These policing practices engaged the evolving discourses of citizenry, security, belonging and border crossings to construct the meanings through which the Western world could identify and understand – immigrant, stranger, foreigner, terrorist – and how they invade, disrupt, threaten and violate the space we call home. As discussed by Balibar (2002):

> external frontiers have to be imagined constantly as a projection and protection
> of an internal collective personality, which each of us carries within ourselves
> and enables us to inhabit the space of the state as a place where we have always
> been—and always will be—"at home."[51]

While America's national ideology has always contained religious signifiers that reference the ever-present connection to a Christian world-view (i.e., "God Bless America," "In God We Trust"), citizenship within this "new" national space became intensely and overtly conflated with religious discourses that bound the American fantasy with righteousness and Christianity. Post-9/11, Americans participated in national prayer services – they "prayed for miracles," they "prayed for the lost and for their families."[52] The end result of this national search for meaning and comfort through Christian convention was/is that crimes against the nation became constructed as sacrilegious and *any* American action or decision could be legitimated as necessary in the fight against evil. Each time the American president speaks about "evil doers" and then asks for God's blessings in the fight against terror, he paints a very clear distinction between his particular *kind* of religious belief/action (Christian/crusader) and those *other* "fanatical" ones (Muslim/terrorist). As suggested by Miles (1989), even before the events of September 11, Christianity had become "the prism through which all knowledge of the world was refracted"[53] and above all else, as suggested by Loomba (1998) it was Islam that functioned as the "predominant binary opposite of and threat to Christianity."[54]

> [T]heological discourse has provided models for the idealization of the nation
> and the sacralization of the state, which makes it possible for a bond of sacrifice
> to be created between individuals, and for the stamp of 'truth' and 'law' to be
> conferred upon the rules of the legal system.[55]

The notion that such "truth" is associated specifically with Christianity is exemplified in the 9/11 example as the events became increasingly framed as both a crime against humanity, and against Christianity itself – a crime, perpetrated by Christianity's polar opposite, Islam. Bernard Lewis, in his historical treatise "The Roots of Muslim Rage" (1990), articulates the differences between Islamic fundamentalism and Judeo-Christianity and clearly foreshadowed a "clash of civilizations" should *either* side be provoked to irrational reactions.[56] That being said, it is important to clarify that these ideas about nationalist practices, citizenship and cultural capital combine to not only construct a kind of universal patriotism (that makes us feel good about ourselves and our nation's "justified," "rational" actions of revenge), but to also produce knowledges that confirm the "deviance" of the *other* while bolstering publicly sanctioned prejudices and discrimination.

Racism "Renewed"

As noted by Dei, Karumanchery and Karumanchery-Luik (2004), because there are a number of "problematics associated with understanding the race concept," we must pay close attention to how meanings are constituted if we want to avoid perpetuating common sense interpretations of the world.[57]

> How, in what contexts and through what processes are racial/racialized meanings acquired? How do such meanings change? How is it that some notions of race emerge as "intrinsically truthful," while others fade? What do these processes tell us about how we are constituted as *other*? What do these processes tell us about how, when and where we are oppressed?[58]

In scrutinizing the social construction of race and racialized identities, it is important to interrogate how our dominant narratives, discourses and "regimes of truth" work to constitute and construct White and non-White bodies. The sign, symbol, text and talk of discursive fields have become increasingly central to the production/reproduction of racism in post-9/11 contexts.

> The manufacturing and molding of the markers and meanings that underlie verbal and social practices of racism largely function through systems of text, talk and communication. So, particularly in contemporary information societies, discourses exist at the very heart of racism.[59]

As discussed earlier, relative to van Dijk's notion of "elite" forms of racism (e.g., political, bureaucratic, corporate, educational and media)[60] it is important to recognize that those who produce such discourses also have the power to enforce/reinforce their validity and scientific status.[61] However, the subtle and implicit mechanisms engaged in this process work to obscure our ability to critically interrogate the politics inherent in the information that we receive through media and other "elite" sources – they simply appear to be real and truthful.

These "regimes of truth" were powerfully active in the media's handling of all things related to 9/11. Looking at CNN's headline webpage image on October 7, 2001, we saw a cloudy, foggy image with a small circle of light. In essence it showed nothing, but the description explained that it was a night-scope view of Kabul. Why are we shown a photo of nothingness when Kabul was a bustling city of 1.4 million people? Why did we not see media representations, footage or interviews with real Afghanis – real people talking, agreeing or dissenting? It becomes much more effective (and perhaps morally reassuring) to present the mysterious illusion and faceless quality of our enemy rather than show actual people – injured, scared or dead by U.S. actions. However vague or ambiguous these images were, when confronted with "the enemy" at "home," America's racialized vision was very clearly articulated and described.

At home, although the enemy may have initially appeared faceless, it was not colorless. The mainstream media didn't need to mention race or color for the public to know which bodies needed extra scrutiny and surveillance. Americans knew their enemies were Brown, and that "Brownness" became almost universally synonymous with fanaticism, inscrutability, foreignness and the suppression of freedom. In fact, while "retaliatory" attacks against innocent people of color (particularly those who looked Arab) exploded in the days immediately following 9/11, those incidents were given scant attention in the media.[62] This retaliation was understood as part of "America's New War"[63] – although the story this war told was not new at all, but an old story made seemingly new. As Stoler states, "one of the most striking features of racism . . . [is] that racism always appears *renewed* and *new* at the same time."[64] When Colin Powell said, "This is a different war"[65] he begged the question: different how? Different in that America was the target? Different in that now we were dealing with what the media dubbed, "A New Breed of Terrorist"?[66] What *old* notions of race and the *other* are alluded to in these messages?

McGreary and Van Biema's (2001) assessment of the "new breed of terrorist" illustrated that they did not fit the typical profile of a suicide terrorist – poor, young, fanatical zealots who were "ignorant of the outside world."[67] In contrast, while the details and histories of the men who piloted the airplanes did little to debunk these stereotypes, the real differences in "breed" arose in that "they did their training right here, among us," again hinting at the incredulity that *we*/Americans could have any part in such evil actions. In fact, the reality of such new internal threats worked to frame certain people as even more "foreign." Again, such media representations effectively widened the divide between those who were considered safe and those who were considered dangerous. How are these messages about *difference* and *breeds* co-opted and enacted in everyday life? What "common sense" forms of knowledge about the *other* do they reinforce? Thobani (2001) asserts that this language is familiar and recognized by people of color around the world; that it is a language rooted in colonial legacy, used to justify colonization by Europe.[68] It is nothing less than racist language that reveals racist beliefs. Hage defines racist beliefs as,

> categories of everyday practice, produced to make practical sense of, and to interact with, the world. Using them, people worry (in a specific, racist way) about their neighbourhood, about walking the streets at night, about where they can do their shopping and what kinds of shops are available to them and so on.[69]

The oppressed are constituted as objects to be positioned and controlled through both micro and macro-power relations. After September 11, we all remember hearing the stories of widespread racial profiling, of particular bodies being stopped on buses and in airports, of mosques and temples being attacked and set aflame, even of murders; of a hyper-alertness and ignitable suspicion existing among people in everyday actions. It was not only that we *couldn't help it*, but also that it appeared *an understandable way to act*. As Razack (2000) states, "if the story of an overtly racist act is transformed into the story of a state forced to defend itself from bodies bent on betraying its trust, then such acts become acceptable and even laudable."[70] I would add that such acts also become "normalized" into the banality of racism in Western contexts.

Normalization involves a complex interplay of processes that work to constitute societal norms of self-discipline, rationality and instrumentalism in specific terms that consequently define the *other* as abnormal.[71] The strength of this normalizing power is that it becomes entrenched as part of our realities and as a part of our consciousness that remains unquestioned. For example, the "preventative war doctrine" recently established by the U.S. government, has become a new norm, unthinkable a few years ago. Similarly, the internment and suppression of Japanese Canadians and Americans during World War II crossed a number of moral and cultural boundaries, but when placed in the context of national security, the government's actions (and the racist vigilante actions of private citizens) were easily sanctioned.[72] As suggested by Chomsky (2003), "such 'norms' are established only when a Western power does something, not when others do. That is part of the deep racism of Western culture, going back through centuries of imperialism and so deep that it is unconscious."[73]

Post-Post-9/11

We are unavoidably side by side. A violent challenge to law and justice in one place has consequences for many other places and can be experienced everywhere.[74]

Now, years after the events of September 11, much of this analysis may seem stale and/or unimportant because we have new things to focus our attention on – new wars to fight, new enemies to hunt and new security measures to enact. However, as researchers, academics and consumers, we have a role to play with regard to the overwhelming and seemingly impenetrable forces and relations of power discussed in these pages. Van Dijk insists that we need to first be cognizant of the power and methods of the media:

> For it is only when we become aware how textual power is wielded, how it rhetorically persuades and seduces, how it produces "common sense", that we can begin to "challenge the dominant ethnic consensus [and] write within an explicitly anti-racist perspective."[75]

Chomsky (2002) suggests that the task is much more impenetrable. He cites four basic observations of the media propaganda model – the fact that the media has been traditionally supported and advocated by elite interests; that its structure has a prior plausibility in that we expect a corporate media to function in particular ways in a capitalist society; that the general public tends to agree that the media are too conformist or subservient; and lastly that this model seems descriptively accurate, that its empirical validity seems to hold up to scrutiny. But, herein lies the point: because the propaganda model *is* valid and the media *does* serve elitist interests, it is for these very reasons that any counter-discussion will be *irrelevant*, "because what it reveals undermines very effective and useful ideological institutions, [it is therefore,] dysfunctional to [the elite culture], and will be *excluded*."[76] This is aptly demonstrated in the anti-war protests that took place around the world in response to the U.S. led invasion of Iraq. Governments still pushed for war and the media-propaganda machine succeeded in substantiating these decisions to the point that the anti-war voice ultimately became irrelevant.

The events of September 11, the backlash that followed and the national fantasy that arose as a result, stand as horrifying and tragic markers of the complex intertwining of power, ideology and racism in a Western context. As advocates for social justice, as educators and as inextricably connected global citizens, we have a responsibility to unravel and expose these underpinnings regardless of the maelstrom in which they reside. We must begin to explore how these normalizing discourses might be questioned, challenged and resisted and in turn, we must work to rupture the production and "renewal" of this racist national fantasy. The answers lie in the choices we make and the tools we use to outwardly or subtly undermine the ideological control systems that work to maintain global inequity and injustice. It is a thin political line we tread when we choose to engage/challenge these relations of power and there is always the possibility of ensuing dangerous consequences. While fearsome, the alternative – those consequences of *inaction* and the possibility of a future unchanged – remain even more so.

Chapter 3

The Ties that Bind

Thinking through the Praxis of Multicultural and Anti-Racism
Education in Canadian Contexts

Carl E. James, PhD
Faculty of Education
York University

Introduction

> The challenge of centering diverse epistemologies within the purview of standard educational practice, requires transcending the notion of multicultural knowledge and "experience" as the ritual of song, dance and food, and instead undertaking a more substantive approach to knowledge production and learning which situates education within a broad global and epistemological frame of reference.
>
> Dei et al., Removing the Margins.[1]

In recent years, probably for more than a decade now, many Canadian educators and school boards have been claiming an anti-racist approach to working with their racially, ethnically and religiously diverse student populations. But insofar as the Canadian multiculturalism discourse is so pervasive – structuring the way in which diversity is understood and taken up in our society – it is questionable whether anti-racism is indeed being practiced in our schools and classrooms. I say questionable because, as I have observed, the "anti-racist" activities and views presented in today's schools are really multicultural education in content, purpose, intent and structure. As such, educators seek to preserve the idea that Canada is a culturally democratic society in which student successes or failures are reflective of individual effort, aptitude, motivation and merit, and divorced from school culture and environment. As such, educators seek to preserve the idea that Canada is a culturally democratic society where individuals' successes or failures in school have little to do with the "culture" of the school, but more with how they apply themselves to their school work. Interestingly, difference is not denied, but it is not seen as playing a crucial role in students' relationship to the school, curriculum materials and to educators. "Difference" is talked about in terms of the ethnicity, race, religion and place of origin that particular bodies represent and the cultures they symbolize. Accordingly, we will sometimes hear such expressions as: "We have a very diversified student population – a united nations" – an indication that students' differences are used as signals that they are from elsewhere, not Canada. There is no stopping to think of the question: different from what or from whom? The thought, then, based on the perspective of multicultural education, is to accommodate – in other words, "celebrate" – the "differences" of students through special events and activities, not incorporate or integrate these differences into the curriculum or the schooling system. So the system, historically structured on Eurocentric, middle class monoculturalism remains intact, leaving little or no space for expressions of students" differences.

The fact is that multicultural education, as framed by the principles of the 1971 federal multicultural policy, operates under the premise that Canada is a culturally neutral society where immigrants (read: ethnic and racial minority group members; people other than English and French) are able to practice and maintain their culture. There is also the logic that when "immigrants" practice their "new," "different" or foreign culture – in relation to their norms, values, customs, languages and/or rituals in the society, tensions between the various cultural groups could result. The aim of multicultural education, therefore, is to promote sensitivity to and recognition of ethno-cultural differences, and assist students in overcoming what the policy refers to as "cultural barriers to full participation" in the society; and in doing so, "promote creative encounters and interchange" among students and parents who are seen as different.[2] To this end, "multicultural" activities such as bringing racial minority "role models" to schools, staging celebrations of Black History Month and Chinese New Year, and expecting some students will be interested in sports and others in mathematics and science,[3] are all considered part of the recognition and facilitation of the students' "culture"; which as many educators would argue, in relation to theirs and the school board's cultural neutrality and color-blindness, has nothing to do with race or racial identification. I refer to this understanding of culture in relation to race, as *race culture discourse*.[4]

In the *race culture discourse*, educators construct racial minority students as "culturally different" not based on their racial "visibility," but on their "observable" behaviors, values, attitudes and aspirations. In other words, consistent with the discourse of multiculturalism, racial minority students' "differences" are understood to be informed by their constructed cultures from elsewhere rather than any societal, structural or institutional inequities due to race, racism and discrimination.[5] Accordingly, their interests and successes in particular school programs and activities are thought to be unrelated to the educational expectations, curriculum content, pedagogical approaches, and performance measures as set out by educators. This conceptualization re-inscribes the notion that the social system is open and meritocratic – that individuals can attain whatever education, occupation and careers they wish through hard work, motivation, abilities, capabilities and by applying themselves. So, in denying that race plays a role in their perceptions and constructions of students, or in claiming color-blindness, educators argue that it is not race or color (not any physical or biological characteristics) but culture that is responsible for the educational performances and outcomes of students. Here culture is understood to be a set of information and observable items and practices that can be identified and communicated, as well as events to be celebrated.[6] As such, expressions of culture are represented in terms of food, "costume" (dress), art, dance, athletic abilities and skills, academic aptitude (e.g., mathematical and science), religious symbols and practices, as well as norms and values governing such things as academic and/or athletic interests and aspirations, motivation to talk in class, and willingness to comply with the rules of schooling. Indeed, as Dion argues with reference to Aboriginals:

> Within the rubric of multicultural education, festivals, religious celebrations, language and customs become the object of dialogue, writing, and research. Students may be asked to participate in a multicultural feast, or in dancing, singing or other culture specific activities. The multicultural discourse sets the culture of aboriginal people as something distinct. . . . It offers non-Aboriginal students the position of respectful admirer. Teacher and students interested in appreciating difference are not required to confront the significance of colonization. . . . Nor does this approach contribute to students questioning the hegemonic voices of dominant ideology. The school books fail to recognize social struggle or class conflict, and instead reinforce a number of myths regarding the nature of political, economic and social life.[7]

If educators are to effectively address the limitations of multicultural education which communicates to students who they are and determines their relationship to the school and the power structure of the society, then they must necessarily have an analysis of students' differences in relation to structural inequities based on race and racism, and of how these operate in the lives of students: privileging some while disadvantaging others.[8] Furthermore, in the context of today's education system, educators must also be *critical participants*, conscious of their own race and/or class privileges, and critically reflecting on (or interrogating) their school activities, curriculum materials, cultural events, and pedagogical approaches in ways that will bring students to a critical understanding and consciousness of their location in the education system in relation to the social power structure thus enabling (or empowering) them to become full participants in their education process.[9]

In this paper, I explore the extent to which these principles are evident in the ideas and practices of a class of teacher candidates with whom I worked some six years ago.[10] Many of the participants tended to believe that they were "ready" to experience the diversity that awaited them in what some called the "inner city" community. In this regard, many understood that their work in such schools required them to be aware of and responsive to the differences and diversity of their students. In doing so, while some argued that their students' needs, interests and aspirations can best be served from a multicultural education approach, others argued for an antiracism education approach. Their respective email exchanges demonstrate the dialogue that might ensue between teachers as they attempt to support their students in a school system informed by the discourse of multiculturalism. The exchanges also provide insights into the tensions that might arise as teachers argue for inclusive education. I start by discussing the participants' respective definitions/interpretations of multicultural and antiracism education and proceed to discuss their theorizations of tolerance and acceptance of students' differences in their attempts to engage in inclusive and equitable teaching. This is followed by a discussion of participants' ideas about celebrations such as Black History Month and Chinese New Year – celebrations upon which they were asked to reflect in terms of what these events contribute to inclusivity and equity. I conclude with reference to the idea of the bind in which teachers find themselves due to the power of the multiculturalism discourse.

Perspectives on Multicultural and Anti-Racism Education

A key aspect of inclusive teaching is to make the curriculum content and pedagogical approaches relevant to the interests and needs of all students.[11] This requires teachers to not only be familiar with or have some understanding of the identities and lived experiences of students within their communities, but also a consciousness of their perspectives, and an awareness of the various positionalities that they bring to the teaching and learning process. For this reason, teacher candidates were asked to take note of the geography and demography of the students' communities, as well as their respective identities. Interestingly, while the usual complications and contradictions arose during our discussions of ethnicity and class, it was the "race-talk" around racial identification and "belonging" that proved the most problematic – particularly for many of the White, and to a lesser extent, some minority teacher candidates.[12] In taking up these topics, we repeatedly returned to the question of perspective: Was multicultural or anti-racism education informing the way we were interpreting and engaging with issues of diversity in terms of ethnicity, race, gender and class identifications?[13] The narratives were most revealing.

For the most part, multicultural education was understood to be the more inclusive of the two approaches to education. Some, like Alena,[14] viewed it "as allowing full development of abilities in all children regardless of their differences . . . [which] may include racial, ethnic, gender, class stratification, etc." As such in the tradition of meritocracy, it was suggested that in a multicultural education program, students' outcomes are not affected or limited by their differences associated with culture based on ethnicity, race, gender and/or class. Alena's statement is instructive:

> I strongly feel that multicultural education should not be taught or implemented just for minority students. I believe that it is just as important for White students to develop a consciousness of ethnicity. White students, too, must learn about the cultures of other students. It bothers me to hear or read about students who were too ashamed and afraid to show the world their "true" identities. They felt they were not good enough to be part of the White Anglo-Saxon society.[15]

In this conceptualization, Alena, like other participants, made an attempt to recognize the complexity of culture and identification, hence going beyond the usual understanding of multicultural education with its primary focus on ethnic minority culture. But at the same time, we still see that there must be a centrality to the ethnic cultures of minoritized Canadians – they must be represented and learned about. Often culture, specifically that of minority groups, is conflated or used interchangeably with ethnicity and race, and seen as something material and observable.[16] Missing from Alena's understanding is the idea that multicultural education operates in a context that is structured by White Anglo-Saxon culture, hence White students are well aware or already conscious of their race and related power and privileges. And it is not that minority students are "ashamed" to show their "true" identity (of course, no such thing exists), but it is that space is not provided for them to do so because of such barriers as racism, ethnocentrism and discrimination. Furthermore, as Lisa explains, when the experiences or works of minority group members are referenced in school settings, they are presented as separate or "outside of the mainstream."

> In [the high school] library, there is a shelf off to the side which is dedicated to multi-cultural literature. On this shelf, you will find books by non-white authors. My question regarding this is: If the literature on this shelf is supposed to be multi-cultural, shouldn't white authors be included too? I mean the very art of isolating non-white authors brings with it the connotation that non-white authors can only be viewed outside of the mainstream while emphasizing the assertion that non-white authors do not and can not belong to the literary canon. Well, if this is the case, I suggest we take the necessary steps to change the canon so that non-white authors do not continue to be shelved in isolation.[17]

This display of "multicultural" books illustrates how the practice of multicultural education tends to be informed by a multicultural ideology of separating out bodies and their literature from the "mainstream." This categorization of these authors' books would suggest a similarity or commonality among them, and a reading that their works are about the same subject matter – *other* Canadians. Their works, therefore, set them apart from those Canadian authors whose writings are "varied" and multidisciplinary, and are categorized accordingly. Picking up on the importance of including the books of minority authors, and calling attention to the complexity and diversity that is missed in the ways such books are categorized, Carmen posted this response to Lisa:

> I agree with you that it's about time all literature was integrated in the canon— when I'm choosing a book to use in the class I'm looking at various categories— themes usually—and all books need to be evaluated for inclusiveness—I'd hate to see a shelf for males and a shelf for females. And just because it's "multicultural" does not make the book suitable. For example my class is doing a novel study of Sword of Egypt at the moment—maybe it was chosen as a multicultural book, but as I see it, it glorifies violence, portrays Bedouins as smelly and evil, Syrians as curly-haired and evil, slaves as stupid, merchants as stupid and self-serving, and females can only position themselves in the text as slaves or members of a harem. And then I looked at the author, and guess what, it was a white male who wrote it. Categorizing literature like this does not address the real issues in what books are used/recommended—that of good quality and inclusive literature.[18]

Lisa, Carmen and several others challenged what constitutes "multicultural books" and the uncritical way in which they are displayed and used in the school system. Their point of reference is noteworthy. Carmen, an Anglo-Canadian, makes reference to gender, indeed, an easy means of identifying with the issue. But she went on to suggest that it is not only a matter of having "multicultural books"; the content and author must also be critically examined. Lisa, an African-Canadian, was concerned with how non-White authors are segregated and categorized. She seemed to suggest that being categorized as "outside the mainstream" and hence not part of "the literary canons," non-White authors are likely to remain outsiders.[19] In this regard, multicultural education has done little to bring non-Whites into the mainstream; something that seems to be implied in Lisa's suggestion that "we [should] take the necessary steps to change the canon." This statement could also be interpreted as an appeal, borne out of her experience and desire for a space where voices like hers can be heard, and where voices of minority group members are not homogenized and trivialized. This point was forcefully articulated about two weeks later in Lisa's follow-up posting:

> Multicultural should be inclusive, not a way of excluding Black authors. So all of the authors and all of their respective subject matters should be included. I mean to have Black authors, simply because they're Black without paying any regard to the subject matter of the book is foolish. Not all Blacks are the same, they don't all have the same thing to say, so why categorize or segregate them as multicultural? I think that by doing that, you trivialize their literature, putting them to one side as if it's some amazing feat that they wrote something.[20]

For both Lisa and Carmen, multicultural programs must do more than merely reposition books and other learning materials if they are to actually address and rupture the status quo. As demonstrated, educational programs and curricula need to integrate[21] the knowledges, traditions and experiences of minoritized students if their diasporic complexities and lived realities are to be truly engaged. On this point, Tam, with reference to Dudley-Marling (1997), argued that teachers should get to "know" their students and not just assume that they are "all the same" because they are minority members or because they might have immigrated from particular parts of the world. In discussing a common error made by teachers in the implementation of "multicultural" programs, Tam critiques the commonly accepted multicultural approach of seeking to support minoritized students through the use of class materials that "match" the students' perceived cultural backgrounds. As Tam pointed out, this practice is highly problematic because the tendency to homogenize group members is based on generalized assumptions that can lead to the "disempowerment" of the minority student. It could also be a form of patronization or tokenism.[22]

Arguing that multicultural education is not able to "address the problematic issues" of curriculum, difference and diversity, Sabra wrote that anti-racism offers a "more progressive" approach to the issues. She said that it is an approach that can "instill in the minds of children" the ability to critically think, question and challenge stereotypes that they might face in educational literature and curriculum. And unlike multicultural literature, anti-racism literature does not present stereotypes or "picture-perfect, 'colorful' images of what goes on" in the communities of "people of color." She went on to identify the salience of race and the effects of racism in the educational experiences of students, particularly, students of color.

> To me, anti-racist education is not necessarily about changing the images of people of color in literature, for example. Rather I think anti-racist education is about consistently identifying, challenging and naming racism in literature or in curriculum, it is important that it be exposed. . . . Through discussions, students can explore what racism can do to people. I think it is very crucial to always look at the immediate context, which for students is the school. If students can identify racism that surrounds them, are aware of racism's dangers, are encouraged to discuss what to do about it, are given the means to tackle the problem on school grounds, they would learn the real essence of what anti-racism is—a principle and not a hand-out by the board.[23]

Continuing from Sabra's discussion around the saliency of race, Wing-Chuan asked: "What is my race?" He recalled that in our introductory discussions, some teacher candidates had identified themselves as White, but because the term did not apply to him, he preferred to think of himself as "part of the human race." To this, Mohan responded:

> That's nice, but let's not neglect the historical and social implications of race which have constructed stereotypes and economic oppression. For many, it is easy (and perhaps simplistic) to say that they are members of the human race. Race as a social construct is unfortunately not about how we define ourselves but how colonialism, slavery, and immigration have determined the relations between various groups that fall into categories of race. As much as we would like to define race on our own terms, we live in a world that has defined race for us, long before our individual existences here. While racial self definition is important in reconstructing problematic notions of race which currently exist, it is a futile exercise to do so without deconstructing race and therein confronting the history and reality which surrounds these ideas.[24]

Arguing from an anti-racism perspective, Mohan explained that identification is not only about how individuals choose – to the extent that they can – to identify themselves, but how the social structure has historically and politically operated to construct and position individuals based on their physical and biological characteristics. In fact, Mohan repeatedly attempted to drive this point home in a number of on-line postings. Arguing that race, racial identification and race privilege must be understood and "confronted" in relation to "historical contexts" and the contextuality of experience, Mohan quite cogently illustrated several of the hidden pitfalls faced by minoritized students. He went on to say:

> Unfortunately we as educators have fallen victim to idealism of a political climate in which entire histories of racism, social, gendered and economic oppression have been neatly glossed over by words such as multiculturalism and equality. How can we possibly promote equality when it has in the past and present never even existed? It seems ludicrous that we can promote "equality" without even acknowledging or addressing the very inequality that is and has been so rampant in our society. Deconstructing race or racism therefore lies in looking at

the problems of history and our society, without patronizing or sheltering our students from the real world. If school is so idealistic in promoting terms such as equality and multiculturalism while neglecting to address our historical and contemporary reality of race, sex and class based oppression, how can we in good conscience stand by and say that we are "educating" our students and how can we in reality call ourselves "teachers"?[25]

Mohan, like Sabra and others, raised many important issues and questions with which teachers struggle. Indeed, racism is a crucial issue that teachers must confront and address if they are to provide students with an education that is relevant to their circumstances and experiences. Anti-racism education, as participants logically reasoned, provided the understanding that was necessary for them to effectively address the structures – race, gender, class and ethnicity – that operated to limit the educational opportunities and possibilities of students in the area.

Engaging "Difference"
– A matter of Tolerance or Acceptance?

As class participants discussed their interpretations of the challenges and possibilities surrounding multicultural and anti-racism education, Helen raised the issue of tolerance and acceptance. In her brief statement, which was reflective of the multicultural discourse, she remarked that we should not be so disapproving of "tolerance" for one does not have to like a person to tolerate him or her.[26] Shortly afterwards, Sabra replied:

> The difference between tolerance and acceptance is that tolerance is like saying 'fine, be yourself. I may not like it, but I'll put up with you." On the other hand, acceptance says "I will respect you for who you are," end of discussion. I think acceptance is far more welcoming of a person than is tolerance. A child will have a significantly more positive self-image in a class that accepts and makes him or her feel valuable. In turn a child will do better in school, and will be able to resist ignorance. . . . Tolerance burdens the child of colour, for example, making him or her feel that he or she is imposing a sacrifice on the individual who is doing the tolerating.[27]

In contrast, Juan did not see tolerance and acceptance as mutually exclusive, nor did he believe that tolerance was necessarily a negative thing. Juan theorized that acceptance includes tolerance, because acceptance necessitates that we must first acknowledge the existence and tolerate the presence of an individual or group before we formulate what we like or dislike about them. Therefore, tolerance, Juan suggests, is a step before an individual begins to accept another person.

> I don't necessarily believe that every time the word tolerance is used, it is with a negative connotation. I'm more likely to say it is mostly used with a conformist attitude. Just think of when one stops tolerating. We usually say "I'm not tolerating this anymore!" in reference to a behaviour. . . . In that context, we stop

tolerating because we can't accept something anymore. If that is the case, then by tolerating we are also accepting. Now in my opinion, accepting can also mean agreeing and even embracing. . . . I therefore think that before one can tolerate something, one must acknowledge what it is that one dislikes (acknowledging existence). That's a very low stage towards acceptance. Sure, we can all tolerate, but tolerating . . . can break at any time. Now acceptance means agreeing to make that conscious effort to work out differences, even if the solution is as simple and complicated as "Let me be. I'll let you be."[28]

Juan went on to suggest that it is selfish individualism, and fear of confronting and acknowledging our differences that prevents people from accepting each other:

The problem then rises in our selfishness, because "letting be," can also mean "being less." It would be nice if we could all accept each other for who and what we are. However, not to be pessimistic but a realist, I must add that the only way to achieve this state is by giving up from within. Unfortunately, this state is utopia. People do not want to admit that everything starts with the person in the mirror, and therefore our problems continue. The real problem is imbalance where balance is required. Everybody talks but no one acts. If we could acknowledge our differences, tolerate them, and accept them also accepting the fact that this works both ways, everything would be nice. However, we tend to think that we are the ones who acknowledge, tolerate and accept, without remembering that we are also acknowledged, tolerated and sometimes, I think . . . also accepted.[29]

While Juan went on to make the point that tolerance carries a subtle, and sometimes blatant assumption/expectation that the marginalized will conform to the mainstream schema, his perspective on the linkages that run between acceptance and tolerance appear to suffer from one major conceptual flaw – the analysis seems to sidestep how applications of power and privilege work to fundamentally mediate the interactions between subjects. In fact, several participants questioned Juan's notion of acceptance. For example, Sabrina asserted that within the context of our stratified society, acceptance might not be the best word to express how we engage with differences among people. Her concern was who had the power to tolerate, who had the power to grant acceptance, and on what basis any such acceptance would be decided? Ultimately, Sabrina and a number of other teacher candidates recognized and asserted that relationships based on tolerance are at best, tenuous.

As noted by Karumanchery (2003), the voice of those in positions of power and privilege tell us what ordinary is, what normal is and that normalcy is always infused and framed through their freedom and sense of safety. We are blinded to the reality that tolerance, as a "multicultural strategy," functions through applications of power that are set within very specific hierarchical structures – structures that are both scrupulously policed and disguised by a "normalizing gaze."[30] Engaging the complexity of these issues, Sabrina is clear in her analysis that with one group having superiority over another, chances are that the expectations and values of those in power will become the basis by which acceptance is decided or granted. Still, even as several other students attempted to ground the discussions within an analysis of power relations – reminding the class of the role of structures in determining and informing relationships between differentially positioned people and groups – the critical anti-racist perspective seemed lost to a number of the class members who continued to make "the individual" the primary, and usually, the only focus of analysis.

Several students made efforts to forestall the discussions all together. Wally, for instance, who had earlier articulated in class that this discussion of terms was merely "about semantics," noted: "I don't believe that human nature, on a wide spread scale, has the ability to unconditionally accept difference. [Humans] only have the ability to politely deal with it."[31] This notion of a "flawed human capacity" inhibiting the individual capacity to mediate difference, is problematic on a number of levels: (a) it overlooks social relations of power; (b) it leaves systemic and structural features of difference and marginalization unrecognized and unaddressed; (c) it minimizes the agency of individuals to act upon thoe structures and relations; and (d) it effectively denies the validity of the work. It is fundamentally important that we engage such discussions as far more than simplistic semantic exercises. As Lori put forth, "Don't our actions depend on the way we interpret the semantics?"[32]

Recognizing the importance of the work being done in and through such discussions, Carmen crystallized some of the most important points being taken up:

> Words are very powerful. They play a significant role in the formation of our thoughts and perceptions and they drive actions. Words are not simply a series of letters strung together, they are tools for communication, and at times, such as in the case of multiculturalism, they can be weapons that inflict a great deal of harm upon those who have been labeled as "inferior."

> Words can be manipulated and applied to achieve any purpose, (e.g. the oppression of underprivileged groups). Thus I think that it is very beneficial and necessary to have discussions which analyze and uncover the meanings associated with these seemingly harmless semantic structures. I for one, would rather be "accepted" and "understood" than simply "tolerated."[33]

Carmen continued to say that in addition to the word understanding, she would add the word "respect" – a word which in Latin meant "to look again, (to *re* – again; *spect* – look)." "Perhaps," she said, "this is where we need to start. We need to 'look again' at what our views and perceptions are about multicultural education and society, and at the words that have been and are being used to define and frame these perspectives."[34] Again, despite the efforts of Carmen and others to call for a closer scrutiny of how multicultural discourse has been framed within the context of today's sociopolitical structures and relations of power, many of the teacher-candidates continued to place a concerted emphasis on interpretations of the individual without interrogating the dilemmas that arise in such Cartesian approaches to understanding human activity and agency.[35]

Looking to understand what was expected of them as educators, many of the teacher-candidates wanted to explore how they might apply what we were talking about to students in their classrooms. For many, the need to understand the discussions at a pragmatic level seriously forestalled their efforts to think abstractly and in relational terms. Helen's thoughts on the importance of educating past differences illustrates this point well:

[T]he solution is education. Many children practice prejudice because it is an already existing practice, sometimes they don't even know why, or where they have even found these feelings of hatred. We, as teachers, need to educate our children on diversity. We need to show them that all individuals, regardless of race, colour, culture, or class are just that, individuals. We all feel the same things, and in essence we all strive for the similar goals. . . . It is the meshing of cultures races, and classes that will benefit society, the idea that we may give each other something which the other lacks.[36]

In suggesting that the solution to "prejudice" and "hatred" might be found in educational efforts at attitudinal change, Helen inadvertently provides a clear illustration of how multicultural approaches to reform fail to engage the sociopolitical contexts at play. Similarly, Mary suggests that "If we give everyone an equal chance to get to know each other, then maybe we can get beyond what we see on the outside, and learn to value what matters – what is on the inside."[37] These and other such statements about the healing power of cultural interchange, and the need to understand our innate similarities, are very much reflective of multiculturalism's inability/refusal to accept that a social pathology permeates and mediates these relations.[38] Although the class' discussions were consistently informed by the critical perspectives of Sabra, Carmen and others, many participants remained committed to the belief that their efforts should still be concentrated at the individual level.[39] In spite of all arguments detailing the sociopolitical and structural factors involved, the online discussions revealed that many of the participants had, and continued to engage a deep-seated belief in multiculturalism's common sense discourse. Ultimately, because multiculturalism and racism operate from an intersecting power base that defines "normalcy" in relation to the concepts of individuality and merit, it makes sense that those ensconced within mainstream racist frameworks would find themselves most comfortable working within multicultural paradigms of theory and practice. Simply put, in the absence of a critical lens, multiculturalism will remain more than just accessible – it will remain the preferred framework for the delivery of "culturally neutral" education and pedagogy.

Additive Measures and Celebratory Approaches to Inclusion

As February approached, our attention turned to discussing the relevance and place of Black History Month in school programs, and moreover, like African-Canadian scholar and literary writer, Althea Prince (1996), we found ourselves asking whether the observance of the month was just a "great Canadian multicultural myth?"[40] Many participants argued that given the Eurocentricity of the existing curriculum, it was the least that schools and educators could do to make "students, teachers, parents and the community aware of the great contributions and past sufferings of Black people."[41] Then again, others students like Betty and Manjit felt that the celebration of Black History in such a fashion was definitely a positive step. Betty saw such celebrations as a positive approach that would serve to raise awareness of the long and diverse history of African people as well as their accomplishments,[42] and similarly, Manjit suggested that having Black History Month would provide opportunities to invite "role models" into schools.[43] That being said, while no one generally disagreed with observing the month, the postings reflected much ambivalence.

On the one hand, several students noted that there were numerous benefits to opening such celebratory opportunities and dialogue. After all, if nothing else, Black History Month recognizes and commemorates the contributions of Black peoples, both to North American societies and to the world.[44] Moreover, such celebrations also provide an opportunity to present "successful Black role models," especially to Black youth who are considered "at risk" and need to be "put right" and supported by other Blacks.[45] Then again, such "time-limited" celebrations clearly serve to establish that true inclusion is only a multicultural myth. Frank spoke to this dilemma:

> Black History Month is good because it recognizes those cultures who contributed greatly to our country's make up (in every way). I think students deserve to know more, and should know more, than the strong Eurocentric voice. . . . This would be an excellent time to introduce this. On the other hand, I feel that Black History Month, with the schools, isn't the best idea in that it promotes a type of segregation, subtle. By doing this you bring light to only a certain set of people but omit others (all of which are important just as well). I don't want to see such segregation within the schools (even if you are promoting a positive celebration). I would like to see an inclusiveness of all cultures within the school, and a celebration of all the cultures.[46]

Much like the ambivalence voiced in the mainstream whenever the topic of racial and ethnic specific celebrations are broached, many participants articulated both support for, and discomfort with, the celebration of the month. In fact, there was a very pointed undercurrent of anxiety and tension that mediated the entire discussion. Many of the students expressed very real concerns around designating a month, or any specific time to any particular group. Like Frank, above, many feared that such measures might ultimately prove segregationist – not only between Blacks and Whites, but between Blacks and other minoritized groups. Echoing these concerns, a number of participants stressed their desire to be inclusive.

> Our job as teachers should not be to celebrate one culture…but to include every culture to promote diversity in Canadian culture.[47]

> What happens to the other cultures that miss out on their heritage?[48]

Importantly, building on these inclusive tenets, several participants also voiced a very serious concern that celebratory efforts of this nature might prove to "trivialize the Black culture and make it seem that they only count one time of the year."[49] Similarly, others were wary of creating a context in and through which Black people's contributions might be identified as outside of what is common place.[50]

Most interestingly, the multicultural discourse remained so persuasive throughout our discussions that participants seemed to pay little or no attention to (or failed to recognize) how the diversity and complexity of the Black population also mediated the issues at stake.

In picking up on this tendency to homogenize and generalize, Norma made the point that the so-called Black activities "may not necessarily reflect the needs of the students being represented." She continued:

> I had a teacher who believed that by placing posters of certain black entertainers [and] celebrities, that somehow I would feel more engaged within my learning. Unfortunately, the images and posters further alienated me, because I did not associate myself with the images presented. Do all blacks, Chinese, Portuguese, Italians share the same identity? Why then do teachers feel that because they have slapped on a cultural representation of a student's culture that they will somehow feel engaged. Without understanding, these practices can be detrimental.[51]

Building on Norma's argument, some participants, like Laura, began to voice the concern that designating a month for any particular group might only increase their sense of alienation by singling them out and making them the voice of the many oppressed.[52] Several students felt that such facile programs were ultimately counterproductive to the inclusive project, and that rather than supporting and empowering administrators and educators to reflect on the relationship between the educational structure, curriculum and the diverse needs and interests of their students, they were actually serving to further obfuscate the real issues involved. After all, as suggested by Laura, if all cultures were celebrated all year long, we might actually proactively decrease the threat of alienating any one particular culture.[53]

Again, despite these protracted and animated discussions, many of the participants continued to minimize and/or sidestep the critical perspectives brought into the online debates. For instance, little consideration was given to Rina when she commented on the European bias of the curriculum. Focusing on the Eurocentrism evidenced in "core subjects such as Math, English or Science,"[54] Rina explained that these normalized perspectives:

> [H]ave been so engraved in us that we don't even realize our ignorance of other cultural perspectives. That is why I think Black History Month is so important, not only to Black students but to other coloured students, because it allows students to see that their culture is acknowledged and hence relevant. The next step however, is to be able to incorporate several cultural perspectives into our curriculum so that ALL students get a more complete understanding of what they need to learn.[55]

This idea of recognizing and including (as opposed to integrating, *see footnote 21*) "other cultures" into the curriculum seemed a stumbling block for a number of the participants. In fact, several of the students wrongly conflated Rina's assertions with the notions of simply expanding Black History Month to incorporate other ethnic and racial celebrations. Falling into this line of reasoning, Nancy raised the question, "If we are to incorporate all cultures into Black History Month, then wouldn't that mean it could no longer be called Black History Month?"[56] Others, in an effort to demonstrate their commitment to democracy and the inclusion of "other cultures" in their teaching, mentioned their own personal efforts to expand celebratory programs to include other cultures. For instance, Betty wrote that she had introduced Chinese New Year to her grade two class. Her activities included:

[L]istening and responding to the story of "Lion Dancer" by Ernie Wan; (2) writing to share how they [the students] celebrate the new year in their culture; (3) reading recipes and making sweet rice balls (one of the types of dessert that people eat during Chinese New year; and (4) making wall hangers with a good-luck message both in Chinese characters and English translation.[57]

In reflecting on how the activities were received, Betty said that almost all of her students enthusiastically participated and shared the ways in which they celebrated new years. "Better still," she continued, "some Chinese students who are usually quiet and shy shared how they like the lion/dragon dance, the red envelopes, sweet rice balls, as they can relate the story to their real life experience. It was an enjoyable learning experience for the students as well as for myself." In response to this posting Wing-Chuan volunteered that he too had similar activities in his class. His students discussed the themes and symbols of fortune, good luck and prosperity; and for art, they made Dragon faces. "They had lots of fun with the vibrant colours on their Dragon faces, and they even learned about symmetry! Integration is great!"[58]

While recognizing that such "culturally celebratory" activities would be fun and interesting for the students, several participants had some issues with these simple multicultural approaches to inclusion. Sabra for instance, acknowledged the receptivity of the students, complemented Betty for her efforts, and went on to say:

> In our efforts to integrate cultural celebrations . . . as part of the curriculum, we must be careful of our approach. For example, we should not only include cultural celebrations that are fun or are considered entertaining. I think that the purpose of integration is to let our students see themselves in the curriculum in the classroom, which [Betty] feels happened. This is great! I truly feel that "understanding" is what is important. . . . Often times, the information we find in books about different cultural groups will not apply to the students in our classrooms, even if they may come from the same country. If I were going to make the class reflective of the students, I would have to be educated by the families and communities to which these students belong, in addition to appropriate written materials. After all, the culture of students is not isolated from their location in Toronto, the . . . school community, in their family. . . . Issues are important. In my high school, people had the chance to learn about Chinese New Year celebrations, Diwali, Kwanzaa and other celebrations. Yet important issues like identity, generation gaps with parents, racism on and off school grounds were never addressed. Don't these issues shape our culture? What we choose to teach our students should reflect the evolving of the culture in Canada.[59]

Here Sabra effectively demonstrates that the recognition of ethno-racial minority students should not simply be about cultural celebrations and entertainment but also, and more importantly, about the realities of their lives in Canada where race and racism affect their educational, social and cultural existence. So whether it is Black History Month or Chinese New Year activities, educators need to be conscious of the ways in which the existing cultural approaches homogenize and essentialize certain bodies. Ultimately, it is fundamentally important that educators and administrators recognize and understand how their cultural practices, as Norma said, can be "detrimental" to a students' self-worth. The fact is, contrary to what Wing-Chuan claimed, integration is not about simply bringing in or getting acquainted with some stable or fixed notion of culture from elsewhere that is believed to be related to students' ethnic, racial and regional origin. Such a culturalist approach leaves unacknowledged the ways in which race and racism structure students' lived cultural experiences as well as their school participation and educational outcomes. Participants needed to be critical; and as anti-racist theorists have long advocated, we need to further interrogate how our European-informed additive approaches to education and educational reform effectively forestall the advance of inclusivity and equity in Canadian schooling.[60]

Conclusion: The Ties that Bind

In light of the online debates on multicultural and anti-racism education that were taking place, Sheva posed this question to the class: "Is multicultural education . . . achieving its purpose which is to educate and empower all students (both minority and majority group members), or is it merely emphasizing a celebration of differences among people in our society?"[61] In response, while many of the students agreed that multicultural education, as implemented in the schools, was "unable to educate and empower ALL students,"[62] they also felt that the multicultural approach would help to address the issues and needs of the students in the schools in which they were practice-teaching. Again, despite the criticisms and practical dilemmas raised in our discussions, a great number of teacher-candidates continued to look past multiculturalism's profound deficiencies. For instance, Kim felt:

> It may not have achieved its ultimate purpose, but what has occurred has definitely made a difference. Imagine if there had been no acknowledgement of the need for multicultural education, most people would not even have known that they were being racist, biased and discriminatory. Things can only get better as we continue to raise everyone's awareness and educate the next generation.[63]

In conceptualizing racism as based primarily in ignorance, Kim and others felt that the systemic marginalization of racialized students could be dealt with, if not overcome, through education and inter-group interactions through cultural events and celebrations. Even though this multicultural approach has been used for years with little success, some participants, like Kerri, saw it as an "ideal." While I disagree with this suggestion, I wonder about the possible merits of Kerri's argument, that naïveté, ignorance, guilt and cowardice are all part of educators' condition, and the main reason for their resistance to changing the status quo and having an inclusive "school atmosphere."

Here is how Kerri articulated this point.

> This [ideal] demands diversity and inclusion to be represented in texts, teachers, school agendas and in community effort. Big changes involve commitment and courage and perseverance. The alternative of accepting the status quo and assigning responsibility for cultural education and acceptance to others (for acceptance

must begin with one's self) would do little and only the naïve or ignorant would deny feelings of guilt in such an act of cowardice.[64]

Reflected in many of these teacher candidates' exchanges is the liberal reformist notion that educational change is possible within the existing structure in which the students they teach are failing to succeed educationally and socially. Their focus of analysis is the individual student, and in so doing, they fail to recognize the links between the micro-dynamics of the classroom and the structural (institutional and societal) inequality and differential social power outside of school.[65] Their understanding of what it would take to have a democratic, inclusive and equitable classroom curriculum in which their teaching and learning is responsive to the needs, interests and aspirations of their diverse student population, is heavily structured by the multicultural discourse in which difference is tolerated and celebrated; for to really accept difference might mean changing the status quo which has afforded many of them the privileges that they have come to enjoy. Interestingly, even as some of the class participants call for change, as Kerri did, the power of the multicultural discourse is evident. For example, while Kerri admits that inclusivity is an important goal, she calls it "an ideal" – something to strive for; a hope or intension which might or might not be attained or materialize. This does not give a sense of immediacy.

Conversely, anti-racism education engages race as a social construct and ensures that racial inequities are made visible and salient in any discussion of inclusivity and educational reform. More than merely difficult to conceptualize and apply to their work, anti-racism stands as somewhat threatening to these teacher-candidates who comfortably rely on color-blind approaches to schooling that allow them to deny their personal implication in the ongoing production and reproduction of social inequities. Accepting anti-racism education requires that these soon-to-be-educators must recognize that power differentials based on race, class, gender, ethnicity, sexuality and other characteristics all mediate the schooling experience of their soon-to-be-students. Moreover, they must be willing to question and interrogate the dominant school culture which functions to legitimize the interests and values of the dominant group, while racializing and marginalizing minoritized students.

Surely, if these teacher-candidates are to develop an inclusive and equitable pedagogy, they will have to be courageous, as Kerri suggested, and recognize as well as confront their ambivalence about difference. This ambivalence, informed by the multicultural discourse and evident through cultural celebrations and tolerance over acceptance, has operated to stifle critical examinations and the disentanglement of multicultural education from its historical and liberal ideological roots. It is possible that the ambivalence, fears and resistance evident in the participants' comments is reflective of the difficulties they have in coming to terms with what the anti-racism requires and expects of them. Their tie to the liberal multicultural ideology so obscures their view of education as color-blind, meritocratic and democratic that it is difficult for them to accept fully the structural argument of anti-racism which asserts that racism and oppression are not only embedded in our education system but in the very fabric of our stratified society. It is this tie to the promise of multicultural education that likely prevents them from the practice of the hard work of anti-racism education, even though they might see anti-racism as relevant and appropriate to fulfilling their own, and their students, needs and expectations. It seems to remain an ideal – an ideal that holds promise for the future if not the present.

In moving forward then, teacher-candidates and teachers will have to acknowledge, contextualize and engage their own privileged and oppressed social positionings in the face of multicultural discourse's banal hold on contemporary educational frameworks. If today's educators, and in particular, classroom teachers who work in heterogeneous communities, continue to provide educational programs without seeking to implement systemic changes, then little will be accomplished in their attempts to meet the needs, interests and aspirations of today's diverse and diasporic students. Ultimately, in today's Canadian contexts, education that addresses issues of diversity must critically challenge entrenched multicultural ideology and provide marginalized students with the anti-racism knowledge and skills to make their schooling related and relevant to their social and political experiences.

Chapter 4

Spectacles of Race
and Pedagogies of Denial
Anti-Black Racist Pedagogy Under the Reign of Neoliberalism

Henry A. Giroux, Ph.D.
Department of Curriculum and Instruction
Pennsylvania State University

Introduction

Race relations in the United States have changed considerably since W. E. B. Du Bois famously predicted in "The Souls of Black Folk" that "the problem of the 20th century is the problem of the color line."[1] This is not to suggest that race has declined in significance, or that the racial conditions, ideologies and practices that provided the context for Du Bois's prophecy have been overcome as much as to suggest that they have been transformed, mutated and recycled into new and often more covert modes of expression.[2] Du Bois recognized that the color line was not fixed – its forms of expression changed over time, as a response to different contexts and struggles – and that one of the great challenges facing future generations would be not only to engage the complex structural legacy of race, but also to take note of the plethora of forms in which it was both expressed and experienced in everyday life. For Du Bois, race fused power and ideology and was also deeply woven into the public pedagogy of American culture and its geography, economics, politics and institutions.

The great challenge Du Bois presents to this generation of students, educators and citizens is to acknowledge that the future of democracy in the United States is inextricably linked "to the outcomes of racial politics and policies, as they develop both in various national societies and the world at large."[3] In part, this means that how we experience democracy in the future will depend on how we name, think about, experience and transform the interrelated modalities of race, racism and social justice. It also suggests that the meaning of race and the challenges of racism change for each generation, and that the new challenges we face demand a new language for understanding how the symbolic power of race as a pedagogical force, as well as a structural and materialist practice, redefines the relationship between the self and the other, the private and the public. It is this latter challenge in particular that needs to be more fully addressed if racism is not to be reduced to an utterly privatized discourse that erases any trace of racial injustice by denying the very notion of the social and the operations of power through which racial politics are organized and legitimated.

When Du Bois wrote "The Souls of Black Folk," racism was a visible and endemic part of the American political, cultural and economic landscape. The racial divide was impossible to ignore, irrespective of one's politics. As we move into the new millennium, the politics of the color line and representations of race have become far more subtle and complicated than they were in the Jim Crow era when Du Bois made his famous pronouncement. And though far from invisible, the complicated nature of race relations in American society no longer appears to be marked by the specter of Jim Crow. A majority of Americans now believe that anti-Black racism is a thing of the past, since it is assumed that formal institutions of segregation no longer exist. At the same time, surveys done by the National Opinion Research Center at the University of Chicago have consistently found "that most Americans still believe blacks are less intelligent than whites, lazier than whites, and more likely than whites to prefer living on welfare over being self-supporting."[4] Contradictions aside, conservatives and liberals alike now view America's racial hierarchy as an unfortunate historical fact that now has no bearing on contemporary society. Pointing to the destruction of the Southern caste system, the problematizing of Whiteness as a racial category, the passing of civil rights laws, a number of successful lawsuits alleging racial discrimination against companies such as Texaco and Denny's, and the emergence of people of color into all aspects of public life, the color line now seems in disarray, a remnant of another era that Americans have fortunately moved beyond. Best selling books such as Dinesh D'Souza's *The End of Racism*, Jim Sleeper's *Liberal Racism*, and Stephan and Abigail Thernstrom's *America in Black and White: One Nation, Indivisible*, all proclaim racism as an obsolete ideology and practice.[5] And a large number of White Americans seem to agree. In fact, poll after poll reveals that a majority of White Americans believe that people of color no longer face racial discrimination in American life. For example, a recent Gallop Survey on "Black-White Relations" observes that,

> 7 out of 10 whites believe that blacks are treated equally in their communities.
> . . . Eight in ten whites say blacks receive equal educational opportunities, and
> 83% say blacks receive equal housing opportunities in their communities. Only
> a third of whites believe blacks face race racial bias from police in their areas.[6]

For many conservative and liberal intellectuals, the only remaining remnant of racist categorization and policy in an otherwise color-blind society is affirmative action, which ironically, it is alleged provides Blacks with an unfair advantage in higher education, the labor force, "entitlement programs," and "even summer scholarship programs."[7]

The importance of race and the enduring fact of racism are relegated to the dustbin of history at a time in American life when the discourses of race and the spectacle of racial representations saturate the dominant media and public life. The color line is now mined for exotic commodities that can be sold to White youth in the form of rap music, hip-hop clothing, and sports gear. African American celebrities such as Michael Jordan, Etta James and George Foreman are used to give market legitimacy to everything from gas grills, to high end luxury cars, to clothes. Black public intellectuals such as Patricia Williams, Cornel West, Michael Dyson and Henry Louis Gates command the attention of *The New York Times* and other eye-catching media. African Americans now occupy powerful positions on the Supreme Court and the highest levels of political life. The alleged collapse, if not transformation, of the color line can also be seen in the emergence of the Black elite, prominently on display in television sitcoms, fashion magazines, Hollywood movies, and music videos. On the political scene, however, the supposedly race-transcendent public policy is complicated by ongoing public debates over affirmative action, welfare, crime and the prison-industrial complex. All of which is to suggest that while the color line has been modified and dismantled in places, race and racial hierarchies still exercise a profound influence on how most people in the United States experience their daily lives.[8] Popular sentiment aside, rather than disappearing, race has not lost its power as a key signifier in structuring all aspects of American life. As Michael Omi keenly observes:

> Despite legal guarantees of formal equality and access, race continues to be a fundamental organizing principle of individual identity and collective action. I would argue that, far from declining in significance (as William Julius Wilson would have us believe), the racial dimensions of politics and culture have proliferated.[9]

Representations of race and difference are everywhere in American society and yet racism as both a symbol and condition of American life is either ignored or relegated to an utterly privatized discourse, typified in references to individual prejudices, or psychological dispositions such as expressions of "hate." As politics becomes more racialized, the discourse about race becomes more privatized. While the realities of race permeate public life, they are engaged less as discourses and sites where differences are produced within iniquitous relations of power than as either unobjectionable cultural signifiers or desirable commodities. The public morality of the marketplace works its magic in widening the gap between political control and economic power while simultaneously reducing political agency to the act of consuming. One result is a growing cynicism and powerlessness among the general population as the political impotence of public institutions is reinforced through the disparaging of any reference to ethics, equity, justice or any other normative referent that prioritizes democratic values over market considerations. Similarly, as corporate power undermines all notions of the public good and increasingly privatizes public space, it obliterates those public spheres where criticism might emerge and acknowledge the tensions wrought by a pervasive racism that "functions as one of the deep, abiding currents in everyday life, in both the simplest and the most complex interactions of whites and blacks."[10] Indifference and cynicism breed contempt and resentment as racial hierarchies now collapse into power-evasive strategies such as blaming minorities of class and color for not working hard enough, or refusing to exercise individual initiative, or practicing reverse racism. Marketplace ideologies now work to erase the social from the language of public life so as to reduce all racial problems to private issues such as individual character.

Black public intellectuals such as Shelby Steele and John McWhorter garner national attention persuading the American people that the subject and object of racism have been reversed. For Steele, racism has nothing to do with soaring Black unemployment, failing and segregated schools for Black children, a criminal justice system that resembles the old plantation system of the South, or police brutality that takes its toll largely on Blacks in urban cities such as Cincinnati and New York. On the contrary, according to Steele, racism has produced White guilt, a burden that White people have to carry as part of the legacy of the civil rights movement. To remove this burden, Blacks now have to free themselves from their victim status and act responsibly by proving to Whites that *their* suffering is unnecessary.[11] Blacks can remove this burden through the spirit of principled entrepreneurialism – allowing themselves to be judged on the basis of hard work, individual effort, a secure family life, decent values and property ownership.[12] It gets worse. John McWhorter, largely relying on anecdotes from his own limited experience in the academy, argues that higher education is filled with African American students who are either mediocre or simply lazy, victims of affirmative action programs that coddle them because of their race while allowing them to "dumb down" rather than work as competitively as their White classmates. The lesson here is that the color line now benefits Blacks, not Whites, and that in the end, for McWhorter, diversity, not bigotry, is the enemy of a quality education and functions largely to "condemn black students to mediocrity."[13]

Within this discourse, there is a glimmer of a new kind of racial reference, one that can only imagine public issues as private concerns. This is a racism that refuses to "translate private sufferings into public issues,"[14] a racism that works hard to remove issues of power and equity from broader social concerns. Ultimately, it imagines human agency as simply a matter of individualized choices, the only obstacle to effective citizenship and agency being the lack of principled self-help and moral responsibility. In what follows, I want to examine briefly the changing nature of the new racism by analyzing how some of its central assumptions evade notions of race, racial justice, equity and democracy altogether. In doing so, I analyze some elements of the new racism, particularly the discourse of color-blindness and neoliberal racism. I then want to address how the denial of racism and neoliberal racism were recently on prominent display in the controversial Trent Lott affair. I will conclude by offering some suggestions about how the new racism, particularly its neoliberal version, can be addressed as both pedagogical and political issues.

Neoliberalism and the Culture of Privatization

The public morality of American life and social policy regarding matters of racial justice are increasingly subject to a politics of denial. Denial in this case is not merely about the failure of public memory or the refusal to know, but an active, ongoing attempt on the part of many conservatives, liberals and politicians to rewrite the discourse of race so as to deny its valence as a force for discrimination and exclusion either by translating it as a threat to American culture or relegating it to the language of the private sphere. The idea of race and the conditions of racism have real political effects and eluding them only makes those effects harder to recognize. And yet, the urgency to recognize how language is used to name, organize, order and categorize matters of race not only has academic value, it also provides a location from which to engage difference and the relationship between the self and the other and between the public and private. In addition, the language of race is important because it strongly affects political and policy agendas as well. One only has to think about the effects of Charles Murray's book, *Losing Ground*, on American welfare policies in the 1980s.[15] But language is more than a mode of communication or a symbolic practice that produces real effects, it is also a site of contestation and struggle. Since the mid 1970s, race relations have undergone a significant shift and acquired a new character as the forces of neoliberalism have begun to shape how Americans understand the notion of agency, identity, freedom and politics itself.[16]

Part of this shift has to be understood within the emerging forces of transnational capitalism and a global restructuring in which the economy is separated from politics, and corporate power is largely removed from the control of nation states. Within the neoliberal register, globalization "represents the triumph of the economy over politics and culture. . . . [A]nd the hegemony of capital over all other domains of life."[17] Under neoliberal globalization, capital removes itself from any viable form of state regulation, power is uncoupled from matters of ethics and social responsibility, and market freedoms replace longstanding social contracts that once provided a safety net for the poor, the elderly, workers, and the middle-class. The result is that public issues and social concerns increasingly give way to a growing culture of insecurity and fear regarding the most basic issues of individual livelihood, safety and basic survival. Increasingly, uncertainty replaces a concern with either the past or the future, and traditional human bonds rooted in compassion, justice and a respect for others are now replaced by a revitalized social Darwinism, played out nightly in the celebration of reality-based television, in which a rabid self-interest becomes the organizing principle for a winner-take-all society. As insecurity and fear grip public consciousness, society is no longer identified through its allegiance to democratic values, but through a troubling freedom rooted in a disturbing emphasis on individualism and competitiveness as the only normative measures to distinguish between what is a right or wrong, just or unjust, proper or improper action. Zygmunt Bauman (2001) captures this deracinated notion of freedom and the insecurity it promotes in his observation that:

> Society no longer guarantees, or even promises, a collective remedy for individual misfortunes. Individuals have been offered (or, rather, have been cast into) freedom of unprecedented proportions—but at the price of similarly unprecedented insecurity. And when there is insecurity, little time is left for caring for values that hover above the level of daily concerns—, or for that matter, for whatever lasts longer than the fleeting moment."[18]

Within this emerging neoliberal ethic, success is attributed to thriftiness and entrepreneurial genius while those who do not succeed are viewed as either failures or utterly expendable. Neoliberalism's attachment to individualism, markets and antistatism ranks human needs as less important than property rights and subordinates "the art of politics . . . to the science of economics."[19] Racial justice in the age of market-based freedoms and financially driven values loses its ethical imperative to a neoliberalism that embraces commercial rather than civic values, private rather than pubic interests, and financial incentives rather than ethical concerns. Neoliberalism negates racism as an ethical issue and democratic values as a basis for citizen-based action. Of course, neoliberalism takes many forms as it moves across the globe. In the United States, it has achieved a surprising degree of success but is increasingly being resisted by labor unions, students, and environmentalists. Major protests against economic policies promoted by the World Bank, International Monetary Fund, and World Trade Organization have taken place in Seattle, Prague, New York, Montreal, Genoa and other cities around the world. In the United States, a rising generation of students are protesting trade agreements like GATT and NAFTA as well as sweat shop labor practices at home and abroad and the corporatization of public and higher education. Unfortunately, anti-racist theorists have not said enough about either the link between the new racism and neoliberalism, on the one hand, or the rise of a race-based carceral state on the other. Neither the rise of the new racism nor any viable politics of an anti-racist movement can be understood outside of the power and grip of neoliberalism in the United States. Hence, at the risk of oversimplification, I want to be a bit more specific about neoliberalism's central assumptions and how it frames some of the more prominent emerging racial discourses and practices.

Neoliberalism and the Politics of the New Racism

Under the reign of neoliberalism in the United States, society is largely defined through the privileging of market relations, deregulation, privatization and consumerism. Central to neoliberalism is the assumption that profit-making be construed as the essence of democracy, thus providing a rationale for a handful of private interests to control as much of social life as possible to maximize their financial investments. Strictly aligning freedom with a narrow notion of individual interest, neoliberalism works hard to privatize all aspects of the public good and simultaneously narrow the role of the state as both a gatekeeper for capital and a policing force for maintaining social order and racial control. Unrestricted by social legislation or government regulation, market relations, as they define the economy, are viewed as a paradigm for democracy itself. Central to neoliberal philosophy is the claim that the development of all aspects of society should be left to the wisdom of the market. Similarly, neoliberal warriors argue that democratic values be subordinated to economic considerations, social issues be translated as private dilemmas, part-time labor replace full time work, trade unions be weakened and everybody be treated as a customer. Within this market-driven perspective, the exchange of capital takes precedence over social justice, the making of socially responsible citizens and the building of democratic communities. There is no language here for recognizing anti-democratic forms of power, developing non-market values, or fighting against substantive injustices in a society founded on deep inequalities, particularly those based on race and class. Hence, it is not surprising that under neoliberalism, language is often stripped of its critical and social possibilities as it becomes increasingly difficult to imagine a social order in which all problems are not personal, in which social issues provide the conditions for understanding private considerations, critical reflection becomes the essence of politics, and matters of equity and justice become crucial to developing a democratic society.

It is under the reign of neoliberalism that the changing vocabulary about race and racial justice has to be understood and engaged. As freedom is increasingly abstracted from the power of individuals and groups to actively participate in shaping society, it is reduced to the right of the individual to be free from social constraints. In this view, freedom is no longer linked to a collective effort on the part of individuals to create a democratic society. Instead, freedom becomes an exercise in self-development rather than social responsibility, reducing politics to either the celebration of consumerism or a privileging of a market-based notion of agency and choice that appear quite indifferent to how power, equity and justice offer the enabling conditions for real individual and collective choices to be both made, and acted upon. Under such circumstances, neoliberalism undermines those public spaces where non-commercial values and crucial social issues can be discussed, debated and engaged. As public space is privatized, power is disconnected from social obligations and it becomes more difficult for isolated individuals living in consumption-oriented spaces to construct an ethically engaged and power-sensitive language capable of accommodating the principles of ethics and racial justice as a common good rather than as a private affair. According to Bauman, the elimination of public space and the subordination of democratic values to commercial interests narrows the discursive possibilities for supporting notions of the public good and creates the conditions for "the suspicion against others, the intolerance of difference, the resentment of strangers, and the demands to separate and banish them, as well as the hysterical, paranoiac concern with "law and order"."[20] Positioned within the emergence of neoliberalism as the dominant economic and political philosophy of our times, neoracism can be understood as part of a broader attack against not only difference, but against the value of public memory, public good and democracy itself.

The new racism represents both a shift in how race is defined and is symptomatic of the breakdown of a political culture in which individual freedom and solidarity maintain an uneasy equilibrium in the service of racial, social and economic justice. Individual freedom is now disconnected from any sense of civic responsibility or justice, focusing instead on investor profits, consumer confidence, the downsizing of governments to police precincts and a deregulated social order in which the winner takes all. Freedom is no longer about either making the powerful responsible for their actions or providing the essential political, economic and social conditions for everyday people to intervene in, and shape, their future. Under the reign of neoliberalism, freedom is less about the act of intervention than it is about the process of withdrawing from the social and enacting one's sense of agency as an almost exclusively private endeavor. Freedom now cancels out civic courage and social responsibility while it simultaneously translates public issues and collective problems into tales of failed character, bad luck or simply indifference. As Amy Elizabeth Ansell points out:

> The disproportionate failure of people of color to achieve social mobility speaks
> nothing of the justice of present social arrangements, according to the New Right
> worldview, but rather reflects the lack of merit or ability of people of color

themselves. In this way, attention is deflected away from the reality of institutional racism and towards, for example, the 'culture of poverty', the 'drug culture', or the lack of black self-development.[21]

Appeals to freedom, operating under the sway of market forces, offer no signposts theoretically or politically for engaging racism as an ethical and political issue that undermines the very basis of a substantive democracy. Freedom in this discourse collapses into self-interest and as such is more inclined to organize any sense of community around shared fears, insecurities and an intolerance of those *others* who are marginalized by class and color. But freedom reduced to the ethos of self-preservation and brutal self-interests makes it difficult for individuals to recognize the forms that racism often takes when either draped in the language of denial, freedom or individual rights. In what follows, I want to explore two prominent forms of the new racism, color-blindness and neoliberal racism, and their connection to the New Right, corporate power and neoliberal ideologies.

Unlike the old racism, which defined racial difference in terms of fixed biological categories organized hierarchically, the new racism operates in various guises proclaiming, among other things, race-neutrality, asserting culture as a marker of racial difference or marking race as a private matter. Unlike the crude racism with its biological referents and pseudo-scientific legitimations, buttressing its appeal to White racial superiority, the new racism cynically recodes itself within the vocabulary of the Civil Rights Movement, invoking the language of Martin Luther King, Jr. to argue that individuals should be judged by the "content of their character" and not by the color of their skin. Amy Elizabeth Ansell, a keen commentator on the new racism, notes both the recent shifts in racialized discourse away from more rabid and overt forms of racism and its appropriation particularly by the New Right in the United States and Britain:

> The new racism actively disavows racist intent and is cleansed of extremist intolerance, thus reinforcing the New Right's attempt to distance itself from racist organizations such as the John Birch Society in the United States and the National Front in Britain. It is a form of racism that utilizes themes related to culture and nation as a replacement for the now discredited biological referents of the old racism. It is concerned less with notions of racial superiority in the narrow sense than with the alleged 'threat' people of color pose-either because of their mere presence or because of their demand for 'special privileges'—to economic, socio-political, and cultural vitality of the dominant (white) society. It is, in short, a new form of racism that operates with the category of 'race'. It is a new form of exclusionary politics that operates indirectly and in stealth via the rhetorical inclusion of people of color and the sanitized nature of its racist appeal.[22]

What is crucial about the new racism is that it demands an updated analysis of how racist practices work through the changing nature of language and other modes of representation. One of the most sanitized and yet pervasive forms of the new racism is evident in the language of color-blindness. Within this approach, it is argued that racial conflict and discrimination is a thing of the past and that race has no bearing on an individual's or group's location or standing in contemporary American society. Color-blindness does not deny the existence of race, but the claim is that race is responsible for alleged injustices that reproduce group inequalities, privileges Whites, and negatively impacts on economic mobility, the possession of social resources and the acquisition of political power. Put differently, inherent in the logic of color-blindness is the central assumption that race has no valence as a marker of identity or power when factored into the social vocabulary of everyday life and the capacity for exercising individual and social agency. As Charles Gallagher observes, "Within the color-blind perspective it is not race per se which determines upward mobility but how much an individual chooses to pay attention to race that determines one's fate. Within this perspective race is only as important as you allow it to be."[23] As Jeff, one of Gallagher's interviewees, puts it, race is simply another choice: "you know, there's music, rap music is no longer, it's not a black thing anymore. . . . [W]hen it first came out it was black music, but now it's just music. It's another choice, just like country music can be considered like white hick music, you know it's just a choice."[24] Hence, in an era "free" of racism, race becomes a matter of taste, lifestyle or heritage but has nothing to do with politics, legal rights, educational access or economic opportunities. Veiled by a denial of how racial histories accrue political, economic and cultural weight to the social power of Whiteness, color-blindness deletes the relationship between racial differences and power, and in doing so, reinforces Whiteness as the arbiter of value for judging difference against a normative notion of homogeneity.[25]

For advocates of color-blindness, race as a political signifier is conveniently denied, or seen as something to be overcome, allowing Whites to ignore racism as a corrosive force for expanding the dynamics of ideological and structural inequality throughout society.[26] Color-blindness is a convenient ideology for enabling Whites to ignore the degree to which race is tangled up with asymmetrical relations of power, functioning as a potent force for patterns of exclusion and discrimination including, but not limited to, housing, mortgage loans, health-care, schools and the criminal justice system. If one effect of color-blindness functions to deny racial hierarchies, another consequence is that it offers Whites not only the belief that America is now a level playing field, but that the success that Whites enjoy relative to minorities of color is largely due to individual determination, a strong work ethic, high moral values and a sound investment in education. Not only does color-blindness offer up a highly racialized (though paraded as race-transcendent) notion of agency, but it also provides an ideological space free of guilt, self-reflection and political responsibility, despite the fact that Blacks have a disadvantage in almost all areas of social life: housing, jobs, education, income levels, mortgage lending and basic everyday services.[27]

In a society marked by profound racial and class inequalities, it is difficult to believe that character and merit – as color-blindness advocates would have us believe – are the prime determinants for social and economic mobility and a decent standard of living. The relegation of racism and its effects in the larger society to the realm of private beliefs, values and behavior does little to explain a range of overwhelming realities-such as soaring Black unemployment, decaying cities and segregated schools. Paul Street puts the issue forcibly in a series of questions that register the primacy of, and interconnections among, politics, social issues and race.

> Why are African-Americans twice as likely to be unemployed as whites? Why is
> the poverty rate for blacks more than twice the rate for whites? Why do nearly

one out of every two blacks earn less than $25,000 while only one in three whites makes that little? Why is the median black household income ($27,000) less than two thirds of median white household income ($42,000)? Why is the Black family's median household net worth less than 10 percent that of whites? Why are blacks much less likely to own their own homes than whites? Why do African-Americans make up roughly half of the United States' massive population of prisoners (2 million) and why are one in three young, black male adults in prison or on parole or otherwise under the supervision of the American criminal justice system? Why do African-Americans continue in severe geographic separation from mainstream society, still largely cordoned off into the nation's most disadvantaged communities thirty years after the passage of the civil rights fair housing legislation? Why do blacks suffer disproportionately from irregularities in the American electoral process, from problems with voter registration to the functioning of voting machinery? Why does black America effectively constitute a Third World enclave of sub-citizens within the world's richest and most powerful state?[28]

Add to this list the stepped-up re-segregation of American schools and the growing militarization and lockdown status of public education through the widespread use of zero tolerance policies.[29] Or the fact that African American males live, on average, six years less than their White counterparts. It is worth noting that nothing challenges the myth that America has become a color-blind post-racist nation more than the racialization of the criminal justice system since the late 1980s. As the sociologist Loic Wacquant has observed, the expansion of the prison-industrial complex represents a "de facto policy of 'carceral affirmative action' towards African-Americans."[30] This is borne out by the fact that while American prisons house over 2 million inmates,

roughly half of them are black even though African-Americans make up less than 13 percent of the nation's population. . . . According to the Justice Policy Institute there are now more black men behind bars than in college in the United States. One in ten of the world's prisoners is an African-American male."[31]

As one of the most powerful ideological and institutional factors for deciding how identities are categorized and power, material privileges and resources distributed, race represents an essential political category for examining the relationship between justice and a democratic society. But color-blindness is about more than the denial of how power and politics operate to promote racial discrimination and exclusion: it is also an ideological and pedagogical weapon powerfully mobilized by the conservatives and the right-wing for asserting that since American society is now a level playing field, government should be race neutral, affirmative action programs dismantled, civil rights laws discarded and the welfare state eliminated.

Within the last twenty years, a more virulent form of the new racism has appeared that also affirms the basic principles of color-blindness, but instead of operating primarily as a discourse of denial regarding how power and politics operate to promote racial discrimination and exclusion, neoliberal racism is about the privatization of racial discourse. Moreover, neoliberal racism is proactive and functions aggressively in the public arena as an ideological and pedagogical weapon powerfully mobilized by various conservatives and right-wing groups. Neoliberal racism asserts the insignificance of race as social force and it aggressively roots out any vestige of race as a category at odds with an individualistic embrace of formal legal rights. Focusing on individuals rather than on groups, neoliberal racism either dismisses the concept of institutional racism or argues that it has no merit. In this context, racism is primarily defined as a form of individual prejudice, while appeals to equality are dismissed outright. For instance, racial ideologues Richard J. Herrnstein and Charles Murray write in *The Bell Curve,*

> in everyday life, the ideology of equality censors and straitjackets everything from pedagogy to humor. The ideology of equality has stunted the range of moral dialogue to triviality. . . . It is time for America once again to try living with inequality, as life is lived.[32]

Arguing that individual freedom is tarnished if not poisoned by the discourse of equality, right-wing legal advocacy groups such as the Center for Individual Rights and the Foundation for Individual Rights in Education argue that identity politics and pluralism weaken rather than strengthen American democracy because they pose a threat to what it means for the United States "to remain recognizably American."[33] But such groups do more than define American culture in racist and retrograde terms, they also aggressively use their resources, generously provided by prominent right-wing conservative organizations such as the Lynde and Harry Bradley Foundation, the John M. Olin Foundation, the Adolph Coors Foundation and the Scaife Family Foundation, to challenge racial preference policies that are not based on a "principle of state neutrality."[34] With ample resources at their disposal, advocates of neoliberal racism have successfully challenged a number of cases before the Supreme Court over the legality of affirmative action programs, campus speech codes, hiring practices, the Violence Against Women Act and the elimination of men's sports teams in higher education.[35] Hence, neoliberal racism provides the ideological and legal framework for asserting that since American society is now a meritocracy, government should be race neutral, affirmative action programs should be dismantled, civil rights laws discarded and the welfare state eliminated. As Nikhil Aziz observes, "The Right argues that, because racism has been dealt with as a result of the Civil Rights Movement, race should not be a consideration for hiring in employment or for admission to educational institutions, and group identities other than 'American' are immaterial."[36]

Neoliberal racism is unwilling to accept any concept of the state as a guardian of the public interest. Motivated by a passion for free markets that is only matched by an anti-government fervor, neoliberal racism calls for a hollowing out of the social welfare functions of the state, except for its role in safeguarding the interests of the privileged and the strengthening of its policing functions. Rejecting a notion of the public good for private interest, advocates of neoliberal racism want to limit the state's role in public investments and social programs as a constraint on both individual rights and the expression of individual freedom. In this view, individual interests override any notion of the public good, and individual freedom operates outside of any ethical responsibility for its social consequences. The results of this policy are evident in right-wing attacks on public education, health-care, environmental regulations, public housing, race based scholarships and other public services that embrace notions of difference. Many of these programs benefit the general public, though they are relied on disproportionately by the poor and minorities of color. As Zsuza Ferge points out, what becomes clear about neoliberal racism is that:

> the attack on the big state has indeed become predominantly an attack on the welfare functions of the state. . . . The underlying motif is the conviction that the supreme value is economic growth to be attained by unfettered free trade equated with freedom tout court. . . . The extremely individualist approach that characterizes this ethic justifies the diagnosis of many that neoliberalism is about the 'individualization of the social.'[37]

By restricting the state from addressing or correcting the effects of racial discrimination, state agencies are silenced, thus displacing "the tensions of contemporary racially charged relations to the relative invisibility of private spheres, seemingly out of reach of public policy intervention."[38]

The relentless spirit of self-interest within neoliberal racism offers an apology for a narrow market-based notion of freedom in which individual rights and choices are removed from any viable notion of social responsibility, critical citizenship and substantive democracy. By distancing itself from any notion of liberal egalitarianism, civic obligation or a more positive notion of freedom, neoliberal racism does more than collapse the political into the personal – invoking character against institutional racism and individual rights against social wrongs – it claims, as Jean and John Comaroff argue, that:

> The personal is the only politics there is, the only politics with a tangible referent or emotional valence. It is in these privatized terms that action is organized, that the experience of inequity and antagonism takes meaningful shape. . . . [Neoliberalism] is a culture that . . . re-visions persons not as producers from a particular community, but as consumers in a planetary marketplace.[39]

Neoliberalism devitalizes democracy because it has no language for defending a politics in which citizenship becomes an investment in public life rather than an obligation to consume, relegated in this instance to an utterly privatized affair. The discourse of neoliberal racism has no way of talking about collective responsibility, social agency or a defense of the public good. But the absences in its discourse are not innocent because they both ignore and perpetuate the stereotypes, structured violence, and massive inequalities produced by the racial state, the race-based attack on welfare, the destruction of social goods such as schools and health-care and the rise of the prison-industrial complex. Furthermore, its attack on the principles of equality, liberty, economic democracy and racial justice, in the final analysis, represents "a heartless indifference to the social contract and any other civic minded concern for the larger social good."[40] Hence, it is not surprising how neoliberal arguments embracing the primacy of individual solutions to public issues such as poverty or the ongoing incarceration of Black males are quick to defend public policies that are both punitive and overtly racist, such as workfare for welfare recipients or the public shaming rituals of prison chain gangs, with an overabundance of Black males always on display. Neoliberal racism's "heartless indifference" to the plight of the poor, and to human suffering in general, is often mirrored in an utter disdain for human suffering as in Shelby Steele's nostalgic longing for a form of Social Darwinism in which "failure and suffering are natural and necessary elements of success."[41]

It is interesting that whenever White racism is invoked by critics in response to the spectacle of racism, advocates of color-blindness and neoliberal racism often step outside of the privatizing language of rights and have little trouble appropriating victim status for Whites while blaming people of color for the harsh conditions under which so many have to live in this country. And in some cases, this is done in the name of a civility that is used to hide both the legacy and reality of racism and a commitment to equality as a cornerstone of racial progress. A classic example of the latter can be found in *The End of Racism* by Dinesh D'Souza. He writes:

> Nothing strengthens racism in this country more than the behavior of the African-American underclass which flagrantly violates and scandalizes basic codes of responsibility and civility. . . . [I]f blacks as a group can show that they are capable of performing competitively in schools and the workforce, and exercising both the rights and responsibilities of American citizenship, then racism will be deprived of its foundation in experience.[42]

Spectacles of Race

Scripted denials of racism coupled with the spectacle of racial discourse and representations have become a common occurrence in American life. Power evasive strategies wrapped up in the language of individual choice and the virtues of self-reliance provide the dominant modes of framing through which the larger public can witness in our media saturated culture what Patricia Williams calls "the unsaid filled by stereotypes and self-identifying illusion, the hierarchies of race and gender circulating unchallenged" enticing audiences who prefer "familiar drama to the risk of serious democratization."[43] In what follows, I want to address the controversy surrounding the racist remarks made by Trent Lott at Strom Thurmond's centennial birthday celebration and how the Lott affair functions as an example of how controversial issues often assume the status of both a national melodrama and a scripted spectacle. I also want to analyze how this event functioned largely to privatize matters of White racism while rendering invisible the endorsement of systemic and state-fashioned racism. The Lott affair functions as a public transcript in providing a context for examining the public pedagogy of racial representations in media and print culture that are often framed within the ideology of the new racism in order to displace any serious discussion of racial exclusion in the United States. Finally, I offer some suggestions about how to respond politically to neoliberal racism and what the implications might be for a critical pedagogical practice aimed at challenging and dismantling it.

While attending Strom Thurmond's 100 birthday party on December 5, 2002, the then Senate Majority leader, Trent Lott, offered the following salute to one of the most legendary segregationists alive: "I want to say this about my state: when Strom Thurmond ran for President, we voted for him. We're proud of it. And if the rest of the country had followed our lead, we wouldn't have had all these problems over all these years, either."[44] Of course, for the historically aware, the meaning of the tribute was clear since Thurmond had run in 1948 on a racist Dixiecrat ticket whose official campaign slogan was "Segregation Forever!"

It took five days before the story got any serious attention in the national media. Once the story broke, Lott offered an endless series of apologies that included everything from saying he was just "winging it" (until it was revealed that he made an almost similar remark as a congressmen at a Reagan rally a few decades earlier) to having found "Jesus," to proclaiming he was now "an across the board" advocate of affirmative action.[45] The Lott story evoked a range of opinions in the media extending from a craven defense provided by conservative columnist Bob Novak, who argued that Lott's racist comments were just a slip of the tongue, to vociferous moral condemnation from all sides of the ideological spectrum. Once Lott's voting record on civil rights issues became public, he became an embarrassment and liability to those politicians who denounced open racial bigotry, but had little to say about structural, systemic and institutional racism.[46] Under pressure from his Republican party colleagues, Lott eventually resigned as Senate majority leader, but retained his senate seat, and the story passed in the national media from revelation to spectacle to irrelevance. The shelf-life of the spectacle in the dominant culture is usually quite long – witness the Gary Conduit affair – except when it offers the possibility for revealing how racist expressions privately license relations of power that reproduce a wide range of racial exclusions in the wider social order.

Lott's remarks cast him as a supporter of the old racism – bigoted, crude and overtly racist. And, for the most part, the wrath his remarks engendered from the Republican party and its media cheerleaders were mainly of the sort that allowed the critics to reposition themselves in keeping with the dictates of the logic of color-blindness and neoliberal racism. In doing so they distanced themselves from Lott's comments as a safe way to attest their disdain for the old racist bigotry and to provide a display of their moral superiority and civility while distancing themselves from what Robert Kuttner has called some "inconvenient truths" when it came to talking about race. As Kuttner observes:

> His stated views made it more difficult for the Republican party to put on minstrel shows and offer speeches dripping with compassion, while appointing racist judges, battling affirmative action, resisting hate crimes legislation, and slashing social outlays that help minorities. Lott made it harder to hold down black voting in the name of 'ballot security' while courting black voters, and disguising attacks on public education as expanded 'choice' for black parents and stingy welfare reform as promoting self-sufficiency.[47]

Of course, singling out Lott also suggested that he was, as an editorial in the *Wall Street Journal* claimed, a one-of-kind bad apple, an unfortunate holdover from a Jim Crow era, which no longer exists in America. David Brooks the editor of the conservative *National Review* proclaimed with great indignation that Lott's views were not "normal Republican ideas" and to prove the point claimed that after hanging out with Republicans for two decades, he had "never heard an overtly racist comment."[48]

Brooks, like many of his fellow commentators, seems to have allowed his ode to racial cleansing to cloud his sense of recent history. After all, it was only ten years ago that Kirk Fordice, a right-wing Republican, ended his victorious campaign for governor – orchestrated largely as an attack on crime and welfare cheaters – with a "still photograph of a Black woman and her baby."[49] Of course, this was just a few years after George W. Bush ran his famous Willie Horton ad and a year before Dan Quayle, in the 1992 presidential campaign, used the racially coded category of welfare to attack a sitcom character, Murphy Brown. Maybe David Brooks was just unaware of the interview that John Ashcroft gave to the neo-confederate magazine, *Southern Partisan*, in 1999 "in which he 'vowed to do more' to defend the legacy of Jefferson Davis."[50] Or as, *New York Times* writer, Frank Rich, puts it in response to the apparent newfound historical amnesia about the overt racism displayed by the Republican Party in more recent times:

> Tell that to George W. Bush, who beat John McCain in the 2000 South Carolina primary after what *Newsweek* called 'a smear campaign' of leaflets, e-mails and telephone calls calling attention to the McCains' 'black child' (an adopted daughter from Bangladesh). Or to Sonny Perdue, the new Republican governor of Georgia, elected in part by demagoguing the sanctity of the confederate flag.[51]

One telling example of how the Trent Lott affair was removed from both the historical record of racialized injustices, realm of political contestation, or any critical understanding of how racializing categories actually take hold in the culture, can be found in a December 23, 2002 issue of *Newsweek*, which devoted an entire issue to the public uproar surrounding Lott's racist remarks.[52] *Newsweek* featured a 1962 picture of Lott on its cover with the caption "The Past That Made Him—and May Undo Him: Race and the Rise of Trent Lott." The stories that appeared in the magazine either portrayed Lott as an odd and totally out of touch symbol of the past, "A Man Out of Time," as one story headline read, or as an unrepentant symbol of racism that was no longer acceptable in American public life or in national politics. *Newsweek* ended its series on Lott with a short piece called "Lessons of the Trent Lott Mess."[53] The author of the article, Ellis Cose, condemned Lott's long history of racist affiliations, as did many other writers, but said nothing about why they were ignored by either the major political party or the dominant media over the last decade, especially given Lott's important standing in national politics. It is interesting to note that Lott's affiliation with the neo-Confederate group – the Council of Conservative Citizens (CCC) – a successor to the notorious White Citizens Council, once referred to as the "uptown Klan," was revealed in a 1998 story by Stanley Crouch, a writer for the *New York Daily News*. Surprisingly, the article was ignored at the time by both prominent politicians and the dominant media. At issue here is the recognition that the history of racism of which Trent Lott participated is not merely his personal history, but the country's history and should raise far more serious considerations about how the legacy of racism works through its cultural, economic and social fabric. While Lott has to be held accountable for his remarks, his actions cannot be understood strictly within the language of American individualism, i.e., as a bad reminder that the legacy of racism lives on in some old-fashioned politicians who cannot escape their past. In fact, Lott's remarks, as well as the silence that allowed his racist discourse to be viewed in strictly personal and idiosyncratic terms, must be addressed as symptomatic of a larger set of racist historical, social, economic and ideological influences that still hold sway over American society. Collapsing the political into the personal, and serious reporting into talk show clichés, Cose argues that the reason a person like Lott is serving and will continue to serve in the Senate or sharing power with America's ruling elite is because "Americans are very forgiving folks."[54] This response is more than simply inane, it is symptomatic of a culture of racism that has no language for, or interest in, understanding systemic racism, its history, or how it is embodied in most ruling political and economic institutions in the United States. Or, for that matter why it has such a powerful grip on American culture. The Trent Lott affair is important, not because it charts an influential Senator's fall from grace and power because of an unfortunate racist remark made in public, but because it is symptomatic of a new racism that offers no resources for translating private troubles into public considerations.

The public pedagogy underlying the popular response to Trent Lott's racist remarks reveals how powerful the educational force of the culture is in shaping dominant conventions about race. Mirroring the logic of neoliberalism, the overall response to Lott both privatized the discourse of racism and restricted the interrogation of a racist expression to an unfortunate slip of the tongue, or a psychological disposition, or the emotive residue of a man who is out of step with both his political party and the spirit of the country. However, such expressions are not simply the assertions of a prejudiced individual, but also modes of exclusion, rooted in forms of authority largely used to name, classify, order, devalue, people of color. As David Theo Goldberg observes:

> As a mode of exclusion, racist expression assumes authority and is vested with power, literally and symbolically, in bodily terms. They are human bodies that are classified, ordered, valorized, and devalued. . . . When this authority assumes state power, racialized discourse and its modes of exclusions become embedded in state institutions and normalized in the common business of everyday institutional life. . . . As expressions of exclusion, racism appeals either to inherent superiority or to differences. These putative differences and gradations may be strictly physical, intellectual, linguistic, or cultural. Each serves in two ways: They purport to furnish the basis for justifying differential distributions or treatment, and they represent the very relations of power that prompted them.[55]

As part of the discourse of denial, the Trent Lott episode reveals how racism is trivialized through a politics of racial management in which racism is consigned to an outdated past, a narrow psychologism, the private realm of bad judgment or personal indiscretion. But racial discourse is not simply about private speech acts or individualized modes of communication; it is also about contested histories, institutional relations of power, ideology, and the social gravity of effects. Racist discourses and expressions should alert us to the workings of power and the conditions that make particular forms of language possible and others seemingly impossible, as well as the modes of agency they produce and legitimate – an issue almost completely ignored in the mainstream coverage of the Lott affair. What was missing from the Trent Lott affair is captured by Teun A. Van Dijk in his analysis of elite discourse and racism:

Racism, defined as a system of racial and ethnic inequality, can survive only when it is daily reproduced through multiple acts of exclusion, inferiorization, or marginalization. Such acts need to be sustained by an ideological system and by a set of attitudes that legitimate difference and dominance. Discourse is the principal means for the construction and reproduction of this sociocognitive framework.[56]

Conclusion

Any attempt to address the politics of the new racism in the United States must begin by reclaiming the language of the social and affirming the project of an inclusive and just democracy. This suggests addressing how the politics of the new racism are made invisible under the mantle of neoliberal ideology. That is, raising questions about how neoliberalism works to hide the effects of power, politics and racial injustice. What is both troubling and must increasingly be made problematic is that neoliberalism wraps itself in what appears to be an unassailable appeal to common sense. As Jean and John Comaroff observe:

> . . . there is a strong argument to be made that neoliberal capitalism in its millennial moment, portends the death of politics by hiding its own ideological underpinnings in the dictates of economic efficiency: in the fetishism of the free market, in the inexorable, expanding 'needs' of business, in the imperatives of science and technology. Or, if it does not conduce to the death of politics, it tends to reduce them to the pursuit of pure interest, individual or collective.[57]

Defined as the paragon of all social relations, neoliberalism attempts to eliminate an engaged critique about its most basic principles and social consequences by embracing the "market as the arbiter of social destiny."[58] More is lost here than neoliberalism's willingness to make its own assumptions problematic. Also lost is the very viability of politics itself. Not only does neoliberalism in this instance empty the public treasury, hollow out public services,and limit the vocabulary and imagery available to recognize anti-democratic forms of power and narrow models of individual agency, it also undermines the socially discursive translating functions of any viable democracy by undercutting the ability of individuals to engage in the continuous translation between public considerations and the private interests by collapsing the public into the realm of the private.[59] Divested of its political possibilities and social underpinnings, freedom finds few opportunities for rearticulating private worries into public concerns or individual discontent into collective struggle.[60] Hence, the first task in engaging neoliberalism is revealing its claim to a bogus universalism and making clear how it functions as a historical and social construction. Neoliberalism hides the traces of its own ideology, politics and history by either rhetorically asserting its triumphalism as part of the "end of history" or by proclaiming that capitalism and democracy are synonymous. What must be challenged is neoliberalism's "future tense narrative of inevitability, demonstrating that the drama of world history remains wide open."[61]

But the history of the changing economic and ideological conditions that gave rise to neoliberalism must be understood in relation to the corresponding history of race relations in the United States and abroad. Most importantly, as the history of race is either left out or misrepresented by the official channels of power in the United States, it is crucial that the history of slavery, civil rights, racial politics and ongoing modes of struggle at the level of everyday life, be remembered and used pedagogically to challenge the historical amnesia that feeds neoliberalism's ahistorical claim to power and the continuity of its claims to common sense. The struggle against racial injustice cannot be separated from larger questions about what kind of culture and society is emerging under the imperatives of neoliberalism, what kind of history it ignores, and what alternatives might point to a substantive democratic future.

Second, under neoliberalism, all levels of government have been hollowed out and largely reduced either to their policing functions or to maintaining the privileges of the rich and the interests of corporate power – both of which are largely White. In this discourse, the state is not only absolved of its traditional social contract of upholding the public good and providing crucial social provisions and minimal guarantees for those who are need of such services, it also embraces a notion of color-blind racelessness. State racelessness is built on the right wing logic of "rational racists" such as Dinesh D'Souza, who argue that "What we need is a separation of race and state."[62] As David Theo Goldberg points out, this means that the state is now held,

> to a standard of justice protective of individual rights and not group results. . . .
> [T]his in turn makes possible the devaluation of any individuals considered not
> white, or white-like, the trashing or trampling of their rights and possibilities, for
> the sake of preserving the right to private 'rational discrimination' of whites. . .
> . [Thus] racist discrimination becomes privatized, and in terms of liberal legali-
> ty state protected in its privacy.[63]

Defined through the ideology of racelessness, the state removes itself from either addressing or correcting the effects of racial discrimination, reducing matters of racism to individual concerns to be largely solved through private negotiations between individuals, and adopting an entirely uncritical role in the way in which the racial state shapes racial policies and their effects throughout the economic, social and cultural landscape. Lost here is any critical engagement with state power and how it imposes immigration policies, decides who gets resources and access to a quality education, defines what constitutes a crime, how people are punished, how and whether social problems are criminalized, who is worthy of citizenship and who is responsible for addressing racial injustices. As the late Pierre Bourdieu argues, there is a political and pedagogical need to not only protect the social gains, embodied in state policies, that have been the outcome of important collective struggles, but also "to invent another kind of state."[64] This means challenging the political irresponsibility and moral indifference which are the organizing principles at the heart of the neoliberal vision. As Bourdieu suggests, this points to the need to restore a sense of utopian possibility rooted in a struggle for a democratic state. The racial state and its neoliberal ideology need to be challenged as part of any viable anti-racist pedagogy and politics.

Anti-racist pedagogy also needs to move beyond the conundrums of a limited identity politics and begin to include in its analysis what it would mean to imagine the state as a vehicle for democratic values and a strong proponent for social and racial justice. In part, reclaiming the democratic and public responsibility of the state would mean: arguing for a state in which tax cuts for the rich, rather than social spending, are seen as the problem; using the state to protect the public good rather than waging a war on all things public; engaging and resisting the use of state power to both protect and define the public sphere as utterly White; redefining the power and role of the state so as to minimize its policing functions and strengthen its accountability to the public interests of all citizens, rather than to the wealthy and corporations. Removing the state from its subordination to market values means reclaiming the importance of social needs over commercial interests, democratic politics over corporate power and addressing a host of urgent social problems that include but are not limited to: the escalating costs of health-care, housing, the schooling crisis, the growing gap between the rich and poor, the environmental crisis, the rebuilding of the nation's cities and impoverished rural areas, the economic crisis facing most of the states and the increasing assault on people of color. The struggle over the state must be linked to a struggle for a racially just, inclusive democracy. Crucial to any viable politics of anti-racism is the role the state will play as a guardian of the public interest and as a force in creating a multi-racial democracy.

Third, it is crucial for any anti-racist pedagogy and politics to recognize that power does not just inhabit the realm of economics or state power, but is also intellectual, residing in the educational force of the culture and its enormous powers of persuasion. This means that any viable anti-racist pedagogy must make the political more pedagogical by recognizing how public pedagogy works to determine and secure how racial identity, issues and relations are produced in a wide variety of sites including schools, cable and television networks, newspapers and magazines, the internet, advertising, churches, trade unions and a host of other public spheres in which ideas are produced and distributed. This means becoming mindful of how racial meanings and practices are created, mediated, reproduced and challenged through a wide variety of "discourses, institutions, audiences, markets and constituencies which help determine the forms and meaning of publicness in American society."[65] The crucial role that pedagogy plays in shaping racial issues reaffirms the centrality of a cultural politics that recognizes the relationship between issues of representation and the operations of power, the important role that intellectuals might play as engaged, public intellectuals, and the importance of critical knowledge in challenging neoliberalism's illusion of unanimity. But an anti-racist cultural pedagogy also suggests the need to develop both a language of critique and possibility and to wage individual and collective struggles in a wide variety of dominant public spheres and alternative counter-publics. Public pedagogy as a tool of anti-racist struggles understands racial politics not only as a signifying activity through which subject positions are produced, identities inhabited and desires mobilized but also as the mobilization of material relations of power as a way of securing, enforcing and challenging racial injustices. While cultural politics offers an opportunity to understand how race matters and racist practices take hold in everyday life, such a pedagogical and cultural politics must avoid collapsing into a romanticization of the symbolic, popular or discursive.

Culture matters as a rhetorical tool and mode of persuasion, especially in the realm of visual culture which has to be taken seriously as a pedagogical force, but changing consciousness is only a precondition to changing society and should not be confused with what it means to actually transform institutional relations of power. In part, this means contesting the control of the media by a handful of transnational corporations.[66] The social gravity of racism, as it works through the modalities of everyday language, relations and cultural expressions, has to be taken seriously in any anti-racist politics, but such a concern and mode of theorizing must also be accompanied by an equally serious interest in the rise of corporate power and "the role of state institutions and agencies in shaping contemporary forms of racial subjugation and inequality."[67] Racist ideologies, practices, state formations and institutional relations can be exposed pedagogically and linguistically, but they cannot be resolved merely in the realm of the discursive. Hence, any viable anti-racist pedagogy needs to draw attention between critique and social transformation, critical modes of analysis and the responsibility of acting individually and collectively on one's beliefs.

Another important issue that has to be included in any notion of anti-racist pedagogy and politics is the issue of connecting matters of racial justice to broader and more comprehensive political, cultural and social agendas. Neoliberalism exerts a powerful force in American life because its influence and power are spread across a diverse range of political, economic, social and cultural spheres. Its ubiquity is matched by its aggressive pedagogical attempts to reshape the totality of social life in the image of the market, reaching into and connecting a wide range of seemingly disparate issues that bear down on everyday life in the United States. Neoliberalism is persuasive because its language of commercialism, consumerism, privatization, freedom and self-interest resonates with, and saturates, so many aspects of public life. Differences in this discourse are removed from matters of equity and power and reduced to market niches. Agency is privatized and social values are reduced to market-based interests. And, of course, a democracy of citizens is replaced by a democracy of consumers. Progressives, citizens and other groups who are concerned about matters of race and difference need to maintain their concerns with particular forms of oppression and subordination. But the limits of various approaches to identity politics must be recognized so as not to allow them to become either fixed or incapable of making alliances with other social movements as part of a broader struggle over not just particular freedoms, but also the more generalized freedoms associated with an inclusive and radical democracy.

I have not attempted to be exhaustive in suggesting what it might mean to recognize and challenge the new racism that now reproduces more subtle forms of racial subordination, oppression and exclusion, though I have tried to point to some pedagogical and political concerns that connect racism and neoliberal politics. The color line in America is neither fixed nor static. Racism as an expression of power and exclusion takes many meanings and forms under different historical conditions. The emphasis on its socially and historically constructed nature offers hope because it suggests that what can be produced by dominant relations of power can also be challenged and transformed by those who imagine a more utopian and just world. The challenge of the color line is still with us today and needs to be recognized not only as a shameful example of racial injustice but also as a reprehensible attack on the very nature of democracy itself.

Section Two

Lessons in Betrayal: Educating the Oppressed

Chapter 5

Empire Building for a New Millennium

State Standards and a Curriculum for Imperialism

Christine E. Sleeter, Ph.D.
College of Professional Studies
California State University Monterey Bay

Introduction

> [I] had long entertained in a vague way the notion that imperialism is a more or less consciously adopted policy. The idea was not clearly formulated, but at the back of my head was the supposition that nations are imperialistic because they want and choose to be, in view of advantages they think will result.
>
> -Dewey, *Imperialism is Easy*[1]

The United States of America[2] is an imperial power: The nation was born of British imperialism, its territories were/are acquired through imperialist methods and its government has always pursued an aggressive policy of expansionism in order to establish an "American" economic and political vision around the globe. All evidence to the contrary, however, most U.S. citizens would still strongly deny the imperial agenda that fuels and frames U.S. interests at home and abroad. As alluded to by Dewey (1927), this seemingly paradoxical denial is firmly embedded in the public's refusal to accept that they themselves are not "innocent of such imperialist desires."[3] In a similar reading of imperialism's functionality, Williams (1991) asserted that any such "intellectual, political, and psychological confusion" would likely be rooted in "our ahistorical faith that we are not and never have been an empire."[4] Importantly, Williams goes on to assert that such denials set the stage for the "use and abuse, and ignoring, of other people for one's own welfare and convenience."[5] Echoing the concerns of these scholars, I contend that such denials only strengthen our implication in the ongoing processes of imperialism today. In order to reverse our perpetration of oppression, we must first "confront our history as an empire."[6] In this paper, I confront that history and its aftermath through a critical interrogation of how state-sponsored discourses effectively construct, support and obscure imperialism in contemporary Western contexts. I will focus this examination on the educational system as one of the State's most powerful apparatus for the transmission of knowledge, culture and values.

My concerns stem from a recognition that our schools do not function as sites through which students are prepared to participate in democratic citizenship. Rather, employing a *curriculum for imperialism*, our educational systems actively discipline students to participate in the maintenance of the dominant sociopolitical and economic order. I realize that educational structures have always reflected the ideologies and beliefs of the sociopolitical spheres in which they develop, but I grow increasingly disquieted by the ways in which "Jeffersonian" notions of democratic citizenship and participation in schooling are pushed to the sidelines of our pedagogical and bureaucratic agendas.[7] Karumanchery and Portelli suggest:

> Walking a tightrope of sorts, contemporary Western educational models have managed to respond to the demands of a competitive world economy while simultaneously espousing a deep commitment to the very values against which they are so often positioned.[8]

Speaking through cultural emblems of freedom, fair play and merit in ways that rarely address the erosion of democracy in education, our schools actively separate equity, experiential knowledge, personal reflection and mutual care from the centrality of schooling. These have become "peripheral" matters in the main business of education, eclipsed by programming and standards that reflect the "special interest politics" of global capital relative to an imperialist schema. So where does this leave our youth and ultimately, where does it lead us as a society? Are our students developing the capacity for critical thought and action? Do prescriptive banking models[9] of education allow students and teachers to dialogue and debate towards the development of knowledge, or are these fundamental aspects of the educational process lost in the streamlined move towards standardization?[10] It is vital that we interrogate these questions with a critical eye towards the politics that inform them. To these ends, I analyze the parallels that run between *California's History-Social Science Framework and Standards*[11] (i.e., as an example of a state-sponsored elite discourse[12] that was developed to drive history and social studies teaching in the State's public schools) and the network of elite-produced mainstream discourses that function to produce a public consciousness that is in line with, and supportive of U.S. imperial interests.[13]

The United States as Imperial Power

While watching TV coverage of the "war on terror" and the subsequent invasion of Iraq, I happened to be examining the *California History-Social Science Framework and Standards* and was struck by the discursive parallels that ran between the two. In fact, as I examined those parallels, it became increasingly clear that many of the government's basic assumptions, as portrayed in the media post-9/11, were also reflected in the framework of the state-mandated curriculum. This is particularly significant in light of today's "educational standards" bandwagon, which has shifted attention from "what knowledge schools should teach," to "how well students learn what the state prescribes." Now, while my intention in interrogating these parallels is not to draw a causal link between California's curriculum and the war on Iraq, it is important, to examine how elite systems and ideologies overlap to produce public opinion and consciousness as "effects" of imperialist discourse. Moreover, it is crucial that we interrogate how the U.S., as a nation in the business of Empire Building, sews its own version of "democracy," "freedom" and "benevolence" into the fabric of society via the media, schools, culture, et cetera.

As suggested by Spivak (1990), one of the most frightening and insidious things about imperialism is its long-term effect – what secures it, what cements it, and how our mass psyche has been infused with the self-representation of imperialist as compassionate and altruistic savior.[14] Like Spivak and other postcolonial scholars, this "long-term effect" occupies much of my attention in such discussions, particularly because we often engage historical readings of imperialism without analyzing the ideological, material and social engagements that reinforce it in contemporary contexts. Importantly, these long-term effects manifest, not simply as resonances of a colonial past, but as ongoing features of an imperialist present. For example, Kenny (2003) contends that the wars on terror and in Iraq are only the most recent cases in a long history of U.S, imperialism:

> The U.S. has officially said that the elimination of weapons of mass destruction is its main objective in using a military option in Iraq. "Regime change," the democratization of Iraq, and fighting global terrorism have been stated as corresponding aims. Missing in mainstream media is much discussion about the role of oil. . . . The history of U.S. efforts to control Middle East oil, the growth of U.S. energy needs and the link between energy supplies and U.S. national security, the enormous profits that U.S. multinational oil companies stand to make with greater access to Iraqi oil, and the additional global power that control of Iraqi oil would give to an aggressive administration in Washington are compelling factors in the debate and should not be ignored.[15]

Why is it that there continues to be so little public debate about the imperialist nature of the Bush Administration's agenda in the Middle East when growing numbers of political commentators, sociologists and economists are asserting that "access to," and "control of" Iraqi oil are the main objectives behind this military campaign? For example, in specific relation to American oil interests in the Middle East, Kenny (2003) notes that (a) the U.S. has been trying to control oil production in the Middle East since 1947, (b) Vice President Cheney's former firm, Halliburton, did active business with Saddam Hussein in the 1990s, (c) U.S. and British oil companies could well net $29 billion per year after rebuilding Iraq's oil infrastructure, which in turn would ensure both (d) American control over a source of cheap energy and (e) the pushing of other oil-producing nations to privatize their oil.[16] With all that being said, I would ask again: why is it that strong majorities of the public in the United States, Britain and Australia, supported military action against Iraq, while far larger numbers around the world condemned it?[17] Moreover, when the United Sates does in fact engage in imperialism, then why is there so little recognition of it here at home?

Arguing that the war on Iraq is part of a larger strategy for expansionism designed to intimidate potential challengers to U.S. global domination, Vltchek (2002) reminds us that imperialist nations sell their own version of the colonization process, while actively discounting or eradicating alternate versions of the "truth."[18] This latest Gulf War has been framed in large part as a humanitarian crusade to liberate the Iraqi people – but illusions need to be maintained, and so news reports about Iraqi deaths continue to be few and far between within U.S. national borders, even though mounting evidence suggests that between 5 000 and 10 000 Iraqi civilians died during the war itself,[19] over 1 million died as a consequence of the U.S.-led UN embargo,[20] and Iraqi deaths substantially continue to outnumber U.S. deaths. Is it a coincidence that so many Americans believe inaccuracies and "half-truths" that serve to justify U.S. military actions in these "foreign" lands (e.g., Afghanistan and Iraq), or are such misconceptions carefully constructed, articulated and managed to further cement the nation's larger imperialist agenda?[21] It would seem that we have been disciplined to turn away from any and all accounts that might make us question the deep-seated imperial nature of the American dream. But where does all this disciplinary work take place and how do we learn to function within these ideological constructs?

Althusser (1971) asserted that the relations of production and exploitation develop in and through the various State apparatus' transmission of repressive ideologies – that each State apparatus would work to maintain the relations of exploitation by transmitting oppressive ideologies into society.[22] Similarly, Bourdieu (1991) argued that elite discourses "impose an apprehension of the established social order as natural (orthodoxy) through the disguised (and therefore misrecognized) imposition of systems of classification and of mental structures that are objectively adjusted to social structures."[23] In other words, because reality doesn't simply speak for itself, but requires interpretation and organization, the symbol systems in elite discourse put some order on the messiness of real life. To the extent that "mental structures" offered through elite discourse overlap with "objective structures" people experience or see (even when that seeing is through the filter of media), elite discourse tends to be taken simply as descriptions of what exists. While it is problematic to define ideological formations as either solely repressive or unidirectional, I still find many of Althusser's and Bourdieu's contentions useful as a starting-point for examining how knowledge and social meaning take shape within the State's various administrative levels and ideological apparatus (e.g., cultural forms and institutions such as churches, schools, families and literature).[24]

Reworking Althusser's notion that ideological formations are bloc specific, Apple (1982) defined ideologies as more than global sets of interests imposed by one group on another. Rather, he argued that ideologies are embodied by our common sense meanings and practices,[25] and that the character of an ideological concept develops in its articulation within a specific bloc discourse and not through its content.[26] This notion of ideological formation helps to reconcile many gaps in Althusser's reading of how various State systems work to manufacture social meaning. For instance, in relation to the educational apparatus specifically, I see State-mandated curricula as an important part of the intersecting web of discourses that frame and construct mainstream worldviews through elite points of reference. It is important to analyze the ideology embedded in such curricula because they manufacture what is to be taken as common sense in the classroom by defining the contours of the subject matter with which teachers work. That being said, while many analysts interrogate how schooling works to produce a regulated and manageable student body as an effect of discourse, my critique here focuses specifically on how the Western educational apparatus promotes perspectives that sustain the needs and utility of U.S. imperialism.

Obscuring U.S. and European Imperialism

As discussed earlier, imperialist nations sell their own version of the colonization process while actively silencing those points of view that might explore or expose their expansionist activities. For example, in a discussion of intellectual property rights, Shiva (1997) contrasts Third World perspectives about economic inequality with those espoused by wealthy nations:

> The economic inequality between the affluent industrialized countries and the poor Third World ones is a project of 500 years of colonialism, and the continued maintenance and creation of mechanisms for draining wealth out of the Third World. . . . Instead of seeing the structural inequality of the international economic system as lying at the roots of Third World poverty, IRP [intellectual property rights] explain poverty as arising from a lack of creativity, which in turn, is seen as rooted in lack of IRP protection.[27]

An enormous number of resources are continuously put towards the active denial of colonialism and its ongoing global effects. To these ends, Imperial powers galvanize various intersecting sociopolitical apparatus like the mass media, education and political pronouncements in order to eradicate, marginalize and sanitize those accounts of imperialism that are perceived through a colonized worldview and/or perspective. *California's History-Social Science Framework and Standards* for instance, works to obscure the fundamental nature of the imperial history and legacy of the U.S. by using place (geography), time (chronology) and specific stories of adventure, hardship and glory as the primary lenses of educational programming and study. Missing from such "selective" analyses are the more critical explorations that might address: (a) the reality of European brutality relative to the genocide of native peoples in the Americas; (b) the ethics surrounding the appropriation of Aboriginal lands; (c) the values and principles that support the use of power to gain wealth and property; and (d) the lived experience of colonized peoples from their points of view.

Rather than focusing on the development of students' critical inquiry skills, current curricular materials and educational strategies are focused on the job of prescribing knowledge. In third and fourth grade, students study local and state history according to a sequence of events that sanitizes the brutal realities of the colonization process: They learn about "the explorers who visited here; the newcomers who settled here; the economy they established; their impact on the American Indians of this region; and their lasting marks on the landscape."[28] It is important to note how landscape provides the context, and sequence provides the structure in which people "visit" and "settle." Moreover, the U.S. acquisition of California from Mexico is also presented mainly as map study and through the use of timelines spiced with dramatizations of events such as gold mining, and the travels of explorers such as Jedediah Smith and John C. Fremont.

Similarly, in both the fifth and tenth grades, European exploration and colonization of the world is presented again mainly through map studies, timelines and the carefully de-politicized telling of frontier stories that mark the heroism and valor of those early explorers and colonists. In fact, even though the early colonial history of the U.S. is marred by violence, racism and oppression, the term "colonist" is only ever used in reference to a category of people who lived in the northeastern U.S. between the 1600s and 1700s, particularly those who fought in the War for Independence. How do such omissions serve to absolve us of collective and individual responsibility for the atrocities of colonial history? Divorcing words such as "colonist" and "settler" from the contexts of trauma, appropriation and genocide that are attached to them effectively cleanses historical accounts into forms that will be more comfortable for us – forms that make it easier for us to justify the power and privilege that we ourselves enjoy today. After all, how much easier is it for us to discuss colonial expansion in the Americas if we avoid discussing what that expansion entailed?

> European contact brought the decimation of the indigenous population, primarily through waves of disease, annihilation, and military and colonialist expansionist policies. The forced social changes and bleak living conditions of the reservation system also contributed to the disruption of American Indian cultures. This painful legacy includes themes of encroachment based on the manifest destiny doctrine and betrayal of earlier agreements and treaties. . . . [T]ribes faced "long walks" where many, if not the majority, died of disease, fatigue and starvation. As the reservation system developed, tribal groups were often forced to live together in restricted areas. When lands were found to be valuable to the government and Whites . . . more ways were found to take them away and resettle the native peoples elsewhere.[29]

Even though European colonization of the Americas is becoming increasingly recognized as an "American Indian Holocaust," our educational system as a whole seems intent on muting that reality. For example, standards 5.2 and 5.3 of the State curriculum address cooperation between "American Indians" and colonists, conflicts between Indians and "settlers" and specific inter-tribal struggles, but throughout these explorations, real in-depth interrogations of the "colonial experience" (i.e., issues of dispossession, the appropriation of native lands and the genocide of the native peoples) are rarely taken-up or engaged from indigenous perspectives. In fact, aside from references to a few historical events, particularly the Trail of Tears, the study of U.S. colonial treatment of indigenous peoples rarely extends beyond calls for sympathy and tolerance. The story that is told is the story of the colonizers, not of the colonized.

By turning world events into a generalized and supposedly apolitical "map study," we can explore the world's shifting geo-political borders without having to get into the nitty-gritty's of "regime change," "globalization," "privatization," "transnational flows" and "world politics." As a case in point, California's grade eight curriculum takes up the mid- to late-1800s by looking at the "changing boundaries of the United States"[30] without interrogating how those borders were extended."[31] In these particular historical treatments, wars such as the Spanish-American War are mentioned, but never in terms of how and why the United States occupied other people's lands. To further illustrate this point, see how *California's History-Social Science Framework and Standards* describes the tenth grade's course curriculum on imperial expansion:

> [S]tudents examine the worldwide imperial expansion that was fueled by the industrial nations' demand for natural resources and markets and by their nationalist aspirations. By studying maps, students will become aware of the colonial possessions of such nations as France, Germany, Italy, Japan, the Netherlands, and the United States.[32]

Following this standards-based curriculum plan, the closest students come to actually studying imperialism as a relation of power is in the framework's "recommendation" that British India should be studied to better understand the cultural conflicts that arise in colonial regimes. The lens for studying this case is one of culture clash rather than power, however; and it is the only case of Western colonialism that is offered as such.

Interestingly, contemporary practices of U.S. imperialism abroad are reframed for public consumption through many of the same discursive strategies used to sanitize California's "colonial" curriculum. Today's global economy is studied mainly in terms of how countries interrelate, specialize for trade, and achieve global stability:

- Elementary school students study the benefits of international trade.[33]

- Standard 10.11 for tenth graders recommends that students study how various Nation States have been integrated into the world economy and how the information, technological and communications revolutions are changing the world (e.g., television, satellites, computers).[34]

- Eleventh graders study the global interrelatedness of national economies and "the establishment of the United Nations and International Declaration of Human Rights, International Monetary Fund, World Bank, and General Agreement on Tariffs and Trade (GATT) and their importance in shaping modern Europe and maintaining peace and international order."[35]

Clearly reflecting the growing demands of the global marketplace, our educational bureaucracies increasingly develop standardized curricula that promote "privatized" discourses as a mainstay of a depoliticized educational context. Thus, while the U.S. has an active history of empire, and while California's students study American history for several years, critical interrogations of imperialism and colonialism are not engaged as part of the core curriculum. In fairness, while some of the standards are sufficiently vague that a teacher with enough background could examine imperialism's links to contemporary globalization and privatization, any such ventures should be understood as extending above and beyond the scope of the State-adopted curriculum.[36] But what then is its scope and purpose if critical thinking has been set to the sidelines? Reflecting on Freire's (1998) assertion that progressive educational praxis should work towards the promotion of a curiosity that is critical, bold and adventurous, it is important to ask-in what direction are we moving?[37]

By minimizing the role of critical thinking in schooling,[38] market-driven educational models work to mute the realities of imperialism while framing alternative educational concerns (i.e., equity considerations) as neither paramount nor central to the interests of a "democratic" education.[39] I would argue that Western educational frameworks and California's specifically, do not engage pedagogical or curricular models that reflect Deweyan traditions of public democracy and critical thinking in education. Rather, we are moving ever-closer to a privatized democracy in schooling – a model marked by systems of standardization, accountability and surveillance.[40] Like Karumanchery and Portelli (2005), I ask:

> Is public education meant to prepare students to compete and succeed in the global marketplace, or is it intended to reflect progressivist frameworks whereby students actively engage the intersections of school, home and community in order to learn how to critically examine and change their society? The reality of contemporary public schooling suggests that dominant strains of Western political thought and institutional practice are so couched in the 'mythos' of liberal democracy that notions of active participation and critical thought in education are becoming increasingly minimized and muted.[41]

If we are to construct and maintain a truly active body politic in our society, it will hinge on the development of a system of public education that is both critically and dialogically[42] engaged. However, as evidenced in the make-up of California's State-mandated history-social science curriculum, normative social paradigms and assumptions about self and world are filtered in ways that are distinctly non-critical, depoliticized and prescriptive. While actively obfuscating the nature of U.S. imperialism, California Public School curriculum works to construct an educational body politic that is compliant and complicit with the needs and designs of national and global imperialism.

In the analysis that follows, I juxtapose the imperialist ontology and approach engaged in *California's Framework and Standards*, with recent political statements made by President George W. Bush in relation to the invasion of Afghanistan, the War on Terror and the occupation of Iraq. Examining what connects these educational and political engagements illuminates the strategic use of ideological and discursive means to effectively construct, obscure and maintain imperialism in contemporary Western contexts. The themes addressed include: (a) the division of the world into we/they binaries; (b) the subsequent characterization of "us" as virtuous and "them" as "our" polar opposite; and (c) the establishment of "our" legitimate entitlement to police the world and solve other people's problems as we interpret them.

Creating Dichotomies: Manufacturing Public Opinion

In the months following the attacks on the World Trade Center and particularly during the U.S. led occupation of Iraq, President Bush has consistently and almost unilaterally framed U.S. policy and military engagements as conflict between freedom-loving peoples (generally non-Muslim) versus terrorist regimes (generally Muslim). For example, in his address to the nation on November 8, 2001:

> We are the target of enemies who boast they want to kill – kill all Americans. ... This new enemy seeks to destroy our freedom and impose its views. We value life; the terrorists ruthlessly destroy it. We value education; the terrorists do not believe women should be educated or should have health care, or should leave their homes. We value the right to speak our minds; for the terrorists, free expression can be grounds for execution. We respect people of all faiths and welcome the free practice of religion; our enemy wants to dictate how to think and how to worship even to their fellow Muslims.[43]

In his address to the Bush-Cheney 2004 Reception:

> In Afghanistan, in Iraq, we gave ultimatums to terror regimes. Those regimes chose defiance and those regimes are no more. Fifty million people in those two countries once lived under tyranny, and now they live in freedom.[44]

And again in his National Prime Time Address on April, 13, 2004:

> Above all, the defeat of violence and terror in Iraq is vital to the defeat of violence and terror elsewhere; and vital, therefore, to the safety of the American people. Now is the time, and Iraq is the place, in which the enemies of the civilized world are testing the will of the civilized world. We must not waver.[45]

Bush has repeatedly placed evil/violent terrorists and civilized/peace-loving peoples in diametrically opposed camps that are marked relative to skin color and religion. In fact, this division of the world into binaries and the related inscription of value and meaning into those differences is a fundamental element of imperial discourse and ideology. By employing discussions about difference rather than power relations, imperialists can establish clear boundary lines between themselves and all that they would oppose – clearly establishing themselves as on the side of righteousness, honor and civilization. Although the exact lines of demarcation and the specific traits assigned to "us" and "them" may shift over time, the process of division and classification does not. For example, echoing Bush's assertions that "countries are either with us or against us," much of the American public has embraced this we/they binary as support for the war has become framed as patriotic, while critiques are clearly denounced as unpatriotic and traitorous.[46]

Forty years ago, at the height of the Cold War, studies show that a majority of U.S. citizens divided the world along Communist and non-Communist lines. Similarly, a recent poll found that a majority of Americans now view the world in Muslim and non-Muslim terms, with most Muslim-majority nations being the least popular.[47] In California's history-social science curriculum, elementary level students learn to compare and contrast "beliefs, customs, ceremonies, traditions, and social practices of the varied cultures."[48] This is problematic in that approaching culture as something to compare and contrast forms a basis for learning we/they binaries. Starting with the sixth grade curriculum, I identified three overlapping binaries that structure such comparisons: Western versus non-Western, Judeo-Christian versus other religions, and democratic political systems/free market economies versus totalitarian systems.

In the sixth and seventh grade history-social science curricula, past civilizations are categorized and taken up along Western and non-Western lines. For instance, the curriculum traces the historical roots of the U.S. back to the "Western" civilizations and cultures of ancient Greece and Rome, and to the moral and ethical traditions of Judaism,[49] confirming that these cultural traditions nurtured the birth and evolutions of "rational thought," Western ethics, values and democracy.[50] Similarly, in grades ten and twelve, U.S. political institutions, the English parliamentary system, the Enlightenment and Western values are again traced back to the ancient Greeks, Romans and Hebrews. Why is it, then, that while these historical and sociocultural linkages are being developed through the curricula, nothing is done to connect "our" culture, values and institutions with Mesopotamia, Egypt, Kush, India, China, Islam, Mali, Ghana or the ancient civilizations of the Americas and Japan? The connective tissue exists, but the California curriculum doesn't make it a priority to study those links. After all, "we" are not interested in how the foundations of Western cultures developed through the early writing systems of Mesopotamia or in the varied influences of Western African civilizations on language, music and religion in the U.S. Simply put, the State curriculum is designed to establish, emphasize and reinforce (through repetition and authority) the "truth" about "our" nation's cultural heritage and lineage – and this "truth" becomes further cemented in our collective understandings of home and world as other similar binaries work to endorse and validate it.

Working in concert with this Western versus non-Western binary, religious dichotomies help to develop an educational sphere in which Judeo-Christian norms are normalized and explored in-depth while *other* belief systems receive minimal and insubstantial treatments. For instance, at the grade six and seven levels, students learn about some of the values and beliefs associated with Buddhism, Confucianism and Judaism, but the history of Christianity, including Old Testament Biblical figures, receives the most attention. In addition, while "Islamic" civilizations are addressed in the *Framework and Standards*, Muslim values and beliefs are not explored and, in fact, the curriculum consistently conflates Islam (religion) and Arab (ethnic group). For students who come from Christian homes, this study of religion reinforces what is familiar, and provides some terminology for *other* religions they might hear about, without providing much depth of understanding.

The third overlapping binary at work here places democratic/free market systems in opposition to systems that are framed as totalitarian/communist. Developed mainly at the high school level, this dichotomy activates a clear distinction between good and bad models of government. As a case in point, tenth grade students study Nazi Germany and Stalinist Russia as examples of regimes that "extinguish political freedom"[51] and twelfth graders learn to compare and contrast various forms of government, particularly dictatorships versus democracies. The political agenda behind these analyses are clear as Communist systems receive considerable attention, emphasizing their poor human rights records, their restrictions on individual liberty, and their general failure, while democracies are conflated with free market economies, freedom and the right to accumulate capital. Thus, in spite of global examples that trouble these socially constructed binaries,[52] the curriculum falsely dichotomizes students into a "we" that is Western, Judeo-Christian and democratic within a free market economy against a "they" that is non-Western, non-Christian, totalitarian and restricted. The origins of the U.S. and the roots of democracy in general are repeatedly and consistently linked to Western (particularly British) traditions that attach "us" to European origins. The United States is, however, a multiracial and religiously diverse nation, and so we must begin to interrogate what this "us" means for *other* peoples who live within our national borders – what does this "us" mean in terms of belonging, safety and a sense of community for those citizens marked, by skin and religion, as outsiders?

The *Framework and Standards* uses the language of multiculturalism to superficially fold diverse peoples into the "we" side of the dichotomy, but such "additive" strategies tend to simply celebrate difference while ignoring the importance of power as the fundamental mediating factor of those differences. In fifth grade, for example, students "learn about the significant contributions that black men and women made to the economic, political, and cultural development of the nation, including its music, literature, art, science, medicine, technology, and scholarship,"[53] but these contributions are neither spelled out nor explored. Similarly, while the various struggles of immigrants and African Americans are recognized in the curriculum, it also emphasizes that opportunities for these groups have far outweighed the struggles. This is the implicit agenda for multicultural policy in California's curriculum: incorporate *other* peoples into the mainstream, but do so in a way that does not disturb that status quo or "our" accepted Eurocentric history, norms and beliefs.

Constructed within an imperialist ideology, California's "multicultural curriculum" teaches culture, race, religion and world civilizations in a way that establishes clear cut "us" and "them" categorizations. Moreover, being written specifically for California's school system, the curriculum manages the study of immigrant and colonized peoples in very specific way:

- It ignores colonized peoples outside of California (e.g., Puerto Ricans and Hawaiians).
- Mexicans are treated mainly within the immigrant paradigm.
- American Indians are treated implicitly as an outsider group, as part of the "they," primarily by being located in history with no lasting legacy and almost no contemporary presence.

As the examples above illustrate, students can learn about racial, ethnic, and religious diversity within the U.S. and at the same time bind that knowledge of diversity to a Western, Eurocentric, Judeo-Christian, capitalist conception of who we are. As Willinsky (1998) points out, while most of us forget the specifics of the history we learned in school:

> [T]he historical distinctions that the imperial powers used to establish colonies, divide races, and distinguish cultures are transformed into universals of nature. These universals then become what people and governments do indeed learn from history.[54]

By developing and nurturing these binary distinctions, the State curriculum does more than inscribe notions of difference, it works to present those differences as attached to similarly dichotomized value sets, pitting the good and virtuous "we" against the bad and immoral "them."

If I'm Gonna be the Hero of the Piece . . .

In his justifications for the war on Iraq, President Bush has frequently evoked virtues that glorify and aggrandize the U.S. and its people. Emphasizing that the future of global freedom and peace depends on American actions, he lauds the U.S. as a "strong," "principled," "courageous" and "compassionate" country and he declares that the nation is "committed to expanding the realm of freedom and peace."[55] But in all these rhetorical speeches, he never unpacks the nature or price of these freedoms, nor does he discuss who defines peace and who benefits from such a peace. How do these value-laden associations cement images of the U.S. as intrinsically connected to notions of freedom, strength and righteousness? Moreover, how do these familiar slogans disguise the imperialism inherent in U.S. foreign policy in order to appear consistent with the nation's understanding of democratic principles?

With these questions in mind while I looked for similar value-laden terms associated with "us" in California's *Framework and Standards*, I found numerous words and phrases that spoke to the intrinsic goodness of the democratic and capitalist systems, rather than of peoples, culture or religions. The terms "free," "choice," "rational" and "liberty" were found interspersed throughout the State curricula and often to specifically mark the benefits and virtues of a free market economy. The seventh grade curriculum links capitalism directly to the Enlightenment through the suggestion that, as Europeans developed rational thinking, they also developed capitalist market economies based on private ownership and free choice. Throughout the grades, students also study democracy as embodied in the Constitution, learning that a representative democracy is the best political system because the government obtains its power from the consent of citizens. Not surprisingly, the terms associated with a representative democratic system are much the same as those associated with market economy: "individual liberty," "rights," "justice," and "freedom."

As noted by Karumanchery and Portelli (2005), by speaking through cultural emblems of freedom, fair play and merit in ways that rarely address the erosion of opportunities and access for the marginalized, related democratic concepts like collective rights and equity are generally omitted in curricular materials.[56] See, for example, this description of the fifth grade curriculum in the *Framework and Standards*:

> This course focuses on one of the most remarkable stories in history: the creation of a new nation, peopled by immigrants from all parts of the globe and governed by institutions founded on the Judeo-Christian heritage, the ideals of the Enlightenment, and English traditions of self-government. This experiment was inspired by the innovative dream of building a new society, a new order for the ages, in which the promises of the Declaration of Independence would be realized.[57]

Since the curriculum associates the same value-laden terms with capitalism and democracy, and since it connects both with the same historical roots, the curriculum implies that they are two dimensions of the same system – the end result of this "indoctrination" is that students are "disciplined" to see America's sociopolitical and economic systems as almost sacrosanct. While the curriculum acknowledges that it is an imperfect system, (i.e., slavery having been a major violation of human rights), capitalism and the bottom-up model of democratic process are still extolled in terms that clearly frame it as the best and only truly just system in human history. The melding of capitalist and democratic philosophies in this way clearly illustrates that the fundamental meaning of "democracy" has changed substantially-to the point that its political dimensions have been almost completely superseded by economic ones.

Encouraging linkages to the discourse of the global marketplace, California's *Framework and Standards* effectively entrench *banking* analogies into the curriculum and apply them to construct schooling and its stakeholders in "capital terms" (e.g., as investments, consumers, beneficiaries,and products). As suggested by Foster (1986), contemporary public schooling in the U.S. is geared to reflect the industrial state's values of efficiency and production. It is a complex discursive interplay that functionally portrays the market, industrialization and "progress" as not only necessary, but natural.[58] Through these interpretive means, California's curriculum presents modern technological progress and development as an additional achievement of Western cultures and nations – emphasizing that while all societies have developed and used technology of some sort, "ours" are distinguished by their sophistication. For example, seventh graders are taught that Western technology emerged from the Scientific Revolution of the Enlightenment, which was part and parcel of European exploration and the growth of democratic institutions (Standard 7.10). Then again in eighth grade, students learn that "progress" was bolstered by new "Western" technological advancements in farming, manufacturing, engineering and the production of consumer goods.[59] Rather than inviting questions about what it means for humans to attempt to control the natural world, the curriculum links the value-laden terms "progress" and "development" to technological change and the Western authors of that change.

There are fundamental problems in social science curricula that are designed to promote national loyalty in this way: they gloss over, ignore or distort injustices, they blunt teaching inquiry and they disrupt possibilities for critical thinking. For example, Takaki (1979) reflects on how the language of progress was used by the U.S. to justify the doctrine of Manifest Destiny: "As white Americans identified themselves with technology and increased in their minds the distance between 'civilization' and 'savagery,' they also viewed westward expansion in terms of technological progress."[60] By illustrating how Western culture was conflated with modernization and the needs of industrial change in order to justify colonial means and ends, Takaki reminds us of how easily progress can be used to rationalize and validate an imperial agenda. As Benhabib (1993) suggests, a democratic state must be wary of elevating economic and capital concerns to the point that they curtail the rights of other competing interests such as those of minorities and dissidents.[61] In light of these discussions, it is clear that although California's public school curriculum advocates teaching inquiry and a "multicultural" approach to schooling, doing so within a story of "us" as the virtuous people makes it impossible to examine injustice squarely, particularly from oppressed points of view.

. . . Then I Guess that Makes You the Bad Guy!

Contemporary imperialist discourses draw upon Orientalist[62] tropes of representation that allow the West to describe, marginalize, rule, humble and denigrate things non-Western. We can see this portrayal in the rhetoric surrounding the war on Iraq. Although most analysts agree that Saddam Hussein can be vilified justifiably, the U.S. administration persistently demonized Iraq and other regimes included in Bush's "axes of evil" as a prelude to attack. For example, Bush repeatedly vilified non-allied nations and particularly those deemed to be a direct threat by referring to them as "enemies of freedom" who could "threaten the world with weapons of mass destruction." A binary analysis of the war and subsequent occupation of Iraq plays out in news reports that frame resistance to the U.S. as loyalty to Saddam Hussein rather than as resistance to imperialism. The fact that a large proportion of U.S. citizens believe that Iraq deployed weapons of mass destruction against U.S. forces during the war in 2003, suggests a mindset that is already conducive to this process of "*other*ing." In my examination of California's *Framework and Standards* for similar portrayals of the *other*, I found four forms of *othering* that work to subtly denigrate specific peoples: (a) the situation of groups as different and disconnected from "normal" Americans; (b) the critiquing of political and economic systems rather than cultures; (c) the evaluation of other countries through the use of U.S. yardsticks; and (d) becoming accustomed to learning about rather than engaging with. I would argue that these forms of *othering* function as effectively as the more blatant forms because they do not appear to be problematic.

Inscribing Difference

American Indians and Islamic peoples are presented as simply different from "us." As noted above, the curriculum locates American Indians in the past. This is also the only American cultural group that is studied through separate units that survey culture, religious beliefs, economic activities, legends and so forth, and only at the elementary level. (Imagine, by way of contrast, a fifth grade unit in which students study the culture, religious beliefs, economy and stories of English-Americans, and then do not study English-American culture after fifth grade.) Further, much of the knowledge of American Indians is termed "mythology," which can suggest to children that it is not necessarily true. When studying Islam, seventh grade students are to learn about intellectual discoveries in various fields in the ancient world and the expansion of Islam in the Middle East, through Africa, and to Spain, India and Indonesia. The portrayal is simply descriptive rather than positive or negative; it is also fairly simple and disconnected from "our" experience" and "our" world.

New Means – Old Ends

Throughout California's curriculum, language is strategically used to convey oppressive meanings through the use of political rather than racial and cultural markers. Peoples and cultures are not specifically denigrated, but political and economic systems are. I found repeated study at the high school level of an amalgamation of totalitarian governments, communist regimes and socialist economies in order to emphasize their severe shortcomings:

- In tenth grade, students study totalitarian regimes to "understand the nature of totalitarian rule and recognize the danger of concentrating unlimited power in the hands of the central government."[63]

- The former Soviet Union and China are examined as communist countries that tried unsuccessfully to modernize by imposing collectivism and communist ideology.

- The Cold War is studied in eleventh grade with particular focus on the shortcomings of the communist system.

- In twelfth grade, while studying World War II, students examine the fascist dictatorships of Germany, Italy, Spain and Portugal, giving attention to "the arbitrary rulings, torture, imprisonment, and executions without trials that attend fascist takeovers and help to maintain their control."[64]

- Studies of genocide make reference to the Ottoman Empire's treatment of the Armenians and Pol Pot's Cambodian regime (U.S. treatment of indigenous people is never taken up in this context).

- Racism is taken up with reference to Nazi Germany (White American treatment of people of color is never taken up in this context).

These kinds of regimes are contrasted very explicitly with democracies, since the curriculum teaches that they represent the antithesis of "us." Along these lines, racist and imperialist discourses that conceptualize right/wrong, good/evil, may do so now under the "liberal" and "multicultural" guise of discussing economics and politics. The means shift, but the racist and imperialist ends remain the same.

Depoliticizing the Lens

The curriculum also views the rest of the world through an American sociopolitical lens. Clearly, "our" Western ontology takes such a stance of authority and normality over every area of the curriculum (i.e., literature, economics, politics, science and imagination) that anyone would be hard pressed to see beyond that politicized veil. Again, the importance of discourse for the study of imperialism and racism helps to drive home the degree to which "our" norms of culture control and constitute every social aspect and meaning attributed to the *other*. Through the use of both implicit and explicit contrasts, the dichotomy between the "we" and the "they" becomes further solidified, and as binary oppositions, the "American norms" are defined and ascribed meaning in direct relation to that which they repress.

- Beginning in second grade, students learn about interdependence among nations, specialization and market exchange in food trade.

- In grade ten, the Middle East, Africa, Mexico, other parts of Latin America and China are studied in relation to examine the dilemmas they face and to study the extent to which they "appear to serve the cause of individual freedom and democracy."[65]

- Tenth graders also analyze the integration of countries into the world economy (but the curriculum does not look to develop a critical analysis of that integration).

- The materials used throughout the public school system are American made and so students learn through practice that it is both appropriate and normal to study other peoples, culture, nations and worldviews through our own frames of reference.

These "depoliticized" meanings are understood in their relation to an established difference and not due to any innate property. But having equated freedom, representative democracy, individualism, capitalism, private property and progress, the curriculum has provided a lens for analysis that reflects a U.S. point of view.

Consuming Rather than Engaging

Throughout the learning process, teachers and students alike are guided in a process of learning about the world that comes from state-produced curriculum guides and state-adopted textbooks. Through such texts, students learn to consume knowledge about the *other*. I would suggest that youth who become accustomed to learning in this fashion will also likely continue consuming pre-packaged imagery of *others* in the future – learning about the world by watching TV – rather than critically engaging it.

Manifest Destiny for a New Millennium

One might argue that it is human nature to divide the world into "us" and "them," and to inflate one's own self-perception while stereotyping and denigrating the *other*. What distinguishes imperialist thinking, however, is the assumption that one's virtues entitle one's country to use power over others. Imperialist nations, attributing their own prosperity to their superior cultural and intellectual systems rather than to any history of exploitation, perceive a duty to name and solve the problems of the *other* (such as famine, inadequate health-care, inadequate education, internal warfare and poverty), even if force is required. In his address to the Bush-Cheney 2004 Reception, for example, President Bush emphasized that "We seek to lift whole nations by spreading freedom." He went on to proclaim that:

> We have duties in the world, and when we see disease, and starvation, and hope-less poverty, we will not turn away. On the continent of Africa, America is now committed to bringing the healing power of medicine to millions of men and women and children now suffering with AIDS. We will lead the world in this great work of rescue."[66]

The terms "rescue," "lift," and "spreading freedom" in the face of "hopeless poverty" are today's version of the so-called "White man's burden." I examined the curriculum for how it might support a sense of U.S. entitlement to apply power globally, given the binary thinking described thus far. The main mechanism I found is the repeated implication that Europeans and U.S. expansionists worked largely in empty territory, and that their actions led to better-ment. For example, consider this passage from the fourth grade curriculum:

> One reason for the Spanish settling in California was to bring Christianity to the native peoples. Students should understand how the introduction of Christianity affected native cultures. . . . Cattle ranches and agricultural villages were developed around the missions and presidios. European plants, agriculture, and a herding economy were introduced to the region.[67]

While the above statements are true, much is also missing. The term "settle," used repeatedly with reference to Europeans and White Americans, sanitizes and legitimates the process of invasion. The concept of bringing Christianity rings with altruism; and the passage ignores perspectives of indigenous people as well as cultural exchanges that flowed in both directions. What Europeans introduced, receives attention; what was already here, does not. In other words, the process of conquest is sanitized, rendered altruistic, and presented as part of a story of development. In high school, the curriculum is more direct about the role U.S. citizens are to learn to play. When studying "Unresolved Problems of the Modern World," tenth grade students are to learn "that the history of the United States has had special significance for the rest of the world, both because of its free political system and its pluralistic nature."[68] "Although democratic ideals first emerged in the West, almost every nation pays them at least rhetorical homage."[69] Thus, the rest of the world wants to be more like the U.S., which suggests some entitlement to use force if needed, to spread its political/economic system.

Polls of the U.S. public have found fairly strong support for intervening in the affairs of other countries, particularly to stop atrocities, address humanitarian problems or track down terrorist groups.[70] But people around the world "divide on whether the US is a positive or negative force on the global economy and on human rights. U.S. citizens, of course, give their country credit for being a positive force in both areas over the past decade," as do other G-7 countries. Asian Pacific countries rate the U.S. as lower, and "in Latin America and the rest of the world, the US is seen as a negative force on both human rights and the economy, especially human rights."[71] As long as U.S. residents believe that U.S. involvement in other countries helps, we tend to feel entitled to name and solve other people's problems, even when much of the rest of the world does not view our involvement in the same way.

State-Mandated Curricula and Free Inquiry

Our colonial literacy model is designed to manufacture the consent of our own people; to discipline and domesticate Americans through the use of an immense and interconnected sociopolitical propaganda model – a truly ironic reality in a nation that espouses the value of freedom of thought.[72] Dimitriadis and McCarthy (2001) point out that U.S. schooling has a long tradition of inducting young people into a colonial way of thinking.

> To a large extent, such a hegemonic approach is deeply informed by the long history of intellectual and academic colonialism in American educational institutions, where Anglos define history and other groups serve as the objects of such definitions. . . . This hegemonic approach constitutes a top-down project that attempts to hold the Eurocentric and establishment core of the curriculum in

place, inoculating it by simply adding on selected, nonconflictual items from the culture and experiences of minority and subaltern groups.[73]

Their description definitely fits the *History-Social Science Framework and Standards* for California Public Schools. I am less troubled by the fact that such a curriculum exists, than I am by the fact that it has been adopted by the state to structure how history and social studies are to be taught in California, and teachers are being directed state-wide to follow it.

Some have told me that at least social studies occupies only a minor part of the current California testing regime, so teachers are not actually bound to follow the history-social science state standards. Recently, for example, I pointed out some of its biases to a Latino principal, who simply shrugged and said that many teachers are spending so much time working to raise test scores in reading and math that they aren't teaching social studies. Not teaching social studies, however, avoids rather than addresses the issue. History and social studies can be taught very differently. There are alternatives to teaching students to divide the world into we/they, or teaching them to compare and contrast cultures and civilizations. Teachers can help students learn to dialogue with others, and learn to see from the points of view of others. Rather than telling stories about the past based on assumptions of the present, which is how the California curriculum is constructed, teachers can help students learn to "see through the eyes of the people who were there," and in the process, "teach us what we cannot see, to acquaint us with the congenital blurriness of our vision."[74] The arts can serve as a venue for teaching from postcolonial perspectives. Artists render complex realities and visions in ways that capture multiplicity, hybridity and complexity. Experiencing complex and nonlinear narratives of postcolonial artists provides a way for students to engage *with* rather than learning *about* others.[75] Young people can learn to dialogue directly with others who differ from themselves culturally, and in the process come to a much richer understanding of what culture is, who one is as a cultural being, and how people think about constructing solutions and answers to the most basic and profound questions humans face.[76]

Young people should be offered multiple narratives and viewpoints about imperialism in history as well as today – from dominant as well as subaltern points of view. Alternative teaching guides can provide readings and teaching strategies that engage new and insurgent narratives and readings about imperialism.[77] For example, Bigelow and Peterson's (2002) text, *Rethinking Globalization*, contextualizes the new global economy in an analysis of colonialism and offers suggestions for teaching at the elementary and secondary level.[78] I believe that this type of exploration is the only way our youth will learn to think critically and imaginatively about forging new relationships based on mutuality rather than control. It is a great irony that some readers may take the questions I raise here as an attack on freedom and democracy. Rather, I believe that state control over what teachers teach and what students are to think serves to undermine freedom of inquiry that is the basis for democratic life. It is essential for educators to challenge and resist the power of the state to define what we teach.

Chapter 6

Racism in Educational Sites

Sustaining Oppression and Maintaining the Status Quo

David Gillborn, Ph.D.
School of Educational Foundations & Policy Studies
Institute of Education, University of London

Introduction

The term *institutional racism* has been around for a very long time. Carmichael and Hamilton (1967) famously used the phrase to describe how White interests and attitudes saturate the key institutions that shape American life.[1] In recent years, the phrase has moved from the realm of political activism and academic debate into more popular usage. However, despite the frequency with which commentators, the media and policymakers use the term, at a fundamental level most White people still ignore the true meaning of institutional racism. For them, racism is assumed to be something that is of declining significance and, if present at all, is perpetuated by a violent minority made up almost exclusively of working class people. That being said, while it is important to remember that the streets of Britain are still dangerous and violently racist places, such vicious and crude forms of racism are not the whole story. Indeed, in the UK recent years have seen a remarkable shift in the public discourse surrounding the existence of institutional racism (arising directly out of an official inquiry into the racist murder of Stephen Lawrence – a young Black[2] man murdered by a group of White youths as he waited for a bus in a part of London where White racism has a particularly murderous history). Unfortunately, the increased frequency with which the term is now used in Britain has not been matched by any significant increase in awareness among the majority of the population.

Racism, in its numerous, changing and sometimes hidden forms, pervades the assumptions and frameworks that shape our sociopolitical systems and institutions. A case in point, while education can be a force for liberation and anti-racism, critical interrogations of educational systems in Britain, Canada and the United States have revealed that racism frames our methods of assessment while producing and reproducing our staff-rooms and classrooms in ways that commonly add to the problem. Indeed, as Paul Gilroy argued more than a decade ago, over-identifying racism with extreme acts and exceptional groups (e.g., the British National Party, National Front and Combat 18 in England, the KKK in the U.S. and the Heritage Front in Canada), has the potential to divert attention from what he called *racism in the mainstream*:

> [S]eeing "race" and racism not as fringe questions but as a volatile presence at the very centre of British politics, actively shaping and determining the history not simply of blacks, but of this country as a whole.[3]

With less gravitas, but no less perception, Marcella (a 14-year-old Black High School student in London) put it this way:

> I don't know how to explain it but I just don't feel that they're fair. . . . It's not blatantly there. I mean, you can't, you wouldn't be able to just walk in the school and say "Oh, the school's racist." You have to take time before you knew that.[4]

Marcella's observations were echoed in the narratives of other participants who took part in Gillborn and Youdell's (2000) two year field study of educational reforms and their impact on (a) the delivery of education; (b) access for marginalized groups; and (c) the channelling of certain students into low status courses. Particularly important in this research was the clear indication that many aspects of the educational reforms were having a markedly negative impact on traditionally disadvantaged groups (i.e., especially Black students and their White working class peers). Generated around the mantra of "raising standards" and operationalized through common sense assumptions about "ability," the most powerful discriminatory effects were amplified and given institutional force through the schools' attempts to raise their profile in the official performance statistics.[5]

This article examines how racism works through the mundane processes of schooling in an atmosphere of high stakes testing and increased calls for ever higher "standards." I argue that racism is a complex, sometimes subtle, but always powerful presence at the heart of contemporary schooling. With these considerations in mind, the following section will explore these processes in relation to the notion of "ability" as a key factor in shaping students' chances of educational success.

Ability and the Myth of Intelligence

The notion of "ability" is of vital importance for several reasons: first, because assumptions about ability (what it is and how it operates) have emerged as a central component of contemporary education policy, and second, because ability is frequently assumed to be a neutral, color-blind category that can be discussed in isolation from wider questions about educational opportunity, social disadvantage and racial inequity. So with these complexities in mind, it is important to first consider how the concept of ability is operationalized (i.e., what it is thought to be, how it is measured and what significance it is accorded) before examining the interconnections that run between ability and disadvantage.

While the word "ability" is used quite frequently, its meaning and significance are rarely discussed in detail. Findings from Gillborn and Youdell's (2000) study suggest that when teachers use the word, they tend to exhibit certain assumptions about the nature of ability. Specifically, they tend to assume that ability is a relatively fixed quality, that it is measurable and that it relates to a generalized academic potential. For example, there is a common belief in the British school system that students who are identified as more (or less) able than the majority of their peers will continue to be distinguished in that way throughout their educational careers. This does not mean, of course, that students ever stop learning; rather, it means that the differentials between students in the same year group (whether at age five, ten, fifteen or whenever) are assumed to remain relatively consistent. In particular, there seems to be a common belief that certain children are simply better at learning than others and that this advantage (and their peers' disadvantage) derives from something which cannot be taught. As one head-teacher put it:

> You can't *give* someone ability can you? . . . You can't achieve more than you're capable of can you?[6]

In this way, ability is commonly assumed to be a characteristic that is generally immutable; leading to differences between peers that are relatively fixed. A second characteristic of ability, in the eyes of many teachers, appears to be its susceptibility to identification and even quantification. Not only can teachers say which students have ability, they can also say how much of it each child possesses. Teachers make judgements about a student's ability in a wide range of different contexts and using a variety of criteria, including test scores, written work, oral presentations and even in relation to behavior. These judgements, and the various labels they produce, are invested with differing degrees of importance, but as evidenced in Gillborn and Youdell's (2000) research, certain criteria have come to command enormous weight in the British school system. Most significantly, the educational system's belief in *ability* taken in concert with its reliance on *standardized tests* (and the scientific facade that supports and bolsters their use), has established a decidedly problematic situation in which such tests have become effectively unassailable as a means of divining children's abilities and deficiencies. These standardized paper-and-pencil tests are generally developed by outside consultants (e.g., the publishing house NFER-Nelson[7]) and sold to schools with the understanding that they will (a) measure students' *Cognitive Abilities*[8] and (b) analyze students' scores to produce a range of predicted outcomes in later test situations (this includes a service that purports to predict students' eventual GCSE[9] performance five years after the completion of the original test). One head-teacher offered this perspective on the tests and their usefulness as predictors of future performance:

> We have found them helpful as indicators of GCSE performance, and in that there is some correlation between the standard tests and the GCSE outcomes. . . . .So for a significant proportion you can be confident that the thing *is* a good predictor of their GCSE results.

The head-teacher assigned great significance to what he called a "correlation" between the test results and students' eventual GCSE performance. Of course, some *association* between the two is to be expected when the school is using the former to decide which students gain access to particular courses and teaching resources.

These tests are accorded substantial status in the systemic process of defining students' capabilities in the short-term and assigning them to ranked teaching groups that will affect their access to resources throughout their school careers. For example, in year nine of the British system (age 13), students are encouraged to meet with senior member of staff to discuss possible career paths and to finalize GCSE subject choices. At this point, the results of the standardized tests stand as one of the most significant pieces of information at the teachers' disposal – it is significant that these meetings takes place more than two years after the original tests were administered. Importantly, every such student-teacher consultation observed in Gillborn and Youdell's (2000) research revealed that while test scores were consulted as a general guide to student ability, teachers' comments as to actual student performance over the previous two and a half years in the school were usually completely absent from the discussion. In this way, the test scores have become one of the principal selection devices upon which teachers prompt students to alter their choices in particular ways to either increase or decrease the academic weight of their studies.[10]

The status and weight given to these tests are such that their authority remains intact even in cases where their predictive power has apparently failed. For example, if a student has been predicted success but ultimately fails, it is assumed that the student has failed to make the most of their ability; that they have not worked hard enough. On the other hand, if a student scores poorly in the initial test but eventually outperforms the school's expectations this is viewed as a statistical anomaly. Although such a performance casts doubt on the assumptions at the heart of school's views of ability and teachers' use of cognitive ability tests, in practice, such occurrences tend to be dismissed as insignificant. One head-teacher suggested:

> [T]here will always be a number for whom the correlation doesn't work, a percentage. But what you don't know is who the individuals are. That's the nature of the statistical analysis.

Assuming that "ability" is a kind of generalized academic quality or potential, the same head-teacher summed up this approach when he said:

> [A]nd they're *indicators* of ability, whatever that means. And obviously indicators of some sort of *general* ability rather than just a sort of subject specific ability. . . . These kind of tests wouldn't necessarily tell you that someone's really good at art. So you might get a good result in art. And you might have a particular *talent* in those areas.

He draws a distinction between a general ability (which he assumes the standardized test is measuring) and a more particularized skill or talent in one curricular area. When teachers describe children by using terms such as "highly able" or "less able," they are encoding these kind of beliefs in a general and relatively fixed notion of ability. Of course that being said, it is important to recognize that such assumptions are not confined to teachers and educational stakeholders alone. While this view of ability as a static, all encompassing quality has long been abandoned by mainstream research, it is echoed in the widespread assumptions that shape public debate about education in many Western societies. Despite the longstanding, and often heated, debate about the usefulness of intelligence testing and other psychometric approaches to education, many sociologists and psychologists have concluded that such approaches offer nothing more than a pseudo-scientific facade that cloaks eugenic thought in supposedly scientific respectability.[11] Interestingly, even within the ranks of psychometric testers themselves (i.e., people who write and administer IQ tests for a living), there is now widespread agreement that there is no single thing that can reliably be termed "ability" nor "intelligence" and that relative scores are not fixed. Robert J. Sternberg[12] (1998) has suggested that:

> [H]uman abilities are forms of developing expertise. . . . [T]ests of abilities are no different from conventional tests of achievement, teacher-made tests administered in school, or assessments of job performance. Although tests of abilities are used as predictors of these other kinds of performance, the temporal priority of their administration should not be confused with some kind of psychological priority. . . . There is no qualitative distinction among the various kinds of measures.[13]

Or to put it more simply:

> The fact that Billy and Jimmy [sic] have different IQs tells us something about differences in what they now do. It does not tell us anything fixed about what ultimately they will be able to do.[14]

Sternberg's central argument, that abilities are a form of developing expertise, is paralleled in the conclusions of the American Psychological Association's *Cleary Committee*:

> A distinction is drawn traditionally between intelligence and achievement tests. A naive statement of the difference is that the intelligence test measures *capacity to learn* and the achievement test measures *what has been learned*. But items in *all* psychological and educational tests measure acquired behaviour.[15] [emphasis added]

Contrary to popular belief, therefore, there is no test of capacity to learn: *every* test measures only what you have learnt so far. Consequently, the view of ability as fixed, measurable and generalized may accord with common sense, but it is actually both factually incorrect and dangerous. Unfortunately, Western educational systems have been fundamentally shaped by this slanted and wholly inaccurate common sense idea of ability – so much so, that it continues to frame current educational policy and practice. For instance, school systems in Britain continue to cling to these outdated and problematic engagements with IQ, intelligence and ability even though the present government espouses an explicitly inclusive agenda. The 1997 Labor election manifesto was entitled "New Labour: Because Britain Deserves Better." One of the defining characteristics of the *new* Labor Party was its readiness to embrace traditionally Conservative ideas and to buy into what Ball (1990) called "the discourse of derision" surrounding state educational standards. The 1997 manifesto stated bluntly that "Children are not all of the same ability, nor do they learn at the same speed."[16] This assertion was used as the basis for a policy that promoted greater use of "setting by ability," a strategy which would supposedly operate to "maximise progress, for the benefit of high fliers and slower learners alike."[17] Subsequent policies have built on this notion and institutionalized perceived differences in ability by championing separate provision to reflect these supposed differences.

These processes include (a) an increased attention to the development of separate teaching groups that would further "set by ability"; (b) the expansion of "gifted and talented" programmes to identify and advantage those students lucky enough to be thought of as the most able; and (c) the promotion of separate vocational education pathways for those students deemed to lack the necessary ability and aspiration for academic study:

> [T]he needs of gifted and talented children in inner city schools are not given the priority they deserve. . . . Secondary schools will be expected to develop a distinct teaching and learning programme for their most able five to ten per cent of pupils.[18]

> Young people should be able to develop at a pace consistent with their abilities, whether faster or slower. Those going faster might skip some examinations or take them early and use the time gained to study some subjects in greater depth or to start new ones. Those progressing more slowly might take GCSEs (or equivalent) later than age 16.[19]

The proposed reforms (unveiled in early 2002) did more than merely reflect the government's belief in a fixed and measurable form of ability. The creation of separate curricular pathways for students of supposedly varying ability seems to be *driven* by a conviction that such differences are both marked and immutable and that attention to those issues offers the only way of raising student achievement. Consequently, we are left in a difficult and dangerous situation. On one hand, the common sense view of ability (as fixed and generalized) is widely discredited by research while on the other hand these reductive and crude notions serve to shape both everyday school interactions and national educational policy. This situation is made even worse by the fact that racially and ethnically minoritized students seem significantly less likely to be viewed as evidencing ability in their teachers' eyes.

Selection and Racial Inequity

There is now a large and growing body of research that draws on work in Europe and North America to explore how the use of selection in educational settings affects different student groups by gender, ethnicity and social class.[20] A consistent finding in this, and other research on ethnic diversity in education, is that Black students are much *less* likely to be seen as *able* in comparison with their White peers. However, they are much more likely to be viewed as disruptive, as lacking motivation and living in unsupportive homes. In fact, even though each of these stereotypes are problematized and challenged by contemporary research evidence, they continue to be powerfully enacted in the classroom. For example, even though research suggests that Black families tend to be more positive about the value of education and more supportive than equivalent White families, classroom studies have generally concluded that: (a) Black students are more likely to be criticized than their White peers who are involved in the same activity; (b) Black students are sometimes criticized for actions that do not break any clear school rule but are nevertheless judged to be "inappropriate" or "threatening" by their teachers;[21] and (c) Black students tend to spend more time on homework and remain in the educational system longer than their White peers of the same sex and social class background.[22]

Unfortunately, the negative interpretations and images of Black deficit find coded expression in many of the comments and beliefs that frame everyday school life. In fact, they are so deeply ingrained in our social and educational spaces that even clear evidence to the contrary does little to lessen their power and/or impact on minoritized peoples. For example, here is a departmental head talking about Black students in his school. Specifically, the teacher is describing the students' reactions when given their *estimated grades*, that is, a prediction by their teachers of their likely performance in the coming GCSE examinations:

> I found that quite strange that the kids had their estimated grades because they then came back at you and gave you earache, you know, would challenge you in the corridor and so you were under threat. You know, 'why have you only given me that grade,' you know? Because kids, you know, have different perceptions of themselves, they have no understanding, you know, and some of them live in cloud cuckoo land. I mean we've got, we had a whole period where we had Afro-Caribbean kids running around with gold rimmed glasses on with plain glass in them because they thought it made them look more intelligent, you know, they really had highly inflated opinions of themselves as far as academic achievement, and this is fact. I mean there were a whole group of kids that put on glasses and wandered round the corridors with gold rimmed glasses on because they really felt that they were sort of A/B.[23]

This is a disturbing glimpse of how racist stereotypes can be sustained and institutionalized, even when the evidence contradicts them. For instance, this teacher *could* have interpreted the episode very differently. After all, the dominant stereotype of Black youth (and especially young Black men) is that they are not interested in academic success and that such commitments are ridiculed as "acting White."[24] But here we have a group of Black students demonstrating a high commitment to success (even to the extent of behaving in ways that the teacher thinks are calculated to make them look more studious) and publicly querying the schools' low estimation of their chances. Faced with such a reaction, some observers might have concluded that the students were highly motivated and hungry for achievement; exactly the opposite of the dominant stereotype. Unfortunately, this departmental head sees no clash with the stereotype. Rather, he casts the episode as further proof of what he sees as their "highly inflated opinions of themselves" and echoing a further part of the dominant stereotype of Black youth as a dangerous presence, he describes their actions as threatening: "they . . . came back at you . . . gave you earache . . . would challenge you . . . you were under threat."

Intelligence, Ability and Racism: The New IQism

More than 25 years ago, Samuel Bowles and Herbert Gintis critically challenged *IQism's* supposition that social inequality was principally a reflection of inherited differences in general intelligence.[25] Although long derided as racist pseudo-science, as I will show in this section, the views critiqued by Bowles and Gintis are alive and well in the Twenty-first Century. Perhaps even more dangerous, however, is a position that could be characterized as a *new* IQism. That is, we have today a situation wherein the old-style language of race, intelligence and subnormality has passed from common usage, only to be replaced by less incendiary terms and assumptions that *implicitly* frame "ability" as relatively fixed and differentially distributed (particularly along lines of social class, race and/or ethnicity).

We have already seen (above) how a crude and regressive view of ability (as relatively fixed, measurable and generalized) can be detected in teachers' perspectives and national policy statements alike. Furthermore, there is growing evidence that White teachers' everyday expectations of Black students reflect a belief that "they" are generally less able and more likely to cause trouble than to excel in their studies. Although coded in talk of "ability" and "aptitude," these views have the same practical consequences as the more obviously extreme notions of "intelligence" and "biological hierarchy" that are peddled by people such as Arthur Jensen, Hans Eysenck, J. Phillipe Rushton, Richard Herrnstein and Charles Murray.[26] These, and other such writers, typically present themselves as pioneering scientists who have the moral courage to seek the "truth" by challenging the flawed assumptions of progressive educators and the forces of political correctness. For example, in a new afterword in the paperback version of *The Bell Curve* (1996), Charles Murray states, "If there is one objective that we shared from the beginning, it was to write a book that was relentlessly moderate – in its tone, science, and argumentation."[27] The relentless nature of Herrnstein and Murray's moderation can be gauged by their views on single parents:

> [W]e want to return to the state of affairs that prevailed until the 1960s, when children born to single women – where much of the problem of child neglect and abuse originates – were more likely to be given up for adoption at birth. This was, in our view, a better state of affairs than we have now.[28]

Herrnstein and Murray's moderation is similarly in evidence when they reflect on the motivation for racist attacks on U.S. campuses which, in their view, arise not from White racism and defence of privilege, but a well-founded sense of White injustice:

> A plausible explanation is that Whites resent blacks, who are in fact getting a large edge in the admissions process and often in scholarship assistance and many of whom, as Whites look around their own campuses and others, "don't belong there" academically.[29]

This "moderate" book made the *New York Times* best-seller list and sparked an international outcry with its conclusion that African Americans (and the White underclass) are genetically predisposed to criminality and stupidity: "*Putting it all together, success and failure in the American economy, and all that goes with it, are increasingly a matter of the genes that people inherit.*"[30] One of the book's principal sources in relation to "race" and "intelligence" was the work of J. Phillipe Rushton of the University of Western Ontario, Canada. Rushton recently summarized his thesis in an online review submitted to internet bookseller Amazon.com:

> We would all be better off by accepting the scientific facts about how biology underlies race differences in sports, crime and school learning . . . evolutionary selection pressures led Europeans (and especially East Asians) to have less testosterone than Blacks. This gives Blacks an edge at sports but makes them restless in school and prone to crime.[31]

This is the clearest possible indication of the kind of reasoning that lies behind works like *The Bell Curve*. Yet Rushton is viewed as a serious scholar by those "experts" who wish to promote a belief in the inevitability of Black academic failure. For example, Arthur Jensen recently cited Rushton's work (along with *The Bell Curve* and the latest book of his own) as recommended texts for those seeking "Fairly comprehensive and scientifically respectable treatments of the topic."[32] Indeed, when one looks more closely at the literature cited among contemporary IQists, it becomes clear that while Rushton may state his views somewhat more plainly than other writers, his beliefs are not uncommon. For instance, in 1994, as the public controversy over *The Bell Curve* raged on, a group of 52 professors (all self-proclaimed "experts in intelligence and allied fields") signed a statement that was published in the *Wall Street Journal* under the title, "Mainstream science on intelligence."[33] Signatories included Rushton, Hans Eysenck, Arthur Jensen and Richard Lynn. Among the many statements of supposedly "mainstream scientific" opinion were the following:

> [G]enetics plays a bigger role than does environment in creating IQ differences among individuals.
>
> The bell curve for Whites is centred roughly around IQ 100; the bell curve for American blacks roughly around 85.
>
> [B]lack 17-year-olds perform, on the average, more like White 13-year-olds in reading, math, and science, with Hispanics in between.

These views are presented as if distilled from numerous scientific studies and the tone of delivery is somewhat dry.[34] But the meaning is clear. First, the authors are stating that intelligence is largely a matter of genetic inheritance. Second, they are saying that most Whites are naturally more intelligent than most Black people. In fact the statement comparing the supposed differences in the "bell curve" (or distribution) between different groups would mean that the average White person is more intelligent than over 80 per cent of Black people.[35]

These explicitly oppressive views, with their deterministic, racist and supremacist consequences, are not overtly present in contemporary education policy. However, the links are closer than is commonly supposed. For example, one of the 52 "experts" backing the above quotes in the *Wall Street Journal* was Julian C. Stanley. One of Stanley's achievements was to found the Center for Talented Youth at Johns Hopkins University in the United States. And that center has been adopted as a model for (and major partner in) the development of an *Academy for Gifted & Talented Youth* which the British Government is establishing at Warwick

University at an annual cost of £20 million[36] (Approximately 44 million Canadian, and 36 million American dollars). I am not suggesting that these links reveal some deliberate conspiracy to advance eugenic pseudo-science in Britain. What I *am* suggesting may be even more dangerous; that is, that the language and assumptions which characterize contemporary British education policy (a *new* IQism) uses an apparently de-racialized (color-blind) vehicle for beliefs and actions that may be just as racist in their consequences as the more overtly rabid views of Rushton and other traditional forms of IQism. To comprehend the scale of the danger, it is necessary to understand the extensive and racialized forms of selection that increasingly characterize education in English schools.

Institutionalizing Racism and "Tiered" Examinations

I have already noted the growing trend towards increased selection in the English education system. There is increased selection *between* schools (through more diversity of type and specialization) and there is increased selection *within* schools (through the use of "setting," the establishment of "gifted and talented" schemes, and the creation of separate vocational routes). These multiple forms of selection offer an institutional means by which supposed differences in ability are translated into different curricular and pedagogic experiences. Students in lower ranked teaching groups receive a restricted curriculum and have access to fewer resources.[37] Their failure is institutionalized. To see how these factors come together it is useful to consider a single example (among the many possible examples): that of *tiered* examinations.

As students near the end of their compulsory schooling in England, the majority are entered for externally moderated examinations in a range of subjects. The majority of GCSE examinations have adopted a system of so-called "tiered" examination papers, whereby students are entered for different question papers within the same subject. Teachers decide which examination a student will take and the decisions are important because each tier only offers a limited number of grades (see Figure 1). The most common system is the two tier model. Here, students in the higher tier can achieve grades A* (starred A) through to D. But if they perform below the level of a grade D, then rather than be awarded a grade between E and G (the remaining "pass" grades) in most subjects they will effectively fall through the tier floor and be awarded a U (ungraded) result. Students entered in the Foundation tier *cannot* exceed a grade C regardless of how well they perform. In mathematics, a subject with a long history of selection, the examination is structured by a *three* tier model (see Figure 1). In this case the best grade available to the Foundation tier is a grade D – which is less than the grade C that is usually taken as the minimum required for study at advanced level or entry to professional training. When these kinds of decisions are taken, it is Black students who are systematically disadvantaged: in comparison with their White peers, young Black people are less likely to be placed in the higher tiers and more likely to be entered at Foundation level.[38] In the two schools studied by Gillborn and Youdell (2000), 66 % of Black students were entered at Foundation level in mathematics. Consequently, *before they had even answered a* *question*, it had been determined that two-thirds of Black children would effectively "fail" their maths exams.

Tiering, and the related differential selection of students by ethnic origin, provides a clear example of how multiple factors can come together to deny educational opportunities. Furthermore, although "race" and ethnicity are rarely (if ever) explicitly positioned as relevant factors in the dominant discourse, they are implicitly at the very heart of the process. Specifically, we have seen that a common sense notion of "ability" is dominant in contemporary schooling even though it is problematic, crude, regressive and ultimately false. Working to the detriment of Black students, who are generally seen as lacking "ability" and prone to disciplinary problems, these practices ask and require teachers to decide which of their students have the most "ability" and potential. This act of selection institutionalizes oppression by presenting marginalized students with markedly different pedagogical experiences and by denying them access to basic educational resources. As highlighted in the *Stephen Lawrence Inquiry*, this, and many other similar educational measures to "raise standards," are clear cut cases of institutional racism.

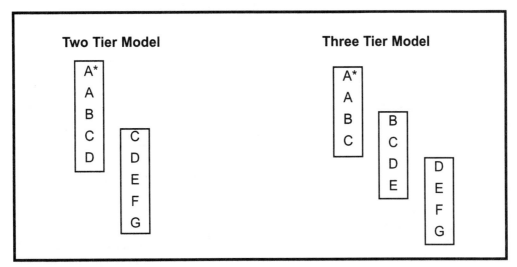

Figure 1: Tiering in GCSE examinations.

Institutional Racism and the Stephen Lawrence Inquiry

"Institutional racism" consists of the collective failure of an organisation to provide an appropriate and professional service to people because of their colour, culture, or ethnic origin. It can be seen or detected in processes, attitudes and behaviour which amount to discrimination through unwitting prejudice, ignorance, thoughtlessness and racist stereotyping which disadvantage minority ethnic people.[39]

The Inquiry into the murder of Stephen Lawrence, and the failed subsequent police investigation, established a definition of institutional racism that has been widely debated in the UK and formally accepted by many organizations, including the National Government and the Metropolitan (London) police force. It is worth taking a few moments to reflect on this definition. First, the Lawrence inquiry condemned the actions both of *individuals* (in their "conduct," "attitudes and behavior") and *organizations and agencies* whose "processes" work against certain groups. In this way the inquiry shifted the focus away from the familiar assumption that racism is limited to the actions of a few "rotten apples."[40] Second, this approach moves away from endless debates about *intent* by explicitly focusing on the *outcomes* of actions and stating that "unwitting" and "thoughtless" acts are equally as problematic as overt racism. This is a familiar element in several previous attempts to define the term and, as already noted, this definition has been formally accepted by the British Government. On the day of publication, the Prime Minster, Tony Blair, stated the following:

> The publication of today's report on the killing of Stephen Lawrence is a very important moment in the life of our country. It is a moment to reflect, to learn and to change. It will certainly lead to new laws but, more than that, it must lead to new attitudes, to a new era in race relations, and to a new more tolerant and more inclusive Britain.[41]

Unfortunately, this "more tolerant and more inclusive Britain" has not been quick to emerge. Indeed, the following months and years have witnessed an increasingly confident and derisive discourse in public and academic life, aimed at undermining the report and reasserting a crude and minimalist definition of racism as relating only to conscious and deliberate acts of violence and discrimination. In fact, just days after the publication of *The Stephen Lawrence Inquiry*, one of Britain's highest circulation Sunday newspapers carried a prominent opinion piece by columnist Stewart Steven entitled, "Don't they know we're no longer a racist society?" Steven acknowledged that racist incidents are common but argued:

> There are no grounds, therefore, for complacency, but that doesn't mean that we should allow the warped imagination of bigoted White low-lifes, whom we have inadequately educated, to destroy that edifice of tolerance which the rest of us have built up over many years. I fear that may happen if Sir William Macpherson's definition of institutional racism is allowed to stand.[42]

On the question of "institutional racism" Steven offered his own view on the definitional issues: "One can't be an unwitting racist any more than one can be an unwitting burglar and to pretend otherwise is to put back the cause of multiculturalism for years."[43]

These views are significant for several reasons. First, Steven reflects the outrage of many White commentators when faced with a definition of racism that might conceivably include their own assumptions and practices. Notice, in particular, how he equates racism with conscious intent and "bigoted White low-lifes." In this way White racism is both minimized (related only to crude and deliberate acts) and it is given a particular working-class character (equating racism with a kind of White-trash/underclass stereotype).

Attacks of this sort have continued alongside claims that the Lawrence definition threatens to paralyze White professionals who can no longer maintain their authority. Such claims are especially pronounced in relation to the police. Now, the facts of race and criminalization are worth considering. For example, in Britain, Black people are more likely than Whites to be the victims of crime.[44] Nevertheless, they are consistently more likely to be stopped and challenged by the police than are their White counterparts. When convicted of similar offences, Black defendants are more likely to be jailed than Whites and once in prison, they are more likely to die in custody than White inmates.[45] Most chilling of all, between 1990 and 1996, just 4% of White deaths in custody were officially recorded as cases where "Police actions may have been an associated factor": the figure for Black deaths was 37%.[46] Despite these facts, police representatives and conservative politicians are quick to argue that the police are now afraid to do their duty for fear of being labelled racist.[47]

Similar complaints are voiced in education. For instance, writing in the *Times Educational Supplement*, a White head-teacher complained:

> Sometimes when I reprimand pupils, they will, in the heat of the moment, suggest that I have done this because I am racist. . . . Under the new regulations this is automatically recorded and I am entered into the statistics as a perpetrator of "racist incidents."[48]

One could be forgiven for thinking that White teachers are living in constant fear of accusation. Or perhaps, to put it more positively, that their professional lives now include a concern to deliver on their promises of equality of opportunity by trying to lessen existing inequalities in attainment. Unfortunately there is no evidence to suggest that teachers are generally any more aware of their potential for racist action. For example, in a study conducted approximately a year after the Lawrence Inquiry was published, Kemp and Gillborn sought to investigate the impact of the inquiry's findings, if any, on teachers' views of education relative to race.[49] The study was conducted in an inner city area with a diverse population and considerable socioeconomic disadvantage – just the sort of location where the inquiry's findings might have been heard the loudest. However, while some schools were noted as enabling good progress among their Black students, the general picture was much less encouraging. Interviews with students (ranging from 8 to 14 years old) revealed that racism between students was a major issue in many schools. Additionally, ethnically minoritized students often complained that they were not treated fairly by their schools because of assumptions based on their ethnicity. Significantly, a number of Black teachers also firmly asserted that racism continues to be a pressing and ongoing concern in the educational experience (e.g., "Racism is evident, it'll always be there," "We talk about racism all the time."). In contrast, for the majority of White teachers in the same schools, the story was very different:

> It's not a problem [here] and I genuinely mean that . . . it's not something we discuss a lot – because it rarely happens.

> I'm not naive enough to think there are no racists. I'd be very surprised if there were any racists on this staff.

The research clearly suggests that despite all the talk of *institutional* and *unintended* racism, a year after the Lawrence inquiry White teachers were still assuming that racism meant actions that are crude and obvious: something they just didn't see in school. This failure to engage with the real thrust of the Lawrence Inquiry is very serious. First, it suggests that White teachers are continuing to hold to a limited and minimalist view of racism (as extreme, obvious and deliberate action). Second, not surprisingly, White teachers see little or no behavior from themselves or colleagues which would match such a limited definition of racism. Consequently, this position strengthens a belief that any failings on the part of minority ethnic children *cannot* be the responsibility of the school: the cause must lie elsewhere. In this way, blame shifts once again onto the victims of institutional racism. This position is made explicit when a child or parent dares to voice the possibility of racist educational policies and practices. As a White teacher told Kemp and Gillborn:

> Black boys and Black parents know, we wouldn't let them use colour as an excuse. The other day a boy called a teacher racist and I said, "We're not allowing you to use your colour as an excuse" and he admitted it . . . it was his cop out.'

Despite all the public rhetoric about engaging with subtle and institutional forms of racism, Black students continue to face a daily reality where any such challenge of power, privilege or oppression is likely to be interpreted as false and malicious.

Backlash

The events of September 11, 2001, triggered a dramatic increase in anti-Islamic feeling in the West, and especially in the USA and Britain. Even before these events, however, Britain witnessed an increasingly vociferous discourse attacking multiculturalism in general (and the Lawrence Inquiry in particular). This was given impetus by a series of disturbances (involving conflict between police and young South Asians) in some of England's northern towns and cities (Oldham, Burnley and Bradford) during the summer of 2001.[50] It was widely acknowledged at the time that each of the English disturbances had been sparked by the activities of White supremacist groups, namely the "British National Party" and the "National Front." However, history suggests that blame has a strange way of shifting sides when "race" is involved. In the late 1950s, for example, White mobs caused widespread damage and launched physical attacks on migrant communities in Nottingham and Notting Hill. Although these, and later disturbances, were clearly started by Whites, they formed the backdrop to immigration controls and wider policy moves that shifted the blame onto the minority communities.[51] Similarly, the protests in 2001 prompted David Blunkett (the Home Secretary) to argue that minority communities must do more to foster a "sense of belonging."[52] He subsequently introduced a policy of *Integration with Diversity* which includes proposals to: (a) discourage marriage outside the so-called "settled community"; (b) speed up deportations; and (c) test the English language skills of new migrants.[53] In the popular media, the events in Oldham, Burnley and Bradford were seized upon by critics of the Lawrence Inquiry. Speaking on the high-profile BBC radio show, the *Today* programme, for example, Marian Fitzgerald argued that the Inquiry had inflamed racial tension:

> [W]e know, from studies of perpetrators of racial harassment, that the sort of people who get involved in this type of activity tend to be alienated young Whites who feel a sense of grievance that ethnic minorities are given preference over them and that their grievances aren't being listened to. . . . Meanwhile, because the [Lawrence] report lacks precision, in terms of defining what the problem actually is, and certainly the term "institutionally racist" I think is a fairly empty phrase. . . . It's hugely divisive, little progress to be shown for it and the danger that the whole thing is going to turn into an unholy mess.[55]

We see here a familiar pattern. First, the Lawrence report's attempt to increase the range and sophistication of anti-racism is rejected and, once again, any engagement with racism is reduced to crude and violent acts such as racial harassment and assault. Second, White racists are again characterized as a particular section of the White working class (i.e., "alienated young Whites who feel a sense of grievance that ethnic minorities are given preference over them and that their grievances aren't being listened to"). This simultaneously assumes that the middle-classes are free from responsibility and erases the long history of working class anti-racism and anti-fascism. Finally, policymakers are warned to tone down their proposals for race equality, for fear of inflaming further White hostility. In this way, as is so often the case, minority voices and concerns are silenced, while White interests and perspectives are reasserted as the natural, mainstream priority.

Conclusion: Back to the Future?

There is no easy way to conclude this account of the current state of race equity policies and practice in Britain and in the British educational system specifically. On the one hand there are encouraging signs, but on the other, certain developments seem to threaten even worse inequities in the future. Among the most important advances are *The Stephen Lawrence Inquiry* itself and the ensuing Race Relations (Amendment) Act 2000. The act places a specific duty on most public bodies to actively pursue race equity. Many of the key parts of the act only came into force in 2002 and so it is too early to judge their effects in practice. These developments provide an opportunity to mainstream race equity in ways that have already been pioneered in some circumstances.[56] Unfortunately, as a good deal of critical scholarship has highlighted, education policy often takes deeply complex and contradictory forms.[57] Certainly the current rhetoric on race equity and social inclusion runs contrary to some very deep-rooted and powerful trends in pedagogic practice and policy making.

Reflecting on the latest reform proposals (promoting separate academic and vocational "routes") it is important to recognize that such a system would likely re-encode existing inequities in opportunity and access, and thereby promote and bolster institutional and systemic racism across the country. What makes the situation all the more frightening is that these possibilities are more than theoretical musings. The lessons should already have been learned from the history of state education in England after the Second World War, when a system of differentiated education was established that separated students on the basis of their results in examinations at age 11 (i.e., with the fortunate going to "grammar" schools and the rest mostly streamed towards lower status "secondary modern" schools). Although that system was scrapped in most parts of England decades ago, the signs are ominous. Take, for example, the following quotations:

> The key-note of the new system is that, so far as is possible, all children should receive the type of education best suited to their abilities and aptitudes.

> Young people should be able to develop at a pace consistent with their abilities, whether faster or slower.

The language is virtually identical. It presents a belief in the existence of different "abilities" and "aptitudes" while arguing for an educational system that separates students on the basis of their perceived strengths and weakness. And yet, despite their linguistic and theoretical proximity, the quotations are drawn from policy statements that are more than half a century apart: the first from the Ministry of Education (1945a)[58] and the second from the 2002 consultation document on reforms to 14-19 education.[59] Have we really learned so little? Is it possible that in the 21st Century we face the re-invention of segregated secondary schooling – albeit beginning at age 14, rather than age 11, and through different *routes* rather than different *schools*? The latest reforms include an assurance that the system will be flexible, so that young people will be able to "choose from both academic and vocational routes and switch between options."[60] But the post-war system came with exactly the same kind of guarantees (e.g., the "free interchange of pupils from one type to another")[61] and it proved to be highly rigid and elitist.

The current system of secondary education manifestly fails to deliver equality of opportunity to many minoritized ethnic groups: differential levels of attainment and rates of exclusion are the most visible part of an iceberg of institutional practices and beliefs that systematically disadvantage minority ethnic groups.[62] There is a very real danger that these inequities will actually worsen in the new emerging system of increased educational diversity, specialization and separation. The dangers are clear. If, as educators, we are serious about race equity, each of us must critically examine our practices and assumptions. *The Stephen Lawrence Inquiry* has exposed how unthinking behavior, even if it is well-intentioned, can add to the problem. Post-Lawrence it is no longer excusable for White power holders to side-step their role in institutional racism on the basis of their ignorance of the facts nor their own good intentions. This approach sets a challenge to the entire education system: unfortunately, the main thrust of contemporary policy and practice suggests that the challenge will be evaded and the future may be as bleak as the past.

Chapter 7

Lessons in Civic Alienation

The Color and Class of Betrayal in Public Education[1]

Michelle Fine and April Burns
The Graduate Center
The City University of New York

Introduction

[T]here are not enough books [and] there's overcrowding. . . . I'm expected to teach a class of 48 to 46 students with only 36 books with only 36 chairs. If those conditions don't improve, education can't improve. Again, go to any other school, and of course you're going to see better academic programs because [they have] more resources for more children, more one on one interaction with student to teacher. And again, I'm only one person. I don't have a TA. I don't have any assistance in the classroom except the other kids....we're expected to perform miracles, part a Red Sea, if you will.

-Vaca, *High School Educator*

As the intersecting rhetoric of bureaucratic efficiency, 'bottom-line' money management and 'democratic values' functionally shifts attention away from equity concerns and towards the normalized interests of power, privilege and the status quo, it becomes increasingly important to address educational change with an eye towards equity and a libratory educational praxis. The success of a democratic education must be seen beyond school's ability to meet the needs of those students able to take advantage of the system. Rather, bringing democracy into schooling means being able to meet the needs of *all* students, and particularly those students who are least able to access available educational opportunities.

-Karumanchery and Portelli, *Democratic Values in Bureaucratic Structures*

California's public schools are crumbling, and that decay is reflected in the anger, frustration and alienation of its poor and working class children of color. Everyday, these marginalized youth and their educators are assaulted in ways that bear serious academic, psychological, socioeconomic and perhaps, even criminal consequences. We write to theorize beyond reproduction theory[2] in order to better understand the personal and social devastation that is cultivated and nurtured when schools are structurally damaged, when teachers are under-qualified and when educational institutions offer little in the way of either instructional materials or rigor. Poor and working class youth of color are reading these conditions as evidence of their social disposability and as markers of public betrayal.

These students see, hear and live social arrangements of class and race stratification every day, and as a result, while neither fully internalizing nor fully resisting this evidence, they come to understand their "place" in the social hierarchy. In this early part of the 21st-century, we are watching as impoverished and ineffective schools transform engaged and enthused students into disheartened youth who recognize that the nation has abandoned and betrayed them. Now, while many have written eloquently on the gentrification of the public sphere and the realignment of public schooling in ways that satisfy and engorge elite interests, few have interrogated how poor and working class youth of color witness, analyze, critique and mobilize in the face of this State realignment. We have set out to explore these issues here.

In examining how marginalized youth of color view both the distributive inequities that now orchestrate the public education system in California, and the procedural injustices through which the State refuses to hear their voices of protest, we are increasingly concerned that the stakes for under-educated youth and for dropouts, are far more severe than they were in the past.[3] While access and opportunity appear to be decreasing for poor and racially minoritized students, the repercussions of such exclusionary policy and practice are growing exponentially.[4] It is clear that these schools are not simply reproducing race and class inequity, but are in effect, and irrespective of intentions, actively streaming poor, working class, immigrant youth and youth of color, away from academic excellence and democratic participation and towards educational failure and civic alienation. There are debates within neoMarxist, feminist and critical race theories that focus on the oppressed as sites of insurgency: Do those on the "bottom" of social hierarchies voice more powerful critique than their privileged counterparts,[5] or do the oppressed learn to see the world through the eyes of their oppressor and actively deny injustice and mimic dominant ideologies?[6] The question is often posed: Can those who have been oppressed really "know" what they haven't seen? If they do, does their critique facilitate hope and/or despair? Recognizing the dangers of working with false dichotomies, this work engages the reality of lived experience and how young people *read/interpret* and come to act on the race, ethnicity and class stratifications that organize their lives in educational contexts.

In preparation to give expert testimony in the case of Williams vs. California, Fine et al (forthcoming) documented and analyzed a series of psychological reactions (e.g., yearning, anger, betrayal, academic motivation, aspirations, relations with educators, civic engagement, speaking out/seeking redress) to these material conditions of education. Analyzing the data within and between elementary, middle and high school levels, we tracked the dialectical relations that ran between: (a) yearning for quality education and anger at being denied; (b) pride in self and community and growing sense of embarrassment and shame over being mis-educated; and (c) the desire to speak out and seek remedy while being actively silenced or disregarded. These three dynamics are crucial in the process of schooling for alienation in that while youth may be strong, resilient and eager to learn, that resolve and desire is continuously set against a backdrop of oppression that tells them that they have been, and will continue to be abandoned, neglected and abused by the State, and for the perceived benefit of their racially and economically privileged peers. The frustration, confusion and anger that arises as an effect of this constant struggle is reflected clearly in the outrage and resentment of students who want to succeed, but "know" that they are denied access to the material resources necessary to engage a quality education.

Cumulative Inequity: Schooling to Alienate

While marginalized youth do indeed see, know and speak about their experience of dissonance and alienation (most often without "naming" it as such), coming to critical consciousness can carry dire consequences for the oppressed. The political "texts" they read (in this case, dilapidated schools) speak to the banality of betrayal in our educational systems and foreshadow brutal ramifications for their educational practice, their civic engagements and their economic trajectories. It is important that we recognize and examine schools as much more than apolitical spaces where "development happens."[7] Rather, schools must be engaged as intimate places where students: (a) construct identity and self-concept; (b) learn to read how they fit into the larger social schema; and (c) develop the capacity to sustain relations and forge the skills to initiate change. These are the contexts in/through which student potential can be either nurtured or extinguished, and too often, we find that potential redirected away from collective mobilization and towards individual survival. Werner and Altman (1998) argue:

> [C]hildren are not separate from their actions or feelings, nor are they separate from other children or the physical, social and temporal circumstances that comprise unfolding events. They are so interconnected that one aspect can not be understood without the others. . . . The street . . . is not separate from its inhabitants.[8]

Recognizing that children who are valued tend to be more positive in self-concept than those who are disparaged, Werner and Altman move beyond this seemingly simple notion to ask how such value is manifested in the everyday.[9] Value, in this respect, is communicated in personal actions or inactions (i.e., compliments and encouragement vs. detractions and discouragement) or in the quality of the very contexts in which we live and develop. Simply put, the "voice" of our surroundings develop into internal voices, constructing much of the core of how children feel about themselves and, in turn, influence how they are perceived and valued by others.[10]

Since the early part of the 20th-century, psychologists and sociologists have argued that human interaction is only one of the avenues through which identity and self-concept are developed and that the structures and institutions around us also send powerful messages about self-worth and social value.[11] Buildings in disrepair are not merely a distraction, they tell a tale about social positioning. So, for youth whose educational environment exposes them to decay, disrepair and filth on a daily basis, these markers of social irrelevance and worthlessness may become internalized in the intrapsychic and psychological frameworks that govern understandings of self or, at least, one's perceived position within social arrangements. Student Alondra Jones[12] details the corrosive effects of a negative structural context on the developing selves of young students:

> It make you feel less about yourself, you know, like you sitting here in a class where you have to stand up because there's not enough chairs and you see rats in the buildings, the bathrooms is nasty, you got to pay.

> I visited Mann Academy, and these students, if they want to sit on the floor, that's because they choose to. And that just makes me feel real less about myself because it's like the State don't care about public schools. If I have to sit there and stand in the class, they can't care about me. It's impossible. So in all honesty, it really makes me feel bad about myself. . . . And I'm not the only person who feels that.

> It really make you feel like you really less than. And I already feel that way because I stay in a group home because of poverty. Why do I have to feel that when I go to school? No, there's some real weak stuff going on.

These conditions both re/produce and exacerbate the emotional, civic and academic troubles faced by youth who are already the least privileged in our nation. With the material gathered for the Williams case, we were able to trace the complex developmental capillaries through which political betrayal filters into the collective subconscious of marginalized youth.

Theorizing Development Inside Contexts of Structural Betrayal

We had the opportunity to interview a series of elementary, middle, high school and graduating college students from the *plaintiff schools*. Across the focus groups, while there was much variation within, it was not difficult to decipher developmental traces of betrayal. Thus, for instance, the elementary school children interviewed from the "plaintiff class" of Williams vs. California were filled, for the most part, with enthusiasm about their schools and were excited about their education. Asked to draw a picture of their ideal schools, they drew pictures of pride and delight, envisioning and documenting a world spread open with possibilities. However, on occasion, some children would speak about the dilemmas they felt were detracting from their schooling experience. When asked what they would like to change about their schools, some responded:

> Bring a lot of security guards and stop the dogs. . . . And no big kids . . . stop the big kids from coming to beat up the little . . . good lunches . . . bathrooms more

cleaner . . . stop people from cussing, trying to beat you up, people telling lies
. . . stop graffiti . . . more books and a bigger library.

Unable to yet name and critically analyze the various racial and class divides that frame their educational experience, these children are, for the most part, enthusiastic about their academic prospects. They ask simply for adults to protect them and provide for a cleaner and more productive school space. However, by the time they have reached middle school, students reflect far more sophistication in their analyses and their narratives begin to reflect a deep skepticism and disillusionment about the nature and consequences of their schooling environment.

Middle School students narrated with significant interpretive skill, the decay, disregard and deficiency through which they are forced to navigate. These young people articulated threads of hope and despair that clearly illustrate the uncertainty between how things are and how things should and could be. While they are distressed about the conditions of schooling and the clear absence of remedy, most, nevertheless, believe that adults would respond appropriately if only they knew about the state of their schools and the effects of those educational conditions. There is still hope in these voices – but it is a hope that seems lost by the time they reach high school.[13]

By high school, students voiced well-articulated, sophisticated and often profound analyses of their school experience (See Table 1). In interviews with high school aged students from the plaintiff class of Williams vs. California, we (Fine et. al., forthcoming) found that students firmly believed their educational needs were being ignored by federal and state governments that were simply serving the interests of the wealthier and White. Recognizing material and economic restrictions, biased curricula and lack of consistent, supportive relations with teachers, these students understand that their educational situation must be looked at in relation to the educational experience of wealthier White students who need not struggle with these same dilemmas. While a discourse of possibility and hope survives even here, that hope is primarily about personal survival in hostile environments. The older students saw these educational inequities as extensions of the disregard and apathy that is directed at them as members of society who live and struggle on the margins and at the bottom of the social hierarchy.[14]

The longer students stay in schools with structural problems, large numbers of unqualified teachers, high teacher turnover rates and inadequate instructional materials, the wider the academic gap will become between those living in the centre and the margins of the social hierarchy[15] These schools of alienation actively reconstruct and bolster a process that limits and constrains personal, educational and civic possibilities for poor and racially marginalized and oppressed youth.

Table 1: How do California students feel about their schools?

Feelings and Opinions about School	Middle School (n = 20) % of interviewed students who agree or strongly agree	High School (n = 66) % of interviewed students who agree or strongly agree
Students feel safe in school	40%	23%
The school building itself is clean	25%	6%
We are a community	45%	6%
All teachers are qualified	45%	17%
We have good books to take home	60%	26%
Teachers listen to our ideas	55%	18%
My classes are too crowded	25%	37%

From Yearning to Anger

I like lab period and [my] algebra teacher . . . he makes you relax, tells you jokes, it kind of calms you off. . . . That's what I like about my teachers.[16]

Right now I have this one teacher . . . he's my English teacher and he's like really trying to help the students right now. We're looking into colleges and stuff. He's really trying to help us, like learn things, because it's like, he'll pull you out of class for a reason. It will be like to learn the stuff.[17]

The students with whom we spoke (Fine, Burns, Payne and Torre, forthcoming), were both frank and eloquent about what they felt constitutes a first-rate education, and while quality curricula and materials were almost always mentioned as part of the puzzle (particularly in the later grades), the issues of support and care were always central in their assessments. Throughout these discussions, as reflected in the narratives above, many students recalled with fondness and gratitude, those teachers who pushed them to excel and/or supported them in hard times. In fact, this sentiment was clearly reflected across focus groups and surveys as respondents expressed genuine appreciation for the benefits that accompany a rigorous curriculum, but that such educational rigor would be most effective if complimented with the support and guidance of caring teachers. When asked to describe what a good and caring teacher was like, students responded by describing someone who holds high standards and helps students reach those standards; someone who listens, asks questions and then listens to student answers; someone who wants to know what students think; and someone who assigns lots of homework but provides the support and time to finish it.

> Lauren: Like he said, we got a lot of substitutes right now. . . . Some of them cap you [put you down], some of them play football. That's not what we come to school for. So we got our teachers there that are pretty cool. But . . . I love the good teachers, but the best ones are like—
>
> Javon: (interrupts) They change the whole school around.
>
> Lauren: They change the whole school.

These students know the difference between substitute teachers who are "pretty cool" and those teachers who "change the whole school around." However, while they value what such dedicated and invested teachers might bring to their schooling experience, they also know that "good teachers" rarely come to their school, and that when they do, they often leave mid-year only to be replaced by long-term substitutes who are unfamiliar with both the curriculum and the students.

> [W]e had a teacher for like the first three weeks of our multi-culture class and then the teacher didn't have all her credentials so she couldn't continue to teach. And since then we've had like ten different substitutes. And none of them have taught us anything. We just basically do what we wanted in class. We wrote letters, all the class wrote letters to people and they never responded. We still don't have a teacher.

The reality for these youth is that while they will have a range of teachers throughout their schooling experience, far too often, their teachers will be neither qualified nor provided with the necessary resources or professional support that would enable them to meet their needs.[18] There is frustration evident in the voices of these students, and it is a frustration that builds on their inability to affect the situation: "When I ask for help, and there's too many kids . . . I know the teacher can't pay attention to me. I'm ignored. That makes me mad."

The hope that framed their schooling experience as children is replaced by a cynicism and anger that grows with each daily reminder that they are expendable and do not matter.[19] However, more than the simple recognition that the educational system is flawed, these youth have begun to realize that the system is "selectively flawed" and that all youth do not receive the same type of education. By the time these students are in high school, they are aware that their wealthier, White counterparts do not share in the deficiencies of their schooling experience and that in turn, they are being denied the opportunities and possibilities they deserve:

> Well, at Tech . . . it is bad . . . they had like another school system inside of it called Phi Beta, like all the smart kids . . . and it's like no minorities in there. And they get all the good instruments and all the other stuff like engineering. And they like, split them up and the rest of Tech, they got their own side of the school. So it's just kind of scandalous how they, you know, put everyone else on the other side of the school or just different classes.

> [M]ost of the "good schools" are majority Caucasian. . . .[I]f they look around the school and they say, "Well we're basically all minorities," and they look at other schools and say "Why they getting treated better than us?" Well we all humans and we have been treated worse. So then that could bring some anger and then they just start lashing out at people, Caucasian people . . . for all the wrong reasons.[20]

What is the psychological effect of this type of "in your face" discrimination and inequity? McCord (2002) contends that these types of disparate facilities would likely convey a message of racial inferiority as implicit in any such policy of segregation.[21] Unlike the hidden aspects of racism and classism that function through subtle forms of systemic oppression (i.e., "normalized" hiring and promotional formulas), these marginalized youth constantly face both explicit and subtle reminders of how they are being abused and as illustrated in the narratives above, the emotional reactions shared by these students are both dramatic and disruptive. Karumanchery (2003) notes that oppressed children in such environments will often respond in aggressive behaviors that allow others to mark them as troublemakers and as "bad seeds." Beyond this, however, we have found from these focus groups, that youth express anger, withdrawal and/or deep skepticism of the public sphere as well. The cumulative effect is reflected in what Crosby (1986) and Leach (1999) called a *relative deprivation*: a substantial discrepancy between what people believe they deserve and what they actually receive; between what they have and what they want; what they have and what they believe they deserve; what they don't have and others do.[22] For example, in discussing his schooling experience, one young high school student explained that:

> Teachers and just people in general underestimate youth, black youth. They think I'm supposed to be speaking Ebonics, hanging out on the streets, dealing drugs and stuff . . . and then when you get in schools and then you go overboard with your assignments because when you first go to school, you really don't know how the teachers grade. . . . With me, I always want to do the best I can. So if they tell me to write a three-page essay, I write a fifteen page essay. So I do and then it's like, well, where'd you get this from? Did you copy out of a book? . . . They're always underestimating your ability to work.

This young man is describing a perceived assault on his dignity. A sense of their criminalization starts early, and as this quote demonstrates, adults often seem suspicious of fraud and duplicity even when disadvantaged students produce quality work. It is an assault enacted through teachers' underestimation of his abilities and the general refusal to recognize and nurture his talents and skills. It is important to be clear that while these youth do not simply reflect or internalize the sense of worthlessness transmitted by their environment and their teachers, they are nevertheless deeply impacted by the systematic attack of deprivation that marks their daily schooling experience.[23]

Despite their willingness (even desperation at times) to engage, they recognize, painfully, that they are being redlined out of the sphere of public education, and corralled, instead, within the grasp of the other – better funded – public sphere: the criminal justice system. These students see themselves being prepared as "inmates" more than "students." Poor and working class youth embody and speak through a critical consciousness that reveals, with sharp and cutting precision, the ways in which their bodies and minds are being exploited in larger schemes of the global economy and the prison-industrial-complex:

> I'm in 10th grade. . . . [T]hey cage us up and they keep putting more gates and more locks and stuff and then they expect us to act like humans and I feel like if you treat us like animals, that's how we're going to act.

> [P]utting all the bad kids in one school, that's just like putting, you know, just like putting them in jail. They're going to be crazy.

A close scrutiny of these narratives suggests an awareness that they are being exploited by, and indoctrinated into, the macro-relations of a global economy. Specifically, they recognize that the systemic push out of the public educational sphere is paralleled and supportive of the systemic pull towards the prison-industrial-complex. These students speak through dual registers of yearning and anger, pride and shame, engagement and alienation, fear and desire; and with the guillotine of high stakes testing overhead, they critically deconstruct the dominant ideologies about urban youth and then reproduce these same concepts when asked to evaluate other students who are having difficulties. This mimicry of the dominant ideology is perhaps the ultimate sign of the duality that frames their "normalized" desire for civic belonging. How do these dilemmas play out in a student's academic potential and what does it mean when academic victories are contaminated by the knowledge that your achievements sit precariously atop a mountain of others who have been failed by the system?

From Pride to Shame

Michael Lewis (1992) argues that the experience of shame requires a self conscious comparison to others, or a recognition that one has failed to live up to a given standard.[24] Importantly, even when narratives evidenced a strong sense of pride in self and community, those positive feelings were almost always accompanied by expressions of embarrassment and shame. Most of the high school students interviewed expressed strength and confidence in relation to their communities and their local worlds. However, while many had plans of going on to college, envisioning hopeful careers as doctors, nurses, lawyers, engineers and teachers, they also worried that they were academically handicapped by opportunities denied, ill-equipped to attend "real" or "serious" colleges and they were embarrassed by their limited vocabulary. These students understand the dilemmas constructed through their mis-education and while they do not necessarily see themselves as less competent, they certainly fear that they can't compete academically with students who have had a more privileged education. One student admitted:

> [If kids from a wealthy school came in here right now] I wouldn't talk because they would be more sophisticated . . . and understand words I don't know and I don't want to be embarrassed.

In discussing their mis-education, many students openly denounced politicians, administrators and teachers as viewing children of color and urban youth as somehow unworthy of a quality education. Many of the student participants believed their schools were purposefully instilling them with shame and embarrassment in the hopes they would leave school, and the resulting increase in the dropout rate would be reflected in decreased class sizes.25 The sophistication of the analysis should not be lost as students are able to recognize the government's political agenda to decrease class sizes while absolving themselves of the responsibility for the loss of student bodies. These interviews revealed a raw sense of social disposability and a penetrating sense of helplessness in their inability to change their schooling conditions.26 This sense of disgust was palpable when student participants discussed the "filth" that constantly reminded them that their needs were not being met and that their school's deficiencies were rarely at the forefront of administrative or governmental interests. When asked to suggest and describe one element that would promote the development of "their ideal school," students were fast to discuss the basic need to have spaces that are clean and healthy. One female student's response was particularly poignant in its simplicity: "If I could have my ideal school, I guess I would have seats on the toilets and enough paper in the bathroom to clean yourself." Another student added: "If you go to a dirty school, you feel like you're dirty, you know, not clean." The candor of these statements and the fundamental nature of the need being expressed cannot be overstated and must not be overlooked.

A number of researchers, among them Duran (2002), Kozol (1991) and Saegert and Winkel (1999), have identified several environmental stressors that are particularly threatening to instruction and the promotion of a healthy sense of self: (a) facilities in disrepair; (b) overcrowding; (c) fluctuations or other problems with temperature regulation; (d) unhygienic or unclean bathroom conditions; (e) excessive or unhealthy noise levels; and (f) exposure to mice, vermin and animal feces.27 Importantly, several of these stressors were found to be prevalent in the structural and environmental settings of the plaintiff class of Williams vs. California. Overcrowding for instance, was a major environmental stressor marked by students as being specifically detrimental to their educational experience. During focus group sessions, several students from the plaintiff class explained:

> Justin: It's way overcrowded. And it's like . . . you don't even have to go there . . . because basically they don't know if we go there, you can just come on campus or whatever. Like right now, we got three different tracks, and they don't know if you don't have an ID. You . . . you can tell them you have to take your ID picture or whatever and just go on in, and they'll believe you, because they don't really know who goes there, because they've got so many kids in that school . . . last year, I had 42 kids in my algebra class.
>
> Rachel: That's a lot.
>
> Justin: And people were standing up and—
>
> Rachel: (interrupts) Sitting on the floor—
>
> Justin: (interrupts) Sitting on the cabinets and stuff . . .

These student concerns are echoed and corroborated in a great deal of contemporary research interrogating the effects of negative environmental factors on mental health. Case in point,

Saegert and Winkel's (1999) study illustrated that higher density environments produce practical and cognitive effects that lead to frequently negative social interactions and affective states in students.[28] The correlations between overcrowding and educational success are striking, but when taken in concert with other detrimental environmental factors such as structural disrepair, the potential for harm becomes exacerbated. For example, in Duran's (2002) study of whether architects' assessments of building quality could be used as predictors of academic success, findings clearly illustrated that building quality could be reliably used as an indirect predictor of academic achievement when race, ethnicity and poverty were controlled for (i.e., structural quality negatively impacts student attendance which in turn directly impacts academic achievement).[29] As mentioned above, the plaintiff class was dealing with the effects and aftereffects of multiple stressors within the same environment. It therefore begs the question, what is the cumulative effect of such mistreatment and neglect on one's capacity to concentrate and produce academic work? Moreover, how does it concurrently induce an elevation in negative emotions such as anger and resentment?[30] In their study of the long-term cumulative physiological and psychological consequences of exposure to multiple environmental stressors, Lepore and Evans (1996) conclude that chronic exposure to such problematics would work to increase one's vulnerability to subsequent stressors, diminish youths' ability to resist oncoming threats.[31] Similarly, Baum, Singer and Baum (1981) concluded that most important aftereffects of such environmental stress would likely be the "simple" effect stress seems to have on the ability to adapt in the future. They go on to warn that "If the amount of adjustment required is large enough, it may render the individual unable to cope and lead to severe consequences."[32]

Self-Blame: Disciplinary Power and the Psychology of Oppression

Marginalized youth are assaulted by a seemingly endless stream of discourses that frame them as responsible for occupying the bottom steps of the social hierarchy, and then in turn, as solely responsible for suffering the psychological and intrapsychic consequences that accompany those oppressed positionalities. The result, as witnessed across the focus group sessions, is a fleeting, infrequent but emotionally powerful discourse of self-blame.[33] Chantal, a graduate of the plaintiff class of Williams vs. California, and one of the few students to continue onto college, explained:

> I didn't do enough at [my high school] to make it better. It pains me to see what my younger brothers and sisters go through at [my old high school]. I feel guilty about my opportunities, compared to others in my community and seriously considered dropping out of college several times. . . . You know, it's hard to know that I am getting an education while other people I know aren't. I guess I'm the lucky one, given all of the students who couldn't beat the stacked odds.

Of these study participants, almost all felt unprepared for the academic expectations at the college level and most expressed the ambivalence of what Lifton (1994) termed "survivor guilt" – a blending of joy at one's accomplishments, tainted by the sense of responsibility to those others left behind.[34]

The oscillation between positive and negative feelings evidenced throughout the narratives, speaks to the intrapsychic dilemma of managing the external social pathology that promote notions of meritocracy and self/victim blame within neoliberal frameworks and the internal psychology that establishes the fundamental emotional need for acceptance, pride, respect, security, support and understanding; the dialectical struggle between wanting to believe that the educational system does and will offer them a fair shot at success, and reading the evidence of sustained structural abandonment. While most of these youth attribute their mis-education to structural inequities, a strong undercurrent of student/self-blame could be heard in focus group conversations. See, for instance, how these student narratives about personal responsibility and educational opportunity echo popular notions that frame institutions and teachers as involved in academic successes, while educational failures are almost always attributed to a lack of student ability and/or effort:

> If I sit in that class and choose to talk, then, hey, that's me. . . . So if that teacher, even if she's teaching a little bit of stuff, I know to sit down and listen to it.

> When I was in middle school . . . I skipped that grade, went right to the ninth grade from seventh grade. I *chose* to mess that ninth grade year up. I *chose* to cut and shoot dice and be doing other things that I'm not supposed to do, you know. So that was *my mistake, my fault.* You know, in my tenth grade year, I *destroyed* it, you know. I *made nothing of it all*, nothing. I passed, I don't know how I passed, you know. So when I look at my transcript, I look at it and say this is where I *failed.* I know I won't be able to make it into a university *because of me*, not because of what peer pressure or what this principal said or what this teacher was teaching me.

Furthermore, as clarified by Dei, Karumanchery and Karumanchery-Luik (2004), the *blame the victim* mentality that runs through mainstream understandings of educational failure serve to ensure that interrogations of the structures for teaching, learning and administration of education become truncated.[35] Holding very low expectations for the effective intervention of adult educators, these students have become cynical about change and they grow increasing doubtful that the government or the school will help them succeed.[36] Recognizing that they have been exempted from the entitlement within the public sphere, California's marginalized students are learning what it means to "swim upstream." The staccato sense of futility that accompanies those efforts manifests itself in a self-fulfilling prophecy of sorts. These youth desperately need (and want) adult guidance and support, but they have learned, and continue to learn that such assistance is rarely forthcoming, and moreover, that seeking adult guidance is a discouraging and often humiliating experience. One student said, "I don't ask the teacher for nothing. I do it all on my own, or ask my friends for help." This student expects his teachers to ignore his requests for help and so he faces this dilemma with a preemptive rejection; a defensive posture that allows him to reject and/or discount his educators as a source of support before they can ignore his request. This defensive stance is paralleled by an internalized and unrealistic belief in personal responsibility, influenced by self-help and criminal justice models of reform where personal responsibility is understood in terms of accepting self-blame (Maruna, 2002) – the end result being that they struggle through these challenges isolated from those who might offer support, and in the likely event of failure, they conclude that those failures are "their fault."

Speaking simultaneously as critics, consumers and producers of meritocratic ideologies, these students seem unaware of the discourses that inform their notions of self-blame, typically asserting a very punitive, super-ego(ish) perspective on their own biographies; feeling that past mistakes do and should dictate a life of impoverished educational, social and economic opportunities (even if those guidelines do not apply for middle- and upper-class White students). While marginalized youth are framed as personally accountable for their "mistakes" and "failings," the disproportionate success of White and middle-class youth is further legitimated by the invisibility of the privatized supports enlisted by privileged students. Importantly, unlike their marginalized counterparts, when privileged youth make mistakes, they tend to be given "second chances" and that disparity carries dire consequences.[37] These youth are constituted in what psychologists term a "characterological personal attribution" or "fundamental attribution error" for past mistakes – when bad outcomes are attributed to personal moral flaws, it tends to be difficult to shed the shame and/or believe oneself entitled to future, positive outcomes.[38]

Liberty and Justice for Some

[S]chools are like mini polities where children can explore what it means to be a member of a community beyond their families, where they learn they are the equal of other citizens, and where they can learn how to negotiate their differences in a civil fashion. . . . [S]chools are settings where children develop ideas about the rights and obligations of citizenship.[39]

In their cross-national study of the correlation between schooling and civic commitment, Flanagan et al. (1998) found that schools act as a proving ground for civic engagement.[40] Similarly, Foster (1986) wrote that schools are "a living statement of the culture and values that form the consciousness of every social member." These scholars are speaking to some of the central dilemmas taken up in this research – the issues of civic engagement and democratic values in education. However, in light of the dilemmas addressed throughout this paper, we must ask ourselves: Who is being engaged and who is being disengaged in and by our schools? And perhaps most importantly, what are the social and psychological ramifications for students who are exploring "what it means to be a member of a community," only to discover that they are in fact, not the equal of other citizens and that their rights are few, if any?

The figures illustrated in Table 2 suggest some troubling answers to the questions posed above. For instance, how are we to interpret the marked decline in almost every category differentiating Middle School and High School student's feelings towards the general ethics of social responsibility and commitment? Moreover, how do we explain the 32% drop in the importance California's students place on serving their country or the 34% decline in the desire to improve their community? As asserted by Karumanchery and Portelli (2004), while the mainstream rhetoric of *democratic schooling* has worked through cultural symbols of freedom, fair play and merit to functionally mute the decline of civic engagement in education and veil the erosion of opportunities and access for the oppressed, the condition is not so easily dismissed by those who feel and suffer its effects on a daily basis.[41] Their response to such chronic abuse can be seen in the marked declines in willingness to extend care and commitment to the larger society – the government that betrays them and the democracy that fails them. Citizenship, membership and partnership are communal notions that require nurturing, and clearly, California's schools are not cultivating this sense of connection among its poor and racialized youth. In fact, we are doing exactly the opposite. Cookson and Persell (1985), Fine (1991) and numerous other researchers have documented how our educational system "teaches" marginalized youth about social stratifications and their place within social hierarchies.[42] These youth reveal a sophisticated analysis of social structures and a broad based understanding of their "place" in society where inequity and social injustice are the norm. Simply put, we are instilling these youth with a profound sense of social isolation and national alienation, so much so that we are damaging their most basic notions of citizenship and belonging and fraying the threads that constitute social relations.[43]

Table 2: What is Important to California Students?

How Important Is . . .	Middle School (n = 20) % of interviewed students who felt the issues were somewhat to very important	High School (n = 66) % of interviewed students who felt the issues were somewhat to very important
Helping my family?	100%	92%
Improving race relations?	71%	58%
Helping those less fortunate?	70%	56%
Working to stop prejudice?	50%	46%
Making my community better?	75%	41%
Leaving my community?	21%	30%
Serving my country?	55%	23%

That being said, because the subject effects are complex and numerous, the consequences of civic alienation are rarely all-inclusive and tend not to result in a complete disengagement from all social fields. Rather, for many similarly oppressed youth, such declines are often paralleled by an increased sense of responsibility to local communities and racial/ethnic in-groups. As Bowen and Bok (1998) demonstrate, it is common for youth of color who graduate from college to display a commitment to give back to their communities and model an ethic of in-group solidarity.[44] What is remarkable in the California youth, however, was the combination of their strong commitments to give back and engage as citizens in local contexts, and their systematic recoiling from, and refusal to engage as citizens in the larger society. While many of the interviewed students voiced a continued commitment to family and community, the overriding message was one of betrayal, bewilderment, anger, disillusionment with, and detachment from, the broader public sphere. In fact, the vast majority of youth directed a considerable degree of anger at the schools that had failed them and towards the government policymakers and leaders who continue to frame their needs as irrelevant. These youth have grown understandably suspicious of the *democratic rhetoric* and *bureaucratic efficiencies* that continue to mark them as expendable. Table 3 illustrates the degree to which their willingness to participate actively with family, neighborhood community and those less fortunate is paralleled by an almost absolute refusal to serve as neglected or disrespected citizens of the State.

Table 3: Attitudes about California, the Government and Society

I Believe That . . .	Middle School (n = 20) % of interviewed students who agree or strongly agree	High School (n = 66) % of interviewed students who agree or strongly agree
It makes me mad when I think of how some people have to live.	80%	71%
No matter how well educated I am, it will be hard for me to get a good job.	25%	42%
The state government is for the rich and not for the average person.	50%	40%
The government doesn't really care about what like me and my family think.	15%	38%
My school is as good as any in the state.	65%	23%
America is basically fair and everyone has an equal chance to get ahead.	65%	23%

How do we justify or support a system that engenders this level of mis-education, mistrust and anger? Again, what does it mean when such a large percentage of the surveyed students believe they will always be hard-pressed to access the labor market's better prospects, that the government functions in favor of the rich and that the needs of poor and racialized people will always go unheard by those in power? In seeking to frame the causal links that engender such anger and suspicion, it is important that we do not focus all our attentions on the impact of environmental deficiencies alone. As illustrated above, the perception of privileged indifference and apathy plays an integral role in how marginalized peoples learn they are being abused and used. It was not simply the case that these youth were denied adequate education and therefore felt helpless. Rather, many of these students had, in the face of overwhelming odds, tried to secure help. They had spoken up, petitioned for their schools to hire "real" teachers and protested to raise awareness of their academic concerns, but few adults listened and even fewer acted. Students in one of the high school focus groups contrasted how their school responded (if superficially) when the State investigated school policies and practices but ignored their requests for quality education:

> We all walked out, 'cause of the conditions, but they didn't care. They didn't even come out. They sent the police. The police made a line and pushed us back in. Don't you think the principal should have come out to hear what we were upset over? But when the state is coming in, they paint, they fix up the building. They don't care about us, the students, just the state or the city.

When these youth have complained, waged grievances or challenged the educational inequities they endure, they have confronted walls of silence. In effect, our educational systems are actively manufacturing a generation of youth who manage to sustain ethical commitments to family, kin and community while divorcing themselves from civic responsibilities to, and connections with, the nation as a whole.[45] Despite the fact that these students are desperately asking for quality educators and a more rigorous curriculum, the evidence suggests that the longer these youth spend in plaintiff schools, the more shame, anger and mistrust they develop; the fewer academic skills they acquire, and the more our diverse democratic fabric frays. The reaction is understandable as these schools actively blunt civic engagement and produce instead, civic alienation. When asked what she would want to tell a judge about her high school experiences, one young graduate of a plaintiff school said eloquently: "Every day, every hour, talented students are being sacrificed. . . . They're [the schools] destroying lives."

Civics Lessons

Given the political economy of the U.S., the devastating invasion of the prison industrial complex into poor communities, the racial stratifications and the social inequities that organized everyday living for poor and working class youth, and youth of color, we must ask: To what extent do these schools reproduce broad social inequities, worsen them or reduce their adverse impact?[46] The evidence presented here suggests that these California schools substantially worsen the already existing social inequities with psychological, academic and ultimately economic consequences, and contrary to much popular opinion, these conditions are not endemic to the public schooling of marginalized youth. There is now a well-established body of evidence, drawn from systematic studies of small schools in Philadelphia, New York City,

Chicago and elsewhere, that demonstrates public schooling can be effectively organized for poor and working class youth of color, to open opportunities, support identity development, offer quality education, prepare for higher education and cultivate a strong ethic of community engagement.

In the last ten years we have conducted research in a number of small public schools in New York, Philadelphia, Chicago and New Jersey with quality faculty and instructional materials, dedicated to rigorous education for students, including poor and working class youth and youth of color. In these schools, all severely under-resourced, students are nevertheless exposed to a rigorous curriculum and they are engaged by educators who work hard to create intellectual contexts of equity and excellence. Interrogating the history and lived experiences of oppression in Western contexts, these students learn about social stratification by researching history, economics and social movements. Youth in these schools learn about both the possibilities for social change and their responsibilities to participate in creating that change.[47] And perhaps most importantly, these youth learn to employ this inclusive and collaborative framework towards a social critique rooted in collective hope and action, rather than individualized despair and alienation. Simply put, these alienating conditions – all too typical in neoliberal societies – are neither natural nor healthy and there is substantial evidence that schools can interrupt the damage of the broader political economy.[48] With the color and class of betrayal in so many of California's (and the nation's) public schools clearly set out before us, the time has come to peel away the layers of rhetoric that frame our notions of "democracy in education," and ask ourselves: Do we actually want democracy in our educational system? If we do nothing to ameliorate the present state of affairs in our public schools, then we are sending a very clear message as to what society we want to be and what type of future we want for these youth.

Section Three

Building Praxical Anti-Racism

Chapter 8

Unmasking Racism

A Challenge for Anti-Racist Educators in the 21st Century

George J. Sefa Dei, Ph.D.
Department of Sociology and Equity Studies in Education
OISE/University of Toronto

Introduction

We are handcuffed. We are constrained. We are kept at arms length from each other and at loggerheads over the question of what, when and how we should fight. As anti-racist pedagogues, activists and students, we too often find ourselves struggling against those *others* who should be our partners in the project. Anti-racists find themselves fighting feminists who find themselves fighting socialists, and so on, and so on. There is an urgent need for all engaged in the pursuit of social justice and equity to work across the differences and intellectual divides that hamper our ability to develop a collective resistance. In fact, if we are to sustain ourselves and our various agendas in the years to come, we must proactively break down the disciplinary boundaries and political frameworks that pit us against one another. Refreshingly, many of today's frontline workers in the struggle for social justice are coming to realize that the intersecting and interlocking nature of oppression necessitates that we work together. However, while anti-racist practice is becoming increasingly informed by this realization, a cooperative project such as this rarely arises without having to face certain challenges – I take this space to engage and address these challenges within a philosophy of hope.

We are faced with numerous dilemmas in our search for a working model of anti-racism that speaks to the demands of solidarity in resistant politics – and chief among those is the question of how we are to manage competing marginalities when they are constantly imposed and exploited in/through/by sites of power and privilege. As community and political/social workers we must develop strategies to foster solidarity in spite of the competing priorities that exist between and within groups because our individual agendas are important and must not be dismissed or muted. First and foremost, those who believe in social justice work cannot deny difference, whether it be structured along the lines of race, ethnicity, gender, sexuality, class, culture, language, religion, ability or age. This discussion is about acknowledging and responding to the relevance of anti-racist practice in the promotion of equity. With that being said, perhaps it would be useful to revisit what anti-racism education is about. Anti-racist education is proactive educational practice intended to address all forms of racism and the intersections of social difference (race, class, gender, sexuality, disability, etc.). As a form of education that makes very explicit the intended outcomes to subvert the status quo and bring about change, the politics and credibility of anti-racism rests in action. After all, theorizing anti-racism does not certify anti-racist work. Today's transnational, global experiences reveal the importance of confronting difference and diversity and coming to grips with how particularly diasporic spaces are claimed and responded to. As our identities become more entangled, myriad social identifications are forged. It behooves anti-racism education to work with the twin notion of difference and diversity as well as the relational aspects of difference in complex ways that speak to how power is negotiated among teachers, administrators, learners and community members. Highlighting the material and experiential realities of minoritized peoples in their dealing with the school system, anti-racism also means learning about the experiences of living with minoritized identities, and understanding how students' lived experiences in and out of school implicate youth engagement and disengagement from school. Anti-racism uncovers how race, ethnicity, class, gender, sexuality, physical ability, power and difference influence and are influenced by schooling processes.

As a racially minoritized scholar in a Western academy, I find the perils and consequences for doing and not doing anti-racist work are very clear. But, rather than enjoy the "benefits" of not speaking out on oppression, I prefer to join others to expose the politics, desires and seductive impetus to remain silent on the privileges and oppressions that frame our lives. Therefore, my academic and political project is to bring a critical gaze on the possibilities of anti-racism for social and educational change. For the purposes of this work, I have framed these issues in the general area of schooling and education in Canada, but more specifically, in the context of the education "crisis" in Ontario.

Competing Marginalities – Contested Space

Writing in *Black Skins, White Masks*, Fanon (1991) cautioned his readers that when we mask our(selves) in denials of difference, we effectively promote the continuance of social oppression.[1] Employing a critical understanding of difference, grounded in what it means to engage a politics of race, our approach to equity reforms must simultaneously draw on both individual and collective complicities/responsibilities to offer praxical strategies for change. Importantly, as ongoing social productions, our identities form in and through their various interactions within society and so, developing a strategic tapestry must involve critical self reflections on how we might manage our own internal marginalities as they shift, struggle and jockey for control. As Bakhtin (1982) asserts, this *dialogical self* is a congress of different times and different knowledges that are constantly being re-inscribed and reassessed within our heterogeneous, multi-voiced and contradictory identities.[2] Not to fall back to Cartesian notions of a unified cognitive self, Kristeva (1974), in her notion of *transpositionality*, theorizes the notion of positionality within the self – which is to say that these multiple *I positions* are dependent on the specifics of the moment: who, where, why and when we are speaking. These internal positionalities emerge, submerge and float as each moment dictates.[3] It is in relation to these internal and external engagements with difference that our thinking about reform must begin. Unfortunately, in today's Canadian educational contexts, multicultural policies and programs functionally side-step self-reflexivity as a starting-point to change.

In North America, the debate on inclusivity and diversity in schooling may be conceptualized in two general categories: diversity as additive vs. diversity as critical.[4] The first approach views diversity in terms of teaching and sharing knowledge about the contributions of diverse cultures. This approach appeals to a liberal humanism wherein diversity is seen to be a safe expression of difference that enriches pluralistic communities. On the other hand, the second approach views schooling as a politically mediated experience in which social, economic, political and historical factors are implicated. Multicultural educational paradigms tend to promote surface level changes to perception and understanding without critically examining the historical complex of disabilities that frame schooling. Within these contexts, we actively do very little to address the various intersecting and interlocking power imbalances that hinder the inclusion of all voices into the mainstream. Rather, multicultural approaches to schooling address neither the pervasive nature of oppression, nor the impact of oppression on the lived experience of marginalized students, families and communities.

Not to downplay the general mainstream resistance to anti-racism praxis, it is important that we recognize at least part of the dilemma that plagues our efforts. Simply put, we do not work within a field that can be understood in Black and White terms. Indeed, critical theory and critical anti-racism praxis specifically, requires us to engage intensely complex phenomena in a manner that can be translated and understood in concrete terms. This is no easy task. Beginning with the recognition that the term *race* itself is hotly contested, the complexity of the struggle for mainstream legitimacy, acceptance and action becomes all the clearer. In fact, the politics that frame resistant struggles always threaten to break down even seemingly lucid attempts at forward movement. Case in point, some authors place quotation marks on the term race (e.g., 'race,' "race") to gesture to its roots in scientific biological racism. Recognizing that race is a socially constructed term, I would add that the practice of "qualifying" the usage of the term by alluding to its problematic origins can be problematic as well. I am concerned with how some might use this practice to de-legitimize race and racism as "real," "knowable" and material phenomena. For example, in Fields' (1990) contention that racial knowledge is imposed upon the oppressed as an *illusion* that does the ideological work of the oppressor, we see how misinterpretations of race's socially constructed nature can be used to downplay and mute its material reality in contemporary contexts.[5] Asserting that the continuation of the race concept exists as a function of society's continued usage and engagement with the term, Fields disparages anti-racists for our part in unwittingly perpetuating racial talk, racial meaning and racial ideology.

Nothing handed down from the past could keep race alive if we did not constantly reinvent and re-ritualize it to fit our own terrain. If race lives on today, it can do so only because we continue to need a social vocabulary that will allow us to make sense, not of what our ancestors did then, but of what we choose to do now.[6]

In her analysis, race has ceased to serve the purpose of justifying racial exploitation and social inequality and so should, by virtue of that immateriality, "fade into the ether."[7] Needless to say, such contentions are at best, naive and at worst, dangerous. This type of theoretical work paves the ground for the equality vs. equity debates and other similarly framed common-sense notions like "color-blindness." These types of analyses always neglect to recognize the fundamental character of race as a social construct that has developed over a millennium or more of diffusion in and throughout every fiber of the social world. As Omi and Winant (1993) point out, whatever race was in its origins, it is now an intrinsic part and fundamental principal of social organization and identity formation. As such, it cannot and must not be trivialized as a mere illusion to be eliminated by the simple "choice" to disencumber ourselves of it.[8] After all, as Bhavnani (2001) clarifies, many terms such as "Black, White, racial, ethnic minorities, culture, cultural difference" exist in such contested space, and so we could dispute any fixed meanings placed on any of these terms.[9] Rather than doing so, we need to acknowledge their relations to power, acknowledge their sociohistorical contextuality and ask ourselves why we feel the need to validate our usage of them.

Race is real, and our engagements with the term must move forward without the need to preface and qualify that reality. While we may claim to denounce the false dichotomies that equate biological differences and cultural differences, it is important to recognize that no corner of the world can claim an escape or sanctity from race knowledge and the discourses that frame it. It may be heresy to state it so bluntly, but racism is a pernicious and vicious social problem, and the brute recourse to biological and pseudo-scientific engagements with race and culture may be cleverly masked, but they are always present. Working to allocate and accord social rewards and punishments, the culture of racial violence (symbolic, physical, material and psychological) works both covertly and overtly to maintain a racial pecking order throughout the world. The scars of racism are obvious, but it takes a critical eye to read race into social narratives when there are no explicit references to race. For example, words such as *immigrant, welfare-mother* and *crime* are all racially coded, but those codes are hidden within implicit social interpretations that are difficult to name and prove. We can see/feel this framework in action as minoritized youth, their families and communities are pathologized and defined in terms of social irrelevance and liability: The challenge is how we might name and rupture these codes. Our exposure to, and inculcation by these systems of dominance may be unmasked and contested – but the question is how? Anti-racism is a project of possibility, a project of change, and if anti-racism education is to offer real hope and a possibility to really effect reform in the face of racism, then we must not reject the challenge as an impossible task. Working from within a "philosophy of hope," we must accept that the reality of applying anti-racism praxis at a systemic level begs the larger question of validity: Who needs it, and who has the power to grant it?

Unmasking Racism: Perils and Consequences

As a pedagogue and community worker I have tremendous respect for school teachers and educational practitioners. Like many, I want to share in the great success stories born in our schools, but at the same time, in order to appreciate those successes, we must be willing to take responsibility for the great failures of that same system. Ultimately, what it comes down to is that the good intentions of educators and administrators can no longer be allowed to stand proxy for student success. Our school systems have failed to support teacher efforts to provide educational equity and curricula appropriate for the most disadvantaged and vulnerable of our youth. With that issue in mind, it is important that we maintain a critical gaze on our work so that we might better understand and appreciate why our good intentions continue to fail minoritized children and their communities.

The search for equity in schooling must be contextualized relative to the experiences of (particularly but not solely) minoritized students who feel excluded by the dominant structures for the delivery of education. But how are we to conduct this search in Euro-American schools looking to address difference and diversity within and among the student population? In order to understand anti-racist educational reform in these contexts, we (as educators, students and community workers) need to embark upon a radical inquiry of social difference that explores how it shapes our ways of seeing, acting and knowing the world. In the current transnational/ global contexts, we must use the power of human imagination to propose alternatives that are informed by how people come to know, understand and experience themselves as members of a community and as citizens of a nation/state.[10] However, with that said, over the last decade, positive changes to administrative and pedagogical approaches in education have still had to contend with the effects of globalization as it reworks, rewrites and re-inscribes the subjugation of certain bodies, experiences and knowledge into schooling.

Today, as "multicultural" efforts at pseudo-reform effectively dilute the potential for real holistic movement in educational praxis, we can take some solace in the knowledge that there are also significant voices of resistance standing in opposition to these trends. Granted, the forced encroachment of global capital in our schools is no small trend to be shrugged off, but still, if there is anything that the discourse of anti-racism brings to the table, it is the recognition that educational reform is not a zero-sum game. If we are to engage anti-racism as part of an organic social movement, it is important that we begin to shift our interests from recognizing the signs, symbols and markers of our oppression, to a pointed concern with the processes through which we ourselves are agents capable of resistance. By this, I mean to say that in some ways, our preoccupation with the physical manifestations of racism and oppression can serve to normalize the very state of oppression through which we suffer. There are multiple sites through which our oppression is manufactured, multiple sites in/through which we are implicated as actors/subjects in those moments, and then again, multiple sites in/through which we might seek to rupture those relations of power. As discussed earlier, I prefer to view the whole of anti-racist work as a tapestry in which each strategy is important and vital. So long as resistant voices stand in opposition to this push to globalize, there is always an insurgent potential for change at work.

Cognizant of these general problematics and possibilities, I want to focus the discussion to address some learning goals and make the case for anti-racist work as being distinct and yet connected to the wider realm of anti-oppression advocacy. First, I would like to pinpoint and establish the challenges of engaging in social justice and anti-racist advocacy within diverse and diasporic populations. Second, I explore some important questions about collective responses towards change. Third, rethink and raise some of the theoretical/philosophical issues related to anti-racist practice and its implications for the pursuit of transformative change.

Difference and Diversity

That Canada is a diverse society is something about which we should all be proud. But taking such pride should necessitate that we also accept a certain degree of responsibility for how our society engages that diversity. Clearly, even though a number of changes are indeed taking place in Ontario's educational system, it is important for us to recognize that our schools have not kept pace with the nation's shifting racial and ethnic make-up. For example, when the demographics of Ontario's Toronto District School Board (TDSB) were examined, a number of staggering linguistic realities were brought to light:

- 53% of secondary school students listed English as their first language while a staggering 41% claimed a first language other than English.

- 70 different languages were being spoken in the homes of TDSB students.

- Secondary schools receive approximately 4000 newcomers every year while TDSB elementary schools (grades 1-8) receive approximately 8000 newcomers per year.

- Students claim a heritage connection to more than 170 countries and 12% of secondary students have been in Canada for only three years or less.

With those staggering statistics in mind, it is important to also acknowledge that TDSB schools are not simply multilingual and multiracial. They are, in fact, diverse along a number of significant markers of difference (e.g., sexuality, religion, gender, social class). Again in TDSB slightly over a half of the students are female, almost one in three students live in poverty, one in ten are gay, lesbian, bisexual or transgender, and one in ten of the students have an identified physical, psychological and/or learning disability. These facts and figures must not be glossed over because our identities are linked to the process of knowledge production and are extremely consequential in terms of schooling outcomes for diverse youth.[11] Although we often get statistics speaking to such demographic shifts and the related dynamics of disengagement for some youth, there is a human side to the experience of marginalization that statistics cannot capture.[12]

Recognizing that the nature of racism is insidious in Western contexts, we would do well to remember that the oppressed and marginalized are all disciplined to see the world through the eyes of privilege. This is the human side of the equation that cannot be captured easily in demographic analyses. Because the oppressed are transfixed within a duality that both rejects and welcomes the oppressor, our constitution within a "privileged reality" works through internalized racism to "oppress from within."[13] As mentioned at the beginning of this paper: "Anti-racists find themselves fighting reminists who find themselves fighting socialists . . ." Simply put, this personal duality shields the "true order" of society from our eyes. As a result, in spite of our pain, we are indoctrinated into a framework that teaches us to both support and deny our own oppression; and in turn, support and deny the oppression of other marginalized peoples. Importantly, this dilemma illustrates clearly that differences alone are not necessarily conducive to the creation of solidarities. Moreover, we must be careful not to expect that the experience of marginality alone should be enough to generate solidarity development between groups. The oppressed are disciplined to see the world through the eyes of privilege; and those eyes are not equipped to perceive marginal matters – not even when they are our own issues.[14] There is a need for us to confront our absorption of White paradigms and internalized racisms because they instill us with a duality that disciplines us to fight those who might be our partners in the project.

There is a great need to engage in political action to break down the barriers that keep us apart. However, with that seemingly simple notion in mind, communicating across differences does not come easily, and particularly not when that communication has to occur across lines of class, sexual orientation, race, ability and the various other positionalities through which we are kept apart. The pleasant poetry of "diversity" and "multiculturalism" would suggest that when we learn about each others' differences, we will learn to appreciate and celebrate what might otherwise be perceived as threatening and unknowable. But these naïve interpretations of difference do not implicate power relations or internalized oppression in the equation. Meeting across differences requires that all involved sink into a certain level of vulnerability in relation to the relative positions of privilege and marginalization inherent in each instance. But as asserted earlier, the fundamentally degrading and destructive nature of oppression ensures that even such potentially supportive and productive encounters can easily become instructive, controlling and directive. As leaders in the anti-racism project, we must take this into consideration and work to establish critical education as crucial to the success of our efforts. However, awareness of racism does not necessitate freedom from it. As Dei, Karumanchery and Karumanchery-Luik contend:

> Awareness alone may allow us to look reflexively at ourselves as 'subjects' within the moment, but it does not necessarily help us to move away from the guilt, solitude, insecurity and pain associated with those moments in which we could not understand 'why.' Why we couldn't defend ourselves. Why we were set apart from the others. It is the paradoxical and painful duality that makes both sense and non-sense out of our oppressor's words. This is why a critical education is so important: because the oppressed cannot be expected to resist without understanding what they are resisting and why they are resisting it.

Consciousness and awareness of racism and oppression will certainly help us to analyze our place within the racist experience, and most importantly to this discussion, it will allow us to engage new possibilities for solidarity with other marginalized groups. There is a collective pain that different marginalized groups share, but it has almost always gone unnamed and unacknowledged. This pain – the pain of our collective past and the pain of our ongoing battles with each other as we jockey for position along the lowest rungs of the sociocultural ladder. Because the multiplicity of social oppressions will almost always lead to the need to negotiate competing marginalities and intersecting identities, the divides that separate us will not be bridged until we ourselves take responsibility for the business of uniting. By sharing our knowledges, experiences, pains and strategies, we will no longer be separated by our differences, and in fact, it will be our differences that join us in a collective resistance.

Collective Responses Towards Social Change

Working with allies allows us to build coalitions towards the development of a progressive politics in schooling, but in doing so we must always recognize how issues of power are to be addressed within these movements. Anti-racist educators must be careful about the intellectual and political paralysis of laboring in "parallel tracks" rather than communicating "across tracks," while also noting (as pointed out earlier) that the collective quest for solidarity in anti-oppression work can mask some underlying tensions and ambivalences. The challenge to us is to see the contingent nature of strategic alliance and the importance of coalition building without compromising the saliency of race in the anti-oppression agenda. Ultimately, anti-racism praxis must be approached as a mutually rewarding and supportive collective. Only then will our work begin to tap into the power of collective action in the face of racism and oppression.

It important to reframe anti-racist conceptualizations of political action to a stance which recognizes that individual and in-group politics alone cannot stand as the lynchpin for social change. As a marker of "healing" or "becoming," individualized movement into politicized spaces of safety and resistance can be powerful, but we must always be hesitant about politics that effectively distance us from other marginalized groups and the potential to develop inter-group politics and action. Again, for clarity's sake, I am not detracting from the importance of solidarity formation among in-groups and I am certainly not suggesting that expressions of such solidarity (i.e., the development of Afrocentric schools) are not powerfully important in the struggle for social justice. What I am saying is that our politics, strategies and practices must recognize the power of collectivities to do work across borders and boundaries of race, gender, class, religion and ability to find the connective tissue that links us in our oppression.

Speaking specifically to the importance of racially and culturally politicized collectivities, the ability to frame ourselves within a space of "normalcy" and a social context of belonging allows us to better place racism as a part of our reality. But this is more than merely being able to see the hidden relations of power at play. It is about the empowering nature of group solidarity, and the propensity for in-group solidarity to allow for reframings of self, and self in relation to society. For me, the notion of communal space stands as a symbols of solidarity that can be accessed when in mainstream contexts – this is a powerful tool. I would draw from this discussion to extend the importance of developing community linkages across oppressed sites. This imperative for the development of inter-community solidarity speaks to the need to bolster oppositional linkages that stand outside the auspices of power and privilege.

Not to paint too rosy a picture, I would reflect on our discussions of diversity and difference to extrapolate the crucial need for "comfort and unity" to stand as the fulcrum upon which these solidarity linkages must be made. Simply put, the decision to enter into such intimate and vulnerable relationships with out-group members is fraught with dilemmas. In fact, while much research shows that marginalized peoples express some confidence in the ability of other minorities to "understand them," the politics of difference and that understanding that strategic essentialisms may be necessary within these private and intimate relationships, always discretely mediates the possibility for safety in these collectivities. There is a sense of comfort and ease that develops in solidarity formations in which one is in the presence of others who have experienced their specific brand of oppression. This "solidarity response" arises because we are socially constructed, constructing and reconstructing individuals. Our accumulated experiential knowledges, what Collins (1998) referred to as our "personal biography," filters through our conscious selves and become linked through repetition over time, revealing that certain interactions are likely to be problematic while others will tend to be positive and beneficial.[15]

For many of the same reasons that marginalized people often try to "pass" within dominant spaces, we find ourselves turning to groups for solidarity and safety. So as useful, beneficial and powerful as inter-solidarities might be to the political and practical applications of anti-racism, we have to always recognize that such collectivities innately carry the potential to be problematic. Paralleling the work of Summers-Effler (2002), Karumanchery (2003) notes that our motivation to feel and develop higher levels of emotional energy pushes us to follow our personal biography's indications as to which interactions tend to be "energy sapping" and which tend to be productive of emotional energy.[16] If possible, we will choose to engage in the latter interactions:

> The history of experiences determines whether an individual is likely to lean towards solidarity or the exertion of power for their source of emotional energy. When all is well, and one's level of emotional energy is not threatened, this process of seeking some interactions over others tends to happen at a level below consciousness.[17]

It is important to note that this notion of commonality extends beyond the "dialogue between physical bodies" and to the dialectics of the metaphysical and the symbolic. Once experienced, the emotional energy generated in the solidarity interaction is taken with the individual into their out-group experiences, and in this fashion, acts as a resource of "emotional capital" to be stored and employed when necessary. This is of pivotal importance to the development of an allied solidarity among marginalized groups. Once these symbols and markers of identity, community and solidarity are established, they become "a shortcut to recreating rituals that will reproduce solidarity and emotional energy." Now, while there are inherent pitfalls that trouble the development of such collectivities of difference, I would suggest that finding commonalities that intersect our differences may in fact allow for powerful allied work that can cross boundaries of positionality.

Engaging such intersections of oppression allows us to tap into a number of oppositional discourses that are not available to us within homogeneous collectivities. For instance, women of color may be able to access more avenues towards resistance, agency and activism than men of color because of their intersecting and interlocking experience of multiple oppressions.[18] As Collins (1990) argues, the nature of African American Women's oppression was conducive of a culture of resistance through which the process of self-definition would assert positive internal relationships with self, and external relationships with community that were specifically female and specifically Black. This sense of community, and feeling of belonging is unique to groups that have undergone the same forms of oppression. Such experiences of community, solidarity, safety, understanding, positionality and shared experience may all work to engender the development of resistant identities framed relative to internal relationships with self, and external relationships with community that are supportive and productive of the development of community. Being mindful of the traps that accompany hierarchies of oppression, and other slippages that problematically set the oppressed against each other, the potential of collective action towards social change is immense and we must look to how these resources might be engaged across lines of social positioning. Difference must begin to be seen in relation to the strengths and possibilities they provide.

Reframing Anti-racist Philosophy and Practice

The failures and resistances of the 1990s must provide a spring board and impetus to rethink anti-racist education in the 21st-century. By expanding our view of what constitutes "education," we can include schools and other formal institutions within broader explorations of the social organization of learning. This open approach will allow us to interrogate the *broad* curriculum with respect to the reproduction of knowledges that shape and transform the social and political world. Contrary to much mainstream discourse surrounding the call for "measurement" and "a return to excellence" in schooling, anti-racism understands that "excellence" must be measured through a critical frame that does not necessarily rely on statistics and/or quantifiable outputs. In truth, the quality of learning environments and the scholarship produced therein increase tremendously with the recognition that equity measures are excellent measures. In critiquing conventional schooling and the trend towards linear banking theories of education, we problematize how today's schools produce, validate and privilege certain forms of knowledge while devaluing and de-legitimizing others.

Critical anti-racist praxis challenges both the dominant processes that constitute what becomes understood as "valid" knowledge, and the relational dynamics that allow some knowledges to become hegemonic along internal and global frameworks. Importantly, as others scholars have noted, because *hegemony* is not limited to the frame of Western knowledges and epistemologies, it becomes a useful notion for understanding the relationship between multiple social values and complex realities. So through an anti-racist prism, we undertake a more rigorous examination of the adequacy of dominant discourses and epistemologies for understanding the realities of people quite different from ourselves; people framed in oppressive positions and in the context of asymmetrical power relations among social groups. In other words, anti-racism is about a search for epistemological diversity in the understanding of the complexity of oppression given the incompleteness of discourse and political practice. Critical anti-racist work requires a redefinition of anti-racism broadly and to situate equity within the anti-racist practice. This means looking at racism in its myriad forms and connecting racism with other forms of oppression. But, as noted already, this practice must be a critical stance that helps us to also address the saliency of specific forms of oppression.

Educators must equip students to understand the historical genesis and political trajectories of race and difference, the historical specificities of racist practices as well as how racisms become institutionalized and normalized in different societies. In the politics of anti-oppression work in general, anti-racism must be quick to offer a counter reading to the liberal notion of pluralism which effaces power relations of race differences. In fact, I would make the specific point that for school teachers, reframing anti-racism is a call to see the perniciousness of anti-Black racism, in particular. While there is no one model of pursuing anti-oppression work, educators cannot separate the "politics of difference" (i.e., the intersections of racial, class, gender and sexual differences) from the "politics of race" (i.e., an acknowledgement of the saliency of race) because this practice helps dominant bodies to deny and refuse to interrogate White privilege and power. Because Whiteness tends to be rendered invisible through a process of normalization, we need to be acutely aware of how "anti-essentialist hegemonic masks can serve to bring white supremacist power and privilege" to the centre of supposedly critical political pursuits.[19] In other words, the emphasis on the individual and dispersed identities can be paralyzing to the extent that it can and does deny the ways centralized dominant systems of power work to establish and sustain particular advantages.

The articulation of White hegemonic power is such that unless Whiteness and the dominant discourse that sustains it is carefully scrutinized, we can be denying and/or silencing the experiential realities of bodies of color. In so doing, Whiteness and the dominant discourse come to assume positions of normalcy. This is reflected in the popular refrains that "working class whites [are] being equally as oppressed as racial minorities" and that "minorities can also be racist towards whites." I would admit that gender, sexuality, ethnicity and indeed class, demarcate Whiteness and that it is problematic to generalize White privilege, but a critical anti-racist approach to understanding the questions of power and difference requires that educators affirm the saliency of race even as we recognize the intersections of race with other forms of difference. In fact, Johal (2000) is particularly instructive when he declares that "as much as white folks across differences of class, gender, sexuality ethnicity or religion may be oppressed in relation to the dominant white middle class male subject – they hold a pigmentary passport of privilege that allows sanctity within the racial polity of whiteness. This is a luxury people [bodies] of color across all our differences do not hold."[20]

As anti-racist educators, we have a unique place in the current climate of school advocacy. This is because of the power of new imaginings that critical anti-racism education offers us. If we believe that the future itself is being hotly contested in the schools, union halls and community forums, then anti-racism has to be part of that struggle because anti-racist educators have unprecedented opportunities to influence many minds and to share and engage different (dominant, privileged, subjugated, subordinated and minoritized) perspectives. The environments in which we work may offer advantages and opportunities depending on our subject positions and politics, so we must be prepared and able to work with and within these specific allocations of space and resources to further the cause of youth education. It all comes to a question of whether an anti-racist educator wants to see current challenges as obstacles or as opportunities and openings to make change happen. This is not a simplistic assertion, and understandably, today many Ontario teachers may feel a bit powerless. But I would suggest that teachers have an option – they may perceive their classrooms as a space where inclusivity, personal narrative and local context can create a "positive learning environment," or they can sink into the frustration and apathy that comes with challenging the monolithics of "the system" and pass on opportunities to develop an insurgent and empowered body politic in their classrooms.[21] Granted, our schools need resources – material, financial, logistical and political – in order to do the necessary work, but the needed resources are not forthcoming. So, while it is understandable to scoff at the official rhetoric suggesting that educators must do more with less, we must engage the daunting challenges of equity and inclusivity to, in fact, do more with less. We owe it to our students and we owe it to our communities.

Conclusion: Finding Anti-Racist Responses to New Questions

There are emerging questions for anti-racist workers to deal with. Educators must address some public disquiet and scepticism about anti-racist practice and its efficacy to bring about changes in schooling. For example, how do we, as anti-racist educators, ensure that our schools respond to the multiple needs and concerns of a diverse body politic? How do we create schools where all students are valued, feel a sense of belonging and have access to instruction that is responsive to the needs of diverse learners? In order to ensure that all students develop a sense of entitlement and connectedness to their schools, there must be a proactive attempt to respond to the needs of all students. Schools have a responsibility to help students make sense of their identities, to build the confidence of all students and remove the fear of confirming lowered expectations. It is also important for an educator to know that the needs of students extend beyond the material to emotional, social and psychological concerns. This is the contemporary challenge for anti-racism – to incorporate these diverse needs into critical educational practice.

To help society deal with these issues, educators cannot extend a helping hand from a distance. We must assist all students to "come to voice," to challenge the normalized order of things and, in particular, the constitution of dominance in Western knowledge production. Because the prevailing notions of "reason," "normalcy" and "truth" are essential to the structuring of asymmetrical power relations in Euro-Canadian society, we must help our students see through ways in which White privilege masquerade as "excellence" and "merit." Moreover, as an extension of this imperative, educators must help students acknowledge and respond positively to difference. That is, to see difference as a site of strength, power and agency. Speaking about difference, it is important to note that our schools are "communities of differences" and no one approach to education will fit all. We must embrace our different identities beyond the constructs of multicultural tasks. Similarly, the notion of "communities of differences" entail that we note how the different identities (race, gender, sexuality, class and physical ability) shape the experiences of the student. Anti-racism education necessitates that we connect these identities with knowledge production and also learn from the diverse knowledges produced by our different bodies. Utilizing subject knowledges, we must start with what people already know, then search for ways to situate the local cultural resource and knowledges into the official curriculum. We are implementing and learning from strategies of local resistance.

With respect to accountability and transparency, anti-racism teachings must move beyond the bland politics of inclusion to holding leaders accountable. This is the only way for educators to establish legitimacy and credibility in the eyes of the local populace. To be accountable is also to be relevant and it is here that the ways of producing relevant anti-racist knowledge becomes imperative. There is a powerful role for anti-racist research in the promotion of educational change. The importance of researching difference and oppression is generally acknowledged by most anti-racist workers. However, today we see a move for more "evidence-based research." While not asking for anti-racism to insert itself in this problematic demand that presents evidence as "objective" and "legitimated knowledge," it is imperative that anti-racism defines its parameters of critical research to make a difference in people's lives. The false split of basic and applied research and the myth of disinterested, non-invested knower or researcher continue to be exposed by critical anti-racism work. Anti-racist educators need to make clear the policy related aspects of our work in an effort to realize material changes. We must not only identify under researched areas and turn our gaze into domination studies, but also highlight what it takes to bring change. Rather than fight for institutional responsibility to support critical work/cutting edge research, anti-racism must strengthen local peoples' capacity to undertake their own research. Last but not least, research must also shift the gaze from the failures to also learn from the strategies of resistance and the success cases.

This discussion started by challenging what appears to be the ostensible harmony espoused by multicultural policies within and beyond the context of schooling. I asserted that the mask of diversity, an additive approach to acknowledging cultural differences, fails to reveal the fundamental power differentials within and across ethno-racial communities as aspects of multicultural Canada. The mandate of anti-racist education, while affirming the salience of cultural diversity with the official Canadian policy of multiculturalism, is also to strive for conditions of equity and excellence for all students. In this era of conservative educational and fiscal policies in Ontario, the challenge becomes one of transgressing a system of differential rewards and punishments. In so doing, the masks of standardization and centralization of educational autonomy may be revealed as sources of inequity that deny excellence for our students and school communities. The struggle for educational change implicates us all. We may be differentially implicated but still we all have responsibilities. Knowledge must compel action and in this era where the political mantra from the powerful is "you are either with us or against us" the perils of speaking out cannot be underestimated. Such binary or dualistic modes of thought are not helpful to anyone. Critical anti-racists scholars will eschew a simplistic "Black-White duality" and also point out that alongside the perceived pressure to racially fit, there is also the desire to racially identify. Educators have always had a responsibility to address these concerns about schooling, but perhaps that imperative is even more so today given that the state appears to have abandoned its obligations to a diversified citizenry. Ironically, the erosion of equity initiatives in various boards of education in Ontario is happening at a time when there is an even greater urgency for educators to engage in this type of work.[22] As the forces of globalization challenge all communities (e.g., the influence of market forces dictating policy responses to difference), anti-racism education has a responsibility to offer a radical critique of our schools. The shirking away of responsibilities by the state, the seduction of "common-sense' discourse must not go uncritiqued and unchallenged. We often hear: "what does anti-racism offer us?" Well, without hesitation, I say, Anti-racism offers us hope.

Chapter 9

Reinventing and Redefining Whiteness

Building a Critical Pedagogy for Insurgent Times

Joe Kincheloe, Ph.D.
Department of Teaching and Learning
Pennsylvania State University

Introduction

It is through the privilege of Whiteness that "difference" continues to be both defined and articulated. Today, while White power and privilege are continuously asserted as a justification for racist practice, claims to White "innocence" and the resulting denial of systemic oppression, serve to leave the mechanisms for racism intact. . . . As many others have demonstrated, it is important that our articulation of Whiteness is seen as more than a sum of White privilege, power and identity. We must connect Whiteness with White racism. . . . But how do we proceed to interrogate and teach about the issues of power, oppression and social control when the very natures of these concepts and the related problematics of privilege are abstract concepts?

-Dei, Karumanchery and Karumanchery-Luik, *Playing the Race Card* [1]

Like the above scholars, I am preoccupied with the question of how to proceed in the struggle to interrupt and rupture the systems of power and privilege that coalesce in articulations of Whiteness. Even though recent years have seen an unprecedented growth in the fields of anti-racism and Whiteness studies, and while most critical educators recognize that the grasp of White power and privilege permeates almost every major issue facing the West today (e.g., affirmative action, intelligence testing, the deterioration of public space, Western imperialism, cultural consumption), we still struggle to define and engage the slippery and elusive concept of Whiteness itself. The dilemma remains a central feature of any critical pedagogy in cultural studies because the concept is continually shifting and re-inscribing itself around changing meanings of race in the larger society.[2] So, while most critical theorists agree that Whiteness is intimately associated with issues of power, privilege and difference, no one at this point really knows what it is. Moreover, although the effort to redefine and reinvent the concept has become the prime directive of today's critical pedagogies of Whiteness, too many of these analyses remain detached, self-satisfied and generally meaningless in the praxical struggle for social justice. As a whole, such efforts leave us questioning where we are going in the evolving sub-discipline of Whiteness Studies. This burning question was at the forefront of my interests as I wrote this paper.

In this article, I explore the sociopolitical and psychological dimensions of Whiteness alongside an analysis of the ideological dynamics of White supremacy and the materiality of power. In interrogating the impact of racism on the White psyche, I argue that the reconstruction of White identity is a fundamentally important step for the future of libratory praxis in the West. The reorganization of "Whiteness" will help to build a "power literacy" capable of simultaneously negotiating and explaining White privilege, the complex nature of Whiteness, the dynamics surrounding the White identity crisis and the formulation of a libratory White identity. In short, it is my hope that in building a critical pedagogy to re-imagine and redefine Whiteness, we will be helping to recast the entire social sphere.

The Future Looks Dim: The Rhetoric of White Supremacy

One of the great paradoxes of Western societies is their ability to deny the fundamentally oppressive nature of democracy as it has come to be practiced today. Drawing on knowledge about equity and "difference" to interrogate how interpretations of democracy are engaged in the West, it becomes increasingly difficult to side-step the oppressive reality of how socially disadvantaged groups are made to struggle within the "normalizing gaze" of power and privilege. In these contexts, the mythical White archetype has become idealized along the lines of his White, male, middle-class, heterosexual and Christian normalcy; and his power echoes and manifests through the intersections and interlocks of those privileges. As Dei, Karumanchery and Karumanchery-Luik (2004) explain, it is through these relations of power that the White standard continues to be reified, imagined and repositioned as the one true gauge against which to measure and define difference, dysfunction and dissidence. In these contexts, marginalized groups are positioned as a threat to the structures and norms of White society[3] while "marginal issues" such as racism, the under-funding of social welfare programs, and the marketization of public schooling actively widen the gap between the privileged and the oppressed.[4] As asserted by Karumanchery (2003), the dogma of democracy plays host to a variety of interconnected discourses that work to sustain a firm denial of racism and oppression while also maintaining and bolstering the charade of White victimization.[5]

> The oppressed that recognize their plight do so exactly because they are marginalized and because they carry the burden of oppression. The privileged, who only benefit as a result of their position in the relations of oppression, have no cause

to look beyond that experience. It is a problematic more complex than simple denial. For the privileged to accept the scope and nature of oppression, they would also have to accept their complicity in that condition. As a defense mechanism, it becomes necessary not simply to deny the reality of oppression, but to see that reality from a perspective that is less personally injurious. The resulting rationalizations of social stratification and inequality invariably function to pathologize victims of oppression as the source of their misfortunes.[6]

Henry et al. (1995) employ the theoretical framework of *democratic racism* to investigate the binary value sets that allow racial oppression to flourish alongside the tenets of liberal democracy.[7] Proposing that racism *should* be addressed, but only through means that *do not* disrupt the present social structures, these discourses work through the intersections of privilege to belie the truth of oppression and fuel mainstream backlashes against any practice, initiative and/or philosophy (e.g., political correctness, affirmative action) that might ameliorate the experience of oppression.[8] Importantly, within democratically racist systems, the firm belief in meritocracy always frames the oppressed as somehow solely responsible for their experience of marginalization.[9] At the same time, the dogmatic belief in equality and fair play acts as a loophole through which resistant Whites might engage in applications of disciplinary power that are openly racist but "socially acceptable."[10] With these issues in mind, we cannot be surprised to encounter Whites who intensely resent and sometimes violently oppose equity based reforms; often arguing that they are "reverse-racist" measures to exact revenge for "past" injustices. Through the democratically racist lens, multicultural initiatives and anti-racist reforms are almost always positioned as "special interest" politics and little more than a "White man's burden." That being said, multiculturalists and anti-racist pedagogues teaching about racism and Whiteness need to be ready to encounter such hostility if they are going to be effective because White students commonly perceive "inclusive" measures as unnecessary, unfair and reverse-racist; and they enter their classes with attitudes shaped accordingly.

This perception of "White victimization" shapes the way many Whites interpret the canon wars, the public conversation about political correctness, feminism and employment equity. For example, within educational fields, efforts to construct academic curricula grounded in the values of inclusivity and social justice have been seen, not as a battle between competing ideologies and pedagogical philosophies, but as a clearly punitive attack on White people. In these contexts, affirmative action and other inclusive reforms are always positioned and portrayed in the mainstream as the manifestations of a liberal/left-wing agenda to punish White people. Today's schools and workplaces are rife with these mutterings about the supposed climate of unfairness that permeates social reforms in the West; and it this brand of anger and denial that propels social regulations that pathologize the oppressed as the root cause of society's ills.[11] In this fashion, "reverse racism" and "liberal" concerns with racial injustice are consistently used as scapegoats to explain the economic declines of the last twenty years and to fear-monger around the "alleged" narrowing of job opportunities for White people. Clearly, White anger, resentment and denial have opened a new racial order to mark the beginning of the twenty-first century. "Leave me alone," they insist. "I've had absolutely nothing to do with racism or racial persecution." Black, Latino and Native American poverty, unemployment and disenfranchisement are not White problems, they argue; they're non-White problems. Such pervasive denials have allowed White civic elites to distance themselves from issues of Black and Latino poverty. In this context the disparity of wealth between White and non-White continues to grow without anyone seeming to care.[12] Having emerged from the chaos of the White identity crisis, this new White consciousness is a serious social phenomenon that must not be dismissed or underestimated.

It is almost as if our White society has been stricken by a case of mass amnesia through which our culture's most dangerous and incendiary memories have been erased by power:

> In the U.S. Ronald Reagan and his handlers adeptly rearticulated old ideologies in a way that reinscribed a racism that camouflaged its racist character. The old ideologies of social Darwinism and Manifest Destiny reassured Whites shaken by the identity crisis that they were the inheritors of the moral capital of the Puritans' "city on the hill" – Reagan invoked the reference frequently during his presidential speeches. The amnesia allows right-wing spokespeople the opportunity to answer any challenge to their efforts to reestablish White hegemony with charges of political correctness. We are victims of political correctness, they have maintained, in the process reversing the rhetoric of racial oppression to the point that non-White victims become the new oppressors of White people.[13]

In this rhetorical universe, affirmative action and employment equity programs have been painted as the ultimate expression of racism; where undeserving individuals drawing upon a distant past of oppression are being "given" advantages in schools and workplaces at the expense of "innocent" Whites. Adeptly deploying this rhetoric of reverse-racism, conservatives hark back to an easier time and a more appealing vision of life in America – before the liberal permissivism of the 1960s and before the nation's greatness had been compromised.[14] Indeed, the Nation at Risk report issued in the spring of 1983 can be viewed as a recovery document outlining the impossibility of seeking educational quality and equality simultaneously. Racial differences in these contexts continue to be framed as a destructive force intent on eroding (White) values and standards in education – declines in test scores and increasing illiteracy are all seen as resulting from our misguided quest for equality and democracy. Ultimately, in education, the recovery of Whiteness meant a return to the little red schoolhouse.

Grounded in an admittedly naive conception of individual equality, the White consciousness of the new racial order challenges the very foundations of critical pedagogies that recognize how power and privilege intersect and interlock within the social sphere. Understanding this dynamic, proponents of a critical pedagogy of Whiteness address both the ideological and interpersonal forces at work in this dangerous context. There is a challenge to difficult knowledge, and while we cannot abandon the study of Whiteness simply because it may anger some Whites, we must take the complex reality of White anger seriously and work to address it at a number of levels. One such level, for example, would involve an examination of how the non-White image has been constructed as dangerous and threatening within the White psyche. Where is the proof for such a belief and where did it come from? How does it shape the way

Whites come to see the world? Acting within this belief system, those with skin color privilege are disciplined to behave both defensively and aggressively towards non-White peoples because they have been constructed as a threat to their very way of life – thus fueling a dynamic of racial conflict. This is a classic example of a self-fulfilling prophecy wherein the built-in assumption of conflict frames any advance in the socioeconomic position of non-Whites as a gain made at White expense. Thus, the flames of White anger are fanned. This White identity crisis and the anger that accompanies it are both manifestations of the growing concern that White power in North America is on the decline. Indeed, in light of today's demographic shift towards increased immigration from the "third world," Whiteness's traditional fear of Blackness is rearticulated in more panic-stricken terms.

Whiteness in decline is being represented as a loss of order and civility. The horror of Africa – so central to understanding the history of the U.S. – reappears in a televised and digitized postmodern guise, taunting Whites with its traditional desire for, and fear of dichotomy. Moreover, this fear is articulated within our integrated neighborhood schools, within their multicultural curriculums, our workplaces with their affirmative action policies, and it is reflected in the supposedly "preferential" and reverse-racist admissions policies being engaged by our universities. This fear paralyzes many Whites, as they grow evermore terrified watching non-Whites become more alienated. The reversal of White victimization plays well at the subconscious level, and the pain of this "new psychological de-privileging" bursts at the seams of the old privilege – it gnaws at our notions of safety and at our sense of belonging in what was once a very Cleaveresque reality.

As I have noted previously (1999) these "absences" loom large in the minds of the White working class, who (as the Whites who gain the least from White privilege) perceive that they lose the most from the non-White exploitation of oppression capital.[15] However, understanding how class clearly mediates these discussions, we must ask ourselves whether there really is a disadvantage to being White in hyper-reality? Is there really a devaluation of Whiteness that permeates the social landscape of the new millennia? And in turn, how might we explore the damage of racism on those it empowers, without diminishing or muting the centrality of the ways racism has harmed its victims? Now, asking these types of questions can be problematic, but answering them moves a pedagogy of Whiteness into dangerous grounds where our intentions can be challenged from a variety of directions – nothing will come easy in a pedagogy of Whiteness.[16]

Recognizing that the last few decades have seen the conservative and "radical right" sharpening their rhetorical skills around discussions of Whiteness and White victimization, we have to be ever cognizant that a pedagogy of Whiteness must do more than simply understand the conservative agenda. More to the point, we must be able to engage in a proactive response to the right-wing's insidious efforts at producing and reproducing White hegemony through a continued exploitation of the White identity crisis. As Gresson (1995) has pointed out, such recovery efforts have been largely successful and work to dismantle the gains made through struggles for social justice.[17] Arguing that "America must learn to live with inequality," right-wing pundits rally around cries of reverse racism in a concerted and effective effort to mask their agenda within calls for "legitimate equity" within a meritocractic and democratic framework.

In this new discursive universe, anti-racist and anti-oppressive struggles are almost always represented in the mainstream, as a form of neo-racism against Whites. The rhetoric continues: since Blacks and Latinos have made so much progress in recent years (at the expense of hard working, honest Whites) racism really isn't an issue anymore. Painting our sociocultural landscape as a Panacea of sorts, the ugly truths of oppression are ignored and downplayed in favor of a "White washed" reality that draws the proof of racism's demise from anecdotal evidence and an almost absolute reliance on the positive imagery of marginalized peoples as found scattered throughout the nation's mediascape. Importantly, while the introduction of marginal matters and "diverse" images into the mainstream has been entirely selective and scrupulously policed, this "inclusion," however limited, has served to permit many Whites to disavow the reality of racism as it exists today at the beginning of a new millennium. Case in point, the White audience of The Cosby Show, often interpreted the program as evidence that racism had been cured. Buying into such popular social readings, when asked, many White students express great anger about Black, Latino and indigenous students speaking out about racism and its impact in their lives, they express confusion as to why "these people" harbor such resentment just because some distant relative was a slave, and they bristle at having to take courses on racism and anti-racism. Again, even with all the research detailing the almost inescapable effects of trans-generational and inter-generational trauma on dispossessed and dislocated peoples, mainstream rhetoric continues to pathologize the oppressed as somehow self-victimizing, and many of us continue to fall in line. Contrary to what is portrayed in the White mainstream, the media landscape does not reflect a social shift towards equity. And in fact, the recovery of White supremacy has been specifically catalyzed by mass media in television and movies. Gresson (1995) noted this same theme in the five *Rocky* movies (1976, 1979, 1982, 1985, 1990) as Sylvester Stallone's character (the great White hope) wins the respect of the "uppity" Black champion, Apollo Creed by fighting him to a draw.[18] Then, in answer to the public outcry for a "happy ending" to the story, Stallone returns in Rocky II to defeat Creed. In fact, we see the title character carrying the flag of Whiteness and American values throughout the Rocky films, and particularly into the fifth installment as he mentors a young White boxer to carry the torch of Whiteness after he retires.[19] Furthering this media analysis of the White recovery theme, Kincheloe (1999) notes:

> In *Soul Man* (1986) a White student (C. Thomas Howell) denied entry to Harvard reinvents himself as an African American and gains admission through affirmative action. Tom Berenger stars in *The Substitute* (1996) as a covert operations soldier who comes home to his girlfriend, a high school teacher in inner city (non-White) Miami. After unruly Latino and Black students hire a Seminole Indian to "kneecap" her with a baseball bat, Berenger's character poses as a substitute teacher in his girlfriend's classes to find the perpetrators. In the process Berenger and his buddies from the Special Forces not only find the guilty kids but also uncover a Latino/Black gang-related drug ring run by the high school principal (an African American) from the basement of the school. Faced with this

non-White corruption Berenger and his men exhibit their answer to school reform: they kill them all and heroically take back the school. In all of these movies a similar message is conveyed: White privilege is under attack from barbaric non-Whites and we (White males) must recover it by acts of heroism.[20]

Most telling, when these racial dynamics are discussed with and within predominantly White groups, a tremendous amount of resistance and disbelief tends to be generated. "You've got it wrong," they tell us. "Blacks and Latinos are heavily represented in the media." Of course, there are indeed more non-Whites on TV and in the movies than there were some thirty years ago. This is certainly not in dispute. However, we rarely, if ever, ask about the nature and centrality of the roles people of color obtain in the entertainment industry. In fact, even when TV and movies dramatize real life events involving African Americans, Latino/as, and other non-Whites, the stars and main characters still tend to be White. For instance, the NBC made-for-TV movie about the Howard Beach case where White youths beat three African American men and chased another one to his death, focused attention on Charles Hynes, the White special prosecutor portrayed by Daniel Travanti. The promos for the movie give a sense of its perspective: as the camera focused for a close-up on Travanti, the voice-over announced that "only one man can unravel the mystery and bring the guilty to justice." The same theme prevails *In Cry Freedom* (1987) as a movie about the Black South African struggle against apartheid focuses its attention on Donald Woods (Kevin Kline) the White journalist who wrote the biography of heroic freedom fighter Steve Biko. One might ask why Woods was the star/hero of the movie if Biko was in fact, the brave figure who led the resistance, underwent torture, and died for the cause. Again, the same theme dominates *A Dry White Season* (1989), *Mississippi Burning* (1988), and a plethora of other movies too numerous to mention here.[21] The themes identified in these movies are not simply interesting readings of a trivial entertainment medium. Rather, in hyper-reality, TV and movies are a central locus for the production of knowledge and the generation of ideological currents that engage the nation's collective psyche. Drawing on an evolving engagement dysgenesis,[22] these racial themes are continuously reinvented in both hyper-reality and cyberspace to shield Whiteness from any blame for the socioeconomic conditions faced by the racially oppressed, and to anoint Whiteness as it reawakens its messianic role. The question then, is how do we respond to, and engage those White youth who are learning to embrace dysgenesis and its concurrent refusal of White complicity in the degradation of marginalized and racially oppressed peoples?

Moments in the Pedagogy of Whiteness

Reflecting on our discussions thus far, it is clear that while many White people have experienced a crisis of identity over the last two decades, the crisis has been, and continues to be inextricably tied to the expanding socioeconomic complex of disabilities that divide us and our counterparts of color.[23] Believing that it is in the best interests of White people to learn about the moral, ethical and civic dynamics involved, I argue that a critical pedagogy of Whiteness must not only interrogate how we are implicated in the relations of oppressive power, but also how we might better formulate progressive and proactive responses to the problem. With that said, there is much work to be done to refute and resist the dogma espoused by the conservative and radical right as we look to gain momentum for the project before we can actively engage any such pedagogy. Again, as right-wing versions of global free market capitalism have gained ascendancy in the last two decades, so too have allies and partners in the project found their best efforts becoming increasingly undermined and forestalled. Indeed, a key dimension of the pedagogy necessitates that we strategize how to resist right-wing efforts that seek to place us in conflict with those who should be our partners in the project. In order to accomplish this difficult task, teachers and cultural workers must examine concepts and processes traditionally ignored in academic settings including invisible power relations and the ways such social forces shape human consciousness. They must develop creative and compelling ways of talking about racial identity, racial privilege and racial discomfort that allow students and other individuals to name their previously unspeakable feelings and intuitions.

The pedagogy of Whiteness proposed here attempts to connect an understanding of the construction of Whiteness to the political and socioeconomic issues previously raised. I recognize that making reference to "feelings" and "intuitions" may convey the image of a "feel good" pedagogy, unconcerned with academic rigor. To the contrary, I would clarify that the curriculum envisioned here is very demanding in its use of analytical methods from history, philosophy, sociology, anthropology, literary criticism, psychology, film studies, political science, economics and educational theory. For instance:

> [S]tudents would engage in a variety of case studies in how color lines are drawn, analyzing historical instances such as California's struggle since the mid-nineteenth century to classify its racial groups and the late-nineteenth century Irish struggle for admission to the fraternity of Whiteness.[24]

Perhaps more importantly, a pedagogy of Whiteness would not be limited by disciplinary boundaries that frame knowledge as valuable in only specific formations and from specific sites. One of the most dramatic moments in teaching Whiteness involves the effort to identify and make sense of White power by encouraging students to understand how the loose alignment of various social, political and educational frameworks functionally establish and maintain White power. For this reason, we would also engage cultural studies, spirituality, indigenous knowledges and other modes of science and thought traditionally deemed unacceptable in the Western contexts.

In seeking to contextualize contemporary power relations, the pedagogy looks to expose the invisibility of White power and privilege without conflating Whiteness as an ideological construction with White people. No easy task as these moments do not present themselves in some convenient linear progression, but are enfolded into the opaqueness of Whiteness itself, expressing themselves here and there like photons in a linear accelerator. Extending the quantum metaphor, the moments are observable only if we ask the "appropriate" questions such as: how Whiteness functions in the lives of White people, how Whiteness as a signifier will be received differently by individuals standing at different intersections of social positioning, and how Whiteness as a norm, shapes the lives of both those who are included and excluded by the categorization.[25]

Another important moment in this pedagogy involves de-normalizing Whiteness. Without trying to elicit guilt and place blame, the attempt to teach students about White power involves the difficult task of tracing oppressive historical frameworks that continue in an ever-evolving form to structure the everyday life of all peoples. Such a process will always be difficult simply because contemporary processes of erasure stifle the free-flow of information that might allow people to gain insight into the workings, maintenance and banality of power. This highlighting of the White power bloc (while intensely resisted and detracted in the mainstream), enables individuals to see the previously invisible role of Whiteness as the standard against which all others are measured. White ways of being can no longer be universalized, White communication practices can no longer be viewed unproblematically and issues of race can no longer be relegated to the domain of those who are not White. Such analyses of Whiteness involve a cultural reassessment and a commitment to rethinking the basis of how we frame and live a multicultural society. Operating on the foundation of such a commitment, White people may begin to work through their discomfort around race-talk – accessing poststructural analyses that engage their Whiteness with discussions of social positioning – to understand that what they "objectively" see may not be as neutral as they originally thought; and that in turn, they may begin to rethink their lives and worldviews accordingly.[26]

Listening – Learning – Changing

The process of inducing White people to listen to non-Whites is one of the key features of a pedagogy of Whiteness, but because Western sociocultural frameworks encourage speaking over listening, those in positions of power and privilege have always been rewarded for their disregard of marginalized positions and experiences. Such anti-racist "meaning-making" requires that White people not only accept the presence of non-White cultures, but that they also actively and proactively interrogate their implication and participation in the maintenance of oppression. Simply put, most White people will find this part of the process to be exceedingly difficult; and given the ongoing right-wing redefinition of Whiteness and the recovery process it supports, the effort to resist such anti-racist reform becomes even more formidable.

The implementation of a pedagogy of Whiteness that induces Whites to listen, learn, and change is a delicate operation because it must balance a serious critique of Whiteness and White power with a narrative that refuses to demonize White people. Teachers and cultural workers must not only negotiate this task but also induce students to form multicultural/racial coalitions that work for structural change. As a note of caution, such inter-racial and multicultural coalitions must be engaged with intense caution on the part of White allies. At a time in history when the universal norm of Whiteness has produced considerable levels of internalized racism and oppression among the oppressed (i.e., self-loathing among minoritized peoples speaks to the internalization of the shibboleths of the White tradition) the White ally cannot assume to engage such spaces in racially neutral terms, regardless of their intended partnership in the project. I contend that as White students come to see themselves through the eyes of racially marginalized peoples, they will find themselves more able to move away from the conservative constructions of the dominant culture, and towards spaces where alternative knowledges and ways of knowing the world can be engaged. Such an encounter with minority perspectives moves many White individuals to rethink their tendency to dismiss the continued existence of racism and embrace the belief that racial inequality results from unequal abilities among racial groups.[27] A pedagogy of Whiteness reveals these power-related processes by exposing how members of both groups have been, and continue to be, stripped of self-knowledge.

As Whites begin to validate and understand the ways in which they are perceived by non-Whites, they will concurrently learn to address social, political and economic structures that perpetuate the cycle of racism. In this process they find that the structures in question are the province of Whiteness, emphasizing once again the importance of studying the social centre as well as multiculturalism's traditional concern with the margins. In this context the work of the coalitions for social transformation does not simply go to racially marginalized neighborhoods and native reservations to do their work; in addition they work with White people and White institutions to develop anti-racist policies and progressive ways of being White. A pedagogy of Whiteness encourages a form of listening that intensely attends to different ways of knowing and their implications for the restructuring of identity. Here White individuals study the insights of Blacks, Latinos, Asians, and indigenous peoples not only into racism and forms of oppression but into others' ways of being, experiencing and living in the world. A pedagogy of Whiteness asks, for example, what are the alternatives to Western modernist rationalism with its emphasis on scientific procedure, the regulation of consciousness, and the division of the world into smaller and smaller categories. Progressive Whites value these alternatives and use them to help extend their imagination beyond a confining monoculturalism. I contend that as White people gain an understanding of the power of Whiteness, White supremacy and the mutating nature of contemporary racism, they will begin to perceive problems with their traditional civics lessons.

Traditional forms of multiculturalism have not offered a space for White people to rethink their identity around a new, progressive, assertive, counter-hegemonic, anti-racist notion of Whiteness. This rethinking of both White identity and the nature of Whiteness itself is a central feature of this pedagogy in that it serves to develop a healthy, hopeful, justice-oriented response to this paradox. I assert that because the asymmetries of racial power do not fit with the American faith in meritocracy and the rewards of hard work, people will have strong reactions to such contradictions – despair, anger at the situation, anger at the messenger, a sense of mission, the development of a moral compass and even efforts to "opt out of Whiteness." Thompson (1996) described her personal effort to escape the responsibility that comes with being White as an "I don't want to be White stage" – a period where she did not want to associate with White people.[28]

> In this mind-set White liberal guilt often leads to an essentialist romanticization
> of non-Whites that grants them a morally superior status. At the same time
> Whites may be essentialized as racist, bland, and undeserving of respect – given

such characterizations what person would want to call herself White? In this context White people may attempt to appropriate the "oppression status" of non-Whiteness, misreading the oppression of others for their own. This, of course, is the space where race traitors enter the Whiteness studies cosmos – some describe the race traitor impulse as the political wing of the academic analysis of Whiteness.[29]

I certainly reject such a labels and agree with Yudice (1995) who troubles "the easy renunciation of Whiteness and privilege" because Whites alone have the privilege of opting out of racial identity by proclaiming themselves as non-raced.[30] Ultimately, no matter how vociferously they may renounce their Whiteness, White people do not lose the power associated with being White. Such a reality renders many White renunciations disingenuous to some extent in that they disconnect with all liabilities of Whiteness while maintaining all its assets. That being said, I would also argue that while such "disingenuous" responses to the crisis of White identity are troubling, they are not, and should not, be seen as the norm. They should be seen as but one possible voice in a chorus of possible responses. Moreover, I might also suggest that while "genuine" efforts at "renunciation" may be of little value in the larger effort to solve the material and spiritual consequences of racism and the inequality it generates, at the very least it illustrates an impetus to reform borne out of the process.[31] Following a great tradition of political theory framed around the position that constructing and maintaining a truly active body politic hinges on the ascendancy of a system of education that engages the capacity for critical thought and action, I argue that a pedagogy of Whiteness is a contemporary adaptation of the Deweyan notion of a progressive education: to gain command of oneself so as to make positive social use of one's powers and abilities. Thus, the pedagogy promoted here is simply a sub-theme of a philosophy of education that concerns itself with cultural identity and the social production of self. In its analysis of White identity, a critical pedagogy of Whiteness seeks a new sociopsychological framework that offers a new vision for a twenty-first century Whiteness.[32]

The redefinition of Whiteness begins with the simple question: what does it mean to be White? How can we answer this question in a way that allows for a critique and rejection of the oppression inflicted in the name of Whiteness but concurrently creates a space for a progressive White identity that transcends some narrow notion of a politically correct orthodoxy? I am not comfortable with the concept of a new oppositional White identity as a "race traitor" who renounces Whiteness. It is unlikely that a mass movement will grow around the race traitor concept, as oppositional Whites would still have little to rally around or to affirm. Anti-racist Whites in search of a new identity in the late 1990s are still walking into a racial netherland with few guides or guiding principles. The netherland can undoubtedly be exciting and affirmational, but it can also be ambiguous and lonesome. One's time in the netherland can nurture creativity while at the same time undermining traditional support systems and emotional stability. A key feature of a Whiteness pedagogy, therefore, involves developing both theoretical and emotional support systems to help courageous White people through this complex transition. Such theoretical and emotional support systems must not be ascetic and punitive but appealing, affirmative, humorous, sensitive and aesthetically dynamic. They must draw upon the emancipatory productions of many cultures while making use of the most progressive aspects of White culture itself.

This reinvention of Whiteness operates outside any notion of racial superiority or inferiority by seeking to transverse the terrain of the netherland of transitional identity. While it confronts White tyranny directly, it avoids the projection of guilt on to White students and in the process, it generates a sense of pride in the possibility that White people can help transform the reality of social inequality and reinvent themselves around notions of justice, community, social creativity and economic/political democracy. These concerns become extremely important in light of the reactions of White students when confronted with the despotism of the White norm and the brutality of White racism. Many White students have understandably encountered great difficulty dealing with such revelations and have in turn reacted negatively to such teaching, not as much out of disbelief or rejection, but out of frustration as to what to do with their new knowledge. Without a vision of racial reinvention and support for the difficulties it entails, such students have nowhere to go. Their frustration in this context often turned to cynicism and a descent into nihilism. Such cold, self-interested realities will always be an impediment to wide-scale efforts to forge new White identities. And this is not the only obstacle, as teachers and cultural workers must deal with a variety of social forces that undermine the effort to reinvent Whiteness. When White students find themselves in a free-fall in these explorations, critical educators must be ready to show them that they understand their struggles, that they can and will be supportive of their journey and that they can offer them a progressive alternative. As teachers teach a pedagogy of Whiteness, they are reminded of how new and unusual such a concept must seem to students and how few models for transcending mainstream embodiments of Whiteness exist, and so, the importance of an anti-racist, positive, creative, and affirmational White identity in this pedagogical context cannot be overstated.

Fashioning White Identities Within a Literacy of Power

The idea of a pedagogy of Whiteness is one of the most compelling notions concerning the struggle for racial justice to emerge in decades and we must position ourselves to take advantage of the possibility it offers. While all pedagogical activity is carefully framed by a commitment to anti-racism, social justice, political and economic democracy, and heterogeneous and egalitarian community building, there is great room for divergence within these categories. Ultimately, the goal of this critical pedagogy involves the construction of an evolving and adaptive White identity that is emancipated from the cultural baggage that accompanies Whiteness. Such pedagogical work requires sophisticated help and support to pull progressive Whites through the social, political and psychological dilemmas associated with the process. Part of the dilemma arises from emerging allies frequently finding themselves at odds with White colleagues and other Whites who are not yet able, prepared or willing to face the harsh truths of oppression. It is for this reason that Whites learning to listen and empathize with racially marginalized peoples will also have to develop collective solidarities with other White anti-racists – individuals in these situations need support groups, if for nothing else, to help them survive emotionally. Importantly, while they need support from White anti-racists who have/are also engaged in these struggles, so too must they ally with people of color who can provide them with other types of insight and support. In this context, alliances can be formed between non-Whites and the White support groups that can address a range of problems in unique and creative ways.[33]

From a critical pedagogical perspective the refashioning of White identity involves an ontological paradigm shift. This re-conceptualization of identity and worldview is first and foremost focused on the critical theoretical notion of emancipatory transformation – not in a modernist sense where the new identity becomes final and authentic, but in a more poststructuralist articulation that speaks of identity as the transitional phase of an ever evolving self. This "emancipatory White identity" is seen as a process of "becoming" that allows for new cognitive possibilities and forms of consciousness that while historically shaped, are not culturally bound. More clearly, as noted by Hall, a self-reflexive engagement with our own critical consciousness must stand as a precursor to such shifts:

> using the resources of history, language and culture in the process of becoming rather than being: not 'who we are' or 'where we are' so much as what we might become, how we have been represented and how that bears on how we might represent ourselves.[34]

Building on Hall's work, I contend a critical pedagogy of Whiteness must encourage and support White students as they take up the critical project of "knowing themselves" as a starting-point to personal and social change. That critical consciousness must entail an ability to interrogate the foundations of oppressive power and the complex interlocks and intersections of power that run through the physical and metaphysical experiences of privilege. This interpretation of libratory theory builds on Fromm's (1965) conception of freedom[35] to suggest freedom for Whites as being: a) freedom from social and psychological sources of power that implicate us in the oppression of others; and b) freedom to pursue a role as ally and partner in the anti-racist project. Without falsely dichotomizing between the internal and external (realizing that they are always connected through experience), this notion of an emancipatory White identity contends that freedom from internal and psychological sources of privilege and power involve a mastering or amelioration of the fears and other psychological phenomena that serve to interfere with a person's ethical and moral imperative towards social justice.

Many who have written about identity and the transformation of identity have used the metaphor of border crossing to characterize this multicultural dynamic. While there is much to recommend the use of such a term in a pedagogy of Whiteness, care must be taken to connect the act of border crossing with a fidelity to critical notions of social justice, democracy, and egalitarian community building. Without such moral and political grounding the border-crosser, like the nomad, can become an agent of the dominant culture who uses his or her knowledge of non-Whites to facilitate their regulation. A pedagogy of Whiteness encourages White students to explore and cross the borders, to take advantage of the benefits of cultural bricolage, to interrogate the new perspectives emerging from the ways traditions are reworked on the cultural borders, to study the manner in which common ground is negotiated in a context where differences are accepted and affirmed, and to analyze the effects of all these border dynamics on identity formation.

While it is clear that the reinvention of Whiteness and the construction of libratory and transformational White identities are steps in the right direction, I would powerfully stress that this conversation about Whiteness and a pedagogy of Whiteness is just beginning. As a form of teaching that carries the potential to engage White students in an examination of their social, political and psychological power, the critical imperative of this pedagogy demands that we continue this work as part of an ongoing and evolutionary process. If not, we risk a lapse into a bourgeoisie self-indulgence that is concerned less with social justice and more with the psychologized attempt to "feel good" about the angst of privilege. As discussed throughout this paper, a pedagogy of Whiteness looks to support White people, and White students specifically in their process of "becoming" partners and allies in the anti-racist project. In this movement, I recognize several general shifts: a) a shift from perceptions of White existence as normal to a more politicized view of Whiteness as normalized within the context of racial oppression; b) a shift from a self-perception of neutrality to one of implication and participation in the relations of power; and c) a shift from oppressor to ally with both agency and purpose. The hope of a pedagogy of Whiteness is that it can arm White people with the critical ability to contextualize their reality in a way that presents them with the agency to walk beside the oppressed in solidarity. Again, this conversation about Whiteness and a pedagogy of Whiteness is just beginning; our job as partners in the project is to ensure that we keep the conversation going.

Chapter 10

Dancing with Turtles

Building Alliances Between Communities and the Academy[1]

Ginette Lafrenière, Ph.D.
Faculty of Social Work
Sir Wilfrid Laurier University

Papa Lamine Diallo, Ph.D.
Department of Sociology
Sir Wilfrid Laurier University

Donna Dubie
Executive Director
The Healing of the Seven Generations

Introduction

Looking back at our collaboration within the Healing of the Seven Generations Project, it seems fitting to frame our journey in relation to the way turtles dance. Those watching from the outside may not see the intricacies of the partnership, and may in fact, see little if any motion at all – it is only when the dance is over that we can see the movement that has occurred. Over the past 18 months, we engaged in a symbiotic partnership within the Healing of the Seven Generation Project, and in doing so, we developed genuine friendships in the community and a new vision of what university and community collaborations might look and feel like. These new alliances moved us to examine our own individual experiences of oppression, and in turn, how many of those same experiences informed our efforts to work across issues of trust, mutual recognition and understanding. By engaging the Aboriginal talking circle (a dialogic form which aims to create spaces for all voices) we have merged both Aboriginal and non-Aboriginal discourses in an attempt to push the limits of traditional academe.[2] That being said, what follows is an exploration of how our practice as anti-racist educators and practitioners has been nourished through this process of alliance-building. Throughout these pages, we have tried to reveal some of the conceptual and experiential truths borne out of this collaborative journey, and we sincerely hope that the reader will be able to find meaning in what we have shared here.

Understanding the importance of situating our imperative to collaborate, we start out by giving some background information on the residential school system and the history of the Healing of the Seven Generations Project. Then, by taking part in a talking circle, we reflexively explore our various social locations and interrogate the determining factors that have shaped our experiences as collaborators and our understandings of what it means to engage in transformative alliance-building across community, academic and cultural borders.

Defining the Residential School System

The residential school system was a politically motivated attempt to systematically assimilate Aboriginal people into Canada's dominant White, European culture. Thousands of Aboriginal children across the country were taken from their homes and institutionalized in residential schools.

> The system was officially in effect between 1892 and 1969 through arrangements between the Government of Canada and the Roman Catholic Church, the Anglican Church, the United Church, and the Presbyterian Church. Although the Government of Canada officially withdrew in 1969, some of the schools continued operating throughout the 70s and 80s.[3]

There, many children suffered sexual, physical and emotional abuse at the hands of the adults who ran the schools.

> Many of these children, in addition to the emotional abuse of being robbed of a family and a culture, were subjected to horrific physical and/or sexual abuse by some of the adults running the schools. Children who tried to escape were beaten, chained, and severely whipped. They were also punished for speaking their language (needles through the tongue was one method used) or for attempting to speak to siblings of the opposite sex.

According to the Aboriginal Healing Foundation, there were approximately 130 residential schools which existed in Canada between 1800 and 1990. In fact, the last school to close its doors was Akaitcho Hall in Yellowknife in the 1990s.[4] The evidence is overwhelming relative to the disastrous long-term effects and legacy of the residential school system in Canada.[5] However, it bears mentioning that the residential system was only one element of a much larger plan to eradicate the "Indian problem" in Canada.

The Indian Act and the Child Welfare, Reservation and Justice systems took over. It is these larger relationships, and the forced assimilationist policy that informs them, which account for much of the varied conditions of Aboriginal life.[6]

A great deal of psychological and psychiatric work has focused on the realities of the multigenerational transmission of trauma in general, and in relation to the traumas of indigenous peoples in their own lands. For instance, Raphael, Swan and Martinek (1998) addressed the legacy of colonialism relative to the traumas of Australian Aboriginal peoples, much as Brave Heart and Yellow Horse-Davis (1998) did in relation to North American Aboriginal peoples.[7] These works are fundamentally important in clearing space to discuss the experience and ongoing cumulative effects of historical context and content, and serve to uncover the pervasive impact of cumulative trauma on Aboriginal peoples who experienced dispossession and dislocation in their own lands. In contemporary contexts, Aboriginal communities are found to display significantly higher rates of suicide, and alcohol and drug dependency, as well as domestic violence and abuse. These serious challenges characterize many urban and non-urban Aboriginal communities alike. And while much mainstream discourse would look to pathologize these communities as self-victimizing, we cannot continue to ignore the colonial pathology that frames Aboriginal experience in today's Canadian context. Simply put, there is an undeniable link between the legacy of the residential school system and the socioeconomic complex of disabilities and inequities faced and experienced by Aboriginal peoples, and those linkages must be exposed and ruptured.

Even though the cultural apartheid which characterizes a large piece of Canada's history (which is rarely problematized in high schools and universities) is unmistakably hideous, it is also a tribute to the resilience of a people who have resisted complete and total cultural annihilation. Fortunately, there are organizations, community groups and individuals across Canada who, as agents of their own healing, have engaged a process of collective recovery in the hopes of addressing the oppressive legacy of the residential school system. The Healing of the Seven Generations is a project which aims to respond to the needs of members of the Aboriginal community in the Waterloo Region in South Western Ontario.

Overview of the Healing of the Seven Generations Project

The Healing of the Seven Generations was conceptualized by Donna Dubie, a First Nations intergenerational survivor of the residential school system. The project aims to address the needs of survivors and intergenerational survivors of the Aboriginal community living within the Waterloo Region. According to the initial proposal to the Aboriginal Healing Foundation, the Healing of the Seven Generations looks to work with all Aboriginal people and community members that are suffering from any of the effects of the legacy of the residential school system. Employing various approaches in their process (e.g., workshops to provide an increased awareness of the Legacy of Physical and Sexual Abuse in Residential Schools, mainstream healing services and traditional therapies such as talking circles, healing circles, sweat lodges and medicine walks) Aboriginal people are encouraged to learn about traditional and non-traditional teachings and ways of both regaining and maintaining holistic well-being. The project's goals are to:

(a) Engage Aboriginal people in a safe and nurturing, culture-based group healing process so they can recognize, address and begin to resolve the healing issues that come from sexual and physical abuse at Residential Schools and/or the intergenerational impacts of such abuse. These impacts can include family dysfunction, addictive behaviors, family violence, abandonment, all types of abuse, low self-esteem, unhealthy relationships, grief and other related problems.

(b) Provide opportunities for learning about Aboriginal traditions, culture and spirituality to Aboriginal people who are survivors of sexual and physical abuse at residential schools or its intergenerational impacts.

(c) Increase the capacity of service-providers to work more effectively with Aboriginal people who are survivors of sexual and physical abuse at residential schools or its intergenerational impacts.

(d) Provide ongoing public education on residential school impacts and sexual assault recovery information.

(e) Initiate community support systems to individuals impacted by sexual assault and the intergenerational effects of the residential schools.

(f) Coordinate and ensure active healing partnerships with individuals, agencies and organizational personnel.

(g) Employ the services of Elders to conduct traditional activities and professional therapists who are culturally skilled and adept at individual and family counselling.

(h) Assist individuals to overcome traumas in their personal lives in order that they stop the cycle of abuse.

It is expected that once members of the community are imbued with understanding and knowledge of the history and legacy of residential schooling on Aboriginal peoples, they will begin to show signs of reciprocal nurturing and positive connections towards their immediate and extended families, as well as towards the community at large.[8]

Engaging the Talking Circle: Donna's Journey

I am an intergenerational survivor; my dad was a residential school kid at the Mushhole in Brantford. Our lives growing up were a mirror of the hell that my father experienced and internalized when he lived at the residential school. I'm proud to say that since my mid-30s, I have managed to get onto a solid path. My kids have all gone to school and are all working in different professions. I'm very proud of them. After working at a manufacturing plant for many years, I went back to school and later worked as an employment counsellor in an Aboriginal organization here in Kitchener.

One day, after receiving a call from my former employer requesting up to 40 clients to come and work at the plant, I realized that I couldn't send even one of my clients to the job because of their personal challenges relative to drugs, alcohol and an assortment of other issues. I became extremely depressed because I felt that the nature of my job was fruitless. I grew increasingly frustrated with the dysfunction of working with unemployed Aboriginal people, sending them off to training programs and job placements, only to see them come back to me months later because they lost their jobs, dropped out of training or renewed their dependency on drugs and alcohol. It was in the Fall of 2002, that I decided that I wanted to do something proactive and positive for the community. Knowing full well that the Aboriginal Healing Foundation was an option for me to create a program for healing, I approached my employer to see if it was possible to develop a program for our clients who would come through the healing program before attempting to engage training or find employment. My supervisor and board were less than thrilled with the idea.

To this day I wonder why they didn't want to support me, but I suspect they were afraid. I quit my job as an employment counsellor, and for almost a year I worked full-time putting together my proposal for what would later be called the "Healing of the Seven Generations Project." I had never put together such a complex proposal and the process of doing so made me realize just how difficult it is for Aboriginal people to access monies for programs. I had to collect dozens of letters of support from people who believed in the project. There is not one Aboriginal organization that I felt that I could go to in order to support this project. Issues of trust or mistrust obviously made my task more difficult. I have to qualify though that while many "individuals" in the Aboriginal community supported my efforts, Native "organization" were not there.

Last Spring I met Ginette from the university and that was when things began to shift for me. She said she was from Northern Ontario and that she had taken her degree in Native Studies in Sudbury. She was bright and funny and easy to be with. I never felt like I had to explain to her why this project was so important. I met with her a few times to strengthen certain pieces of the project; it was different for me to be working with someone who was in a university setting. I had never worked with anyone from the university before and it was fun to come to campus and work with Ginette. She invited me as a guest speaker in a few of her classes and slowly I became integrated as a resource person for the Faculty of Social Work. I was invited by another professor in the Faculty to speak to her class on therapeutic relationships. Again, it was interesting to speak to young social workers and describe to them how much Native people distrust social workers and other so-called helping professionals. My colleague, who works in Restorative Justice, and I were also guest speakers at a conference held at the university last year. Again, I felt there was value in what I was doing and that people seemed really supportive and interested in my project.

Getting someone to *sponsor* my project was difficult. I was not incorporated as a non-profit and funders necessitated that the project fall under the supervision of an established organization. Ginette's partner at the time was the Executive Director of the Social Planning Council (SPC) in Cambridge and when I approached him with the project, he said that he would bring the idea of supporting the project to his board. Apparently after much debate, the board agreed to sponsor my project. I was thrilled. I never realized, however, how difficult it would be to get the project off the ground. There were many revisions to the budget as well as the way we were to deliver the project. We finally had our grand opening this past April (2005) and I'm very excited. I feel enormous responsibility for it to be successful and as it stands now, we've surpassed our expectations for participants. I have a team of dedicated volunteers as well as two psychologists who have many years of experience working with Aboriginal people. As for the collaboration with the university, I believe that it's been helpful for all kinds of reasons. We have access to physical space to hold meetings and we're doing a conference there next February. We have the support of professors when we need them and we feel strong as an organization by having them as partners. We've become friends over time and that transcends much of what we do.

Engaging the Talking Circle: Ginette's Journey

I am originally from Sudbury, Ontario. When I say this, I am usually greeted with feeble attempts at humor relative to the ever-present story of astronauts practicing on barren land-scapes in the 1960s – practicing for eventual scientific invasions of outer space. I mention this because like Sudbury, which is now an international model for re-greening efforts and environmental turnarounds, I too have changed since the early 1980s when I was a young student in the Native Studies program at Laurentian University. My social location as a feminist and Franco-Ontarian in a Native environment taught me much in terms of White privilege. I was also taught, however, that I can be an ally. I remember on the eve of my grad-uation, one of my Native Studies professors encouraging me to keep on working in the realm of social justice and to work at letting "White folks" know about Aboriginal issues. Truth be told, I wasn't very pleased with this advice because I knew full well that he was gently encour-aging me to abandon my pursuit of becoming a constitutional lawyer for the Aboriginal community. It was only a few years later that I realized his advice was invaluable and I ventually understood that the Aboriginal community didn't need me as much as I thought I needed it.

As a mature adult, I carved a space for myself as a community organizer within the Francophone community in a career which I most enjoyed. Through my work, I would at times collide socially and professionally with members of the Aboriginal community and various ethnocultural communities. When called upon to do so, I would give workshops on a variety of themes. In fact, it is through my work as a community organizer that I grew into my role as an "ally." I have worked in Ontario, Quebec and abroad, and while I have purposefully chosen not to work exclusively within minoritized spheres, I have collaborated on a good many projects with a wide variety of people.

When my students ask me how I harmonize my *raison d'être* within various social and minoritized locations, I explain to them that my presence can only be counted on if I am invited. My pedagogy as an educator and community organizer is etched in the belief that I, as an indi-vidual, may have something to offer another individual. As such, if an individual chooses to call upon me as an ally and if I feel that I can contribute something, then I do. If this individual is coming from an Aboriginal or ethnocultural community I think very hard before engaging in a relationship with this individual. If I do, I am always cognizant of my social location as a White, Franco-Ontarian feminist; hence I came to be an ally for the Healing of the Seven Generations Project. In May 2003, I met Donna at a diversity training workshop where she was part of a panel discussing the challenges of diversity within the Region of Waterloo. Shortly after this chance encounter, we met at the university to discuss her proposal for an Aboriginal healing program. It was Donna's first attempt at putting together such a document and as such, we spent much time poring over the language and requirements for this most ambitious endeavor.

Given the fact that she needed a sponsor (as she was not yet incorporated) I suggested that we strategize around one who would understand the depth and magnitude of the project. I was surprised to learn that her project did not receive much support from neighboring Aboriginal services (I would soon learn about the notion of "trust" within the Aboriginal spaces she negotiated). New to the Waterloo community I suggested that the only person whom I believed would understand and welcome the opportunity to nurture her project was my partner Lamine Diallo. At the time, he was working as the Executive Director of the Social Planning Council of Cambridge and North Dumfries. As an African professional who had worked extensively as a community organizer with both Aboriginal and non-Aboriginal communities, I thought a meeting with him would be helpful. At this point, it is important to note that my role as an "ally" is often challenged relative to issues of intercommunity racism and violence, mistrust and, at times, corruption. I know as an organizer and as an ally that these challenges are often by-products of colonial and oppressive spaces. However, as an ally, and specifically with regards to being "of service" to others, I have come to a space where I recognize all I can do is my best.

By colliding socially with Donna, I was able to be of service to her and pull her into the world of academia. As such, we have established a connection of mutual recognition relative to navigating both community and academe. Often times, I am called upon to assist when needed on funding proposals, or to give advice which may or may not be taken relative to a certain initiative, and, inversely, she is called upon to play the role of "resource person" to our students in Laurier's social work program. She has been invited to several forums at the university and has established a rapport with several of my students and colleagues at the Faculty of Social Work. Research is key in our working relationship because it enables Donna to show people the evidence of the incredible work in which she is involved. Ultimately, through my involvement in this project, I have come to believe that the message which ought to be shared with non-native allies is that the best way to "assist" native service providers and community developers is to simply create spaces whereby our alliance-building might encourage and support Aboriginal people in the process of becoming agents of their own change. Anit-oppressive praxis and resistance cannot, must not, be something that we do for the oppressed. Rather, such work must be engaged as a collaborative effort that nurtures the development and growth of agency and healing from within.

Engaging the Talking Circle: Lamine's Journey

I am African and originally from St-Louis in Senegal. I came to Quebec via France as a student in 1989 and collided academically with Ginette at the University of Sherbrooke. Her feminism combined with my impatience with colonial discourses made for interesting discussions and debates. Fifteen years later and a beautiful son in our midst, I'm happy to say that our debates are still ongoing. One thing which we do agree upon is our commitment to community and our understanding of why Donna's project was so important for the Aboriginal community. As a community organizer and educator I have often reflected on the common denominators which both Africans and Aboriginal people share in terms of our parallel colonial histories. Like my colleagues in the Aboriginal community who still grapple and resist the colonial infrastructures and legacy of colonization, I too observe how Africa continues to battle the economic colonization which even now chokes any real possibility of economic emancipation. I have fought in my own way to contribute to the African diaspora in Africa, Europe, Quebec and Canada and as such, am ideologically predisposed to collaborating with my colleagues in the Aboriginal community.

When Ginette asked me if I would meet with Donna, I hesitated. Given the fact that I was very new to my position as the Executive Director (ED) of the Social Planning Council (SPC), I was unsure of how the Board would react to a request to sponsor an Aboriginal project. I agreed to meet with Donna and after our first meeting, was committed to helping her. I argued successfully to our Board that the SPC should sponsor the project as it was part of our mandate as a planning council. Linda Terry (who is now the ED of the SPC) was president of the Board at the time, and was instrumental in convincing the Board that this was an important project for the SPC and the community. Now that I am teaching at Wilfrid Laurier, I have continued my association with the project as a member on the Board of Directors of the Healing of the Seven Generations. I am the only African on the board and I feel most comfortable and welcome amongst my colleagues. Admittedly, while I find many similarities between my volunteer work here, and within the African community in Kitchener-Waterloo, there are still important issues of trust which often impede our ability to move forward on certain projects and programs.

Another challenge is attempting to navigate between Aboriginal and non-Aboriginal "ways of doing." Given the fact that this is a new project there has been an enormous learning curve for the staff and volunteers with regards to the roles and responsibilities of board members as well as the importance of having by-laws and committees to enhance the work being done within the project. Clearly, our collaborative efforts have certainly helped to develop the viability of the project, but I would also stress that much of the "success" is primarily due to Donna's vision and personal investment. Having said that, I would also note that success cannot only be measured in the outcomes of the project goals themselves, but also must be framed in relation to the bonds of friendship and collegiality developed throughout the process. I believe that the process itself has been mutually beneficial for Donna, Ginette and me. Engaging in this working relationship as academics and community organizers has allowed us to grow and learn within our respective fields and work environments. Moreover, as a result, our students benefit from Donna's lectures, and as researchers we are learning much with regards to community-based healing and organizing.

It is very clear to me that what binds us as a team of collaborators are our own lived experiences relative to racism, sexism, marginalization and oppression. While we enjoy varying degrees of privilege (aware that the notion of privilege is one which is relative given the diversity within our group), ultimately, we as a trio realize the importance of building alliances in order to move forward on this very important project. Our common denominator is etched in the belief and traditions of engaging in anti-racist work. I am acutely aware that while there may be curious reflections and even ingrained racism towards me and my involvement within this project, (Ginette also enjoys the benefits of this curiosity but for very different reasons) I continue to believe that in order for marginalized communities to move forward in their quest for empowerment and self-reliance, the only way in which we can do this is through our capacity to engage in healthy and equitable alliance-building. I believe that our collaboration is a model for aspiring allies and partners in the anti-racist project.

University and Community Collaboration

The critical literature is quite clear as to how Aboriginal peoples have suffered through colonization, its effects and the subsequent cultural atrophy generated within the residential school system.[9] Importantly, this reality informs our praxis as partners and as allies whenever we work with and/or within native communities. However, just as we feel it crucial that resistant politics and strategies are informed by such critical knowledge, so too are we pointed in our belief that any such strategies must be engaged within a philosophy of hope. That being said, while there has been much written about Aboriginal efforts at reclamation, self-empowerment and self-healing, very little has been written about the hopeful efforts of allies and allied institutions working in partnership with Aboriginal communities. One such gap in the literature exists in relation to how universities can, and have, acted as viable partners working with culturally determined groups, and how in turn, these groups have demystified and redefined their communities.

It occurs to us that the nature of the project, in its mandate to reach out to all Aboriginals healing from the "residential aftermath," is most interesting given that it operates from a standpoint of "community" even thought the notion of "Aboriginal community" has long been challenged. After all, what does the notion of "community" mean to urban Aboriginals living in Kitchener-Waterloo? The dissonance associated with notions of community in this context begs several key questions: How can a community-based project recreate "community" when many of its participants have never experienced the safety of a nurturing, healthy kinship or solidarity group? Is it possible to recreate and redefine the notion of community for Aboriginal people seeking respite and assistance? And finally, what role, if any, does an academic institution have in this process of redefinition? We contend that the common denominator in engaging these questions must be a belief in the legitimacy of alliance-building and a commitment to anti-oppressive praxis.

Like Mullaly (2001) we argue that progressive social work praxis must engage an anti-oppressive framework as a moral imperative. Ultimately, unless we understand and recognize how social relations of power are implicated in the ongoing challenges faced by marginalized communities, we have no way to break out and away from the social pathology that positions them as *other*. In this same vein, both Valtonen (2001) and Gramsci (1988) argue that while ideological power is an insidious type of oppression given the fact that it can permeate the way that we learn and integrate knowledge, those who are marginalized can still become instruments and initiators of their own anti-oppression interventions.[10] In an article on academic and community partnerships, Gronski and Pigg (2000) argue that such collaborations are fundamentally important to efforts aimed at supporting marginalized peoples in their self-reflexive explorations of oppression and resistance. Moreover, they contend that there is a very real need for renewed collaboration between various stakeholders in the community towards these ends:

> The multiple and often messy needs of families and communities require a renewed collaboration among business, government, nonprofit services and local groups.[11]

As collaborators within the Healing of the Seven Generations Project, we believe that the symbiotic relationship which has emerged between the project and Wilfrid Laurier University has served to create an energy which has been mutually satisfying; from both an intellectual and practical standpoint. This is not to say there have not been challenges. In fact, given that the development and implementation of the project lasted a full year, we had our share of queries from colleagues questioning the legitimacy of engaging in such a labor intensive "unfunded" endeavor. After all, as Marullo and Edwards (2000) remind us, "the academic reward system . . . values most highly the science of discovery and offers fewer incentives for faculty to engage in the scholarships of application, integration and pedagogy."[12] As new academics, we were constantly being reminded about the value of publishing and significance of engaging in intellectual labor that was considered meaningful and important. But ultimately, we had to ask: Who gets to decide what is meaningful? Who gets to decide what is important? We would argue that this is precisely what we have done here. For over a year, we have been documenting the trials and tribulations associated with getting such a project off the ground and reflexively examining the role that we ourselves have played as academics in terms of facilitating this process. Echoing Boyer (1999) who speaks to the notion of a "scholarship of engagement," we qualify this work as an "academic respositioning" whereby universities are inevitably reshaped as they enter into partnerships with various actors within the community.[13] Marullo and Edwards (2000) support this idea:

> [T]he engaged scholar weaves together local or regional constituencies . . . [and] they must also play the role of organizer among their university colleagues so that networks of interested faculty, administrators, and staff can collaborate with enduring community-based constituencies and develop innovative "win-'win" projects for all parties.[14]

Part of what makes our collaboration with the Healing of the Seven Generations a win-win situation is the free flow of information, expertise and learning that has occurred in the past year. Certainly our students have benefited from Donna Dubie's presence within the university and we anticipate that in the future Donna's program may well benefit from the presence of progressive and dynamic Aboriginal placement students within her program. As academics, we have learned a great deal, much of which has moved us to challenge even some of our most basic and long held assumptions about community organizing. For example, the issue of intercommunity violence and notions of trust are prevalent themes which we have discussed at great length with members of the Healing project. As academics, we are forced to consider the enormous complexities of community organizing and development within a community which does not have a long tradition of trust or collaboration. This makes for difficult outreach when attempting to initiate a healing project.

There is certainly much room for reflection and research in terms of how to address and redress the conceptualization and delivery of community projects which are mutually nurturing and supportive within Aboriginal spheres. While much has been written on the issue of modern anthropology theoretically shaped by colonial conquest and imperialism, we would highlight the writings of Celia Haig-Brown (2001) who states the following:

> Perhaps it is my white skin privilege which leads me in the final analysis to an incessant desire to contribute to a project of rebuilding the university in a way which acknowledges its strengths, recognizes its historic shortcomings, and feels a need to shift priorities and redefine its "business" in an effort to address some conception of social justice.[15]

We would offer that our collaboration utilizes its various strengths as feminist and minoritized researchers within academe to create spaces for community projects like the Healing of the Seven Generations in order to enhance the Aboriginal community's capacity to be designers of their own healing and empowerment. Inversely, the creation of such space also means that our students and colleagues are sensitized to the needs of Aboriginal people and that these needs are articulated by Aboriginal people themselves.

This brings us to what motivates us to engage in such a process in the first place. Firstly, even though we come to this work from very different social locations (African, Franco-Ontarian and First Nations), as social justice advocates, we share a common understand and critical lens when it comes to issues of oppression and marginalization. Through our research and our work in the community, we hope to support and encourage marginalized communities to feel secure in their attempts to be agents of their own transformative community work. It is most important to us, as allies and as partners in the project, to work *with* the oppressed towards these ends and towards their liberation and healing.

As mentioned earlier, our relationship as social justice advocates and educators with the Healing of the Seven Generations Project is etched in an anti-oppressive framework. As such, our work is guided by the values of empowerment, feminism and agency. We believe that what has made our collaboration noteworthy and relatively successful is our understanding and commitment to encouraging a culturally-specific Aaboriginal project. The notion of a culturally-specific project is important to us as Francophone academics because we believe there is legitimacy in creating culturally homogenous spaces in order to fortify marginalized communities.[16] As Dei, Karumanchery and Karumanchery-Luik note:

> We learn to establish reference groups—out-groups with whom we feel a sense of alienation and in-groups with whom we feel a certain affinity. Through our daily experiences of oppression, we learn to recognize those 'others' who are also positioned as deviant, 'less than' and violable, and they come to represent a 'solidarity reference group'. Over time, as we mature in Western contexts, our chain of oppressive and inclusive interactions will indicate to us, strategies for survival. Some strategies for survival will reflect a need to identify with and engage in solidarity interactions with our fellow oppressed and other strategies will move us to identify with our oppressor.[17]

There is a healing power in community and we have seen the evidence of what projects like the Healing of the Seven Generations can do to contribute to people's sense of well-being. Yalom (1985), in relation to the healing potential of group psychotherapy, referred to this sense of empowerment through solidarity as an experience of "universality." He noted that this experience was especially penetrating and powerful for victims of trauma who had felt particularly isolated by shameful secrets.[18] Within this project, we have certainly worked with a number of people who struggle to externalize and do away with the ugly messages which they have received from the cultural asphyxiators of the residential school system. While it is far too early to speak with any legitimate or credible authority on the positive effects of the project on the lives of its clients,[19] we certainly can attest to the overwhelming demand for its services. Originally conceived to service a pilot group of only 15 individuals, the Healing of the Seven Generations presently has over 100 active members and clients who seek cultural refuge within the confines of its small space. To us, this is a sign of the gap which our collaboration has managed to fill within our community.

Enhancing Collaboration

As academics that have both, in our respective ways, felt the effects of a type of "pedagogical oppression" (a Franco-Ontarian feminist and an African male) while attending university, we are committed to engaging in work with the community which attempts to turn the academic table. We are guided by an anti-oppressive framework because it is one which makes sense to us as individuals who have experienced marginalization but have also been empowered by such marginalization. Working with Donna has allowed us to see the evidence of the importance of having a culturally-specific Aboriginal project run by and for Aboriginal people. We have no illusions as to how difficult this can be, but we have seen evidence that while it is difficult to conceptualize and sustain such a program, it is not impossible. The collaboration between our academic space and Donna's community space has allowed us to reflect on what has made our collaboration effective.

Like Dei, Karumanchery and Karumanchery-Luik (2004) in their critical analysis of the notion of "in-group solidarity and politicized partnerships," we attempt to draw upon the teachings of Freire (1993) to inform how we work with the oppressed.[20] In this case while we are not all coming from Aboriginal spaces, what binds us is our relative understanding both personal and collective of oppression and marginalization. We have developed an allied space that not only affords us the potential to nurture and mentor each other, but also the safety to challenge and push each other. Our differences, both cultural and political, strengthen our collaboration and so while all three of us are acutely aware of our relative privileges and social locations, we make no excuses for the fact that we have developed a deep friendship over time and that the notion of *la reconnaissance mutuelle*[21] is the strongest element of our alliance. The following details what we would qualify as determining factors which have positively enhanced our collaboration:

1) Our initial collaboration grew out of a common denominator of social justice and solidarity and as such a resulting friendship emerged.

As mentioned several times throughout this article, since all three of us have had a long history of working in spheres of social change and social action, the "buy-in" was easy. But with respect to the notion of "alliance-building," it has been our experience that taking the time to get to know one another as allies was important for our relationship. Thompson, Story and Butler (2002) assert that "collaborative relationships take time, and persistence signals sincere and serious intention."[22] Our working relationship was forged over a long period of time which permitted us to get to know one another and as a result a friendship ensued. While some may think that merging friendship and collaboration is inadvisable, we would respect-fully submit, as would Shragge, E. (2003), that the basis of many collaborations for social action and change are etched first and foremost in personal relationships.[23]

2) What brought us together were individuals not institutions.

It is important for us to highlight that while we are connected to academic and community institutions, we are quite clear on the concept that the chemistry which we have as individuals was what brought us together initially and what sustains our mutual enthusiasm to keep on working as a collaborative. Alliance-building for us is not so much about dealing with the *other* in an "institution" but with individuals with whom we believe we can get along. While this may sound simplistic (and we recognize that it is) we also recognize that after 17 years of community organizing both in Canada and abroad, what we have learned on our journey is that the notion of an "ally" on the purest and simplest level has to do with the individual and not the institution which s/he represents.

3) There was a strong common denominator with oppression and marginalization as experienced between someone who is African and Aboriginal.

Not to negate Ginette's experience of oppression and marginalization (or her contribution to the collaboration) it is most legitimate to state that given our respective experiences with the devastating effects of colonization both in Africa and here in Canada, there is a silent and recognizable mutuality of experience relative to the experience of colonization. There is very little research which points to alliance-building between African and Aboriginal people in Canada but we would submit that we are "natural" allies even though the present-day effects of colonization in our respective geographic spheres may be quite different. As such, our collaboration with the Healing of the Seven Generations is a way to manifest solidarity for indigenous people everywhere who continue to suffer, but more importantly, resist the colonizer's design of cultural and economic suffocation.

4) *There was strong leadership on the part of the initiator of the project and as such, partners were very clear about mutual expectations.*

Without a doubt, Donna Dubie's vision and strong leadership has brought the Healing of the Seven Generations to a space of respect and much solicitation. At the beginning of our alliance, Donna was very clear as to what her expectations were: she required some assistance with the mechanics of submitting a proposal and needed a sponsor until she was incorporated as a non-profit. Upon reflection, the key determining factor which influenced the initial journey was the fact that Donna was able to take a risk and ask for help. She also knew instinctively that there was perhaps some merit in developing an alliance with an academic institution.

Another key determining factor which has permitted us to sustain our alliance, is that we, as academics, have been very clear about what we can or cannot contribute to the project. At the beginning of our working relationship, we articulated that we had no experience whatsoever working on any aspect of residential school system redress. We are not clinicians and as such could not and cannot offer anything in terms of how to deal with the effects of sexual abuse for example. What we did articulate is that we were interested in university and community collaboration and as such we would be most interested in documenting the relationship between the project and the university. We would also assist in accessing funding to help sustain the project and would also create spaces whereby we could mentor members of the Healing of the Seven Generations Project in matters of research and data collection. We also offered our services to shoot a short documentary on the project in order to facilitate dissemination of information relative to the project. As a result of our alliance, we have identified people who are videographers as well as individuals who are involved in arts-based social development work. Inversely, our university has benefited much in terms of having members of the project and the larger Aboriginal community help our students and colleagues understand the devastating effects of the residential school system on Aboriginal people in Canada. For us as academics, we certainly have been challenged and encouraged to reflect upon Eurocentric ways of writing and engaging in meaningful community-based research.

5) *Academic partners had for the most part very supportive academic work environments which encouraged such community-based work.*

We feel that it is important to mention that if allies working in academic institutions wish to collaborate with Aboriginal communities in any type of manner, we believe that a strong determining factor which would enhance the success of this type of alliance would be nurturing and supportive work environments. It is very important that academic workplaces show great flexibility in order to accommodate community partners. A simple task such as providing parking passes for community partners can be most helpful in creating accessible spaces for collaboration. Larger issues such as valuing community-based research is also key in sustaining the enthusiasm for one's commitment to this type of research.

Conclusion

Since the beginning of this journey, our alliance has been both intellectually and personally satisfying. Given that this collaboration is still in its infancy, there is much room for future research as to how the work has evolved and how it has been shaped by our mutual collaboration.[24] What we do know is that we firmly believe this alliance works because of the determining factors that have been listed above. Importantly, while these influences are specific to this particular alliance and should be viewed and appreciated as such, we believe they may be useful in inspiring and guiding others in academic and non-academic communities engaged in similar types of partnerships. Of particular importance is the attention which we, as a collective, have purposefully attributed to our own social locations and how our experiences with marginalization have informed the way we are committed to this project. It is noteworthy to say that we firmly believe that our personal friendships, and the friendships made with other members of the project, were/are a fundamental feature of what made this alliance an honest success for us and for the community. Our work on this project has certainly helped to develop our critical view of the superficial attention being paid to diversity issues in academic and political institutions in English Canada, not to mention the gross and arrogant neglect of the larger community amongst many Canadian universities. We feel it is important to state that where we were employed in Quebec prior to coming to Ontario, our university had an entire department entitled: "*Service aux collectivités*" which loosely translates into "services to and for communities." We believe our work in this project is beginning to illustrate the benefits that arise through the building of linkages between academic institutions and community partners.

In conclusion, we realize that future research into the project's impact on the community and its evolving relationship with Wilfrid Laurier will inevitably mean opening up our alliance to fellow collaborators. Regardless of the inevitable shifts and repositionings to come, what is important to us as allies is that we continue in our commitment to create spaces for academia and community to work together towards the betterment and the healing of Aboriginal peoples living in the Region of Waterloo. True anti-oppressive praxis encourages and supports people in their efforts to become agents of their own empowerment. We believe our collaboration facilitates this process in our community, and we are hopeful that it will do so for many years to come.

Chapter 11

Implications for Anti-Racist Education

A Pedagogical Needs Assessment

Leeno Luke Karumanchery, Ph.D.
Executive Director
Diversity Solutions, Inc.

Introduction

Black(ness) as a social, cultural and historical construction has powerful meaning in society. To 'be black' as a racial identity and/or 'becoming black' as a politicized identity is/are reproduced, experienced and addressed in a multitude of ways. As students construct, appropriate, negotiate and shape racial identities, they take on a political agency and collective resistance.

-Dei and James, *Becoming Black*[1]

Discovering the futility of his alienation, his progressive deprivation, the inferiorized individual, after this phase of deculturation, of extraneousness, comes back to his original positions. This culture, abandoned, sloughed off, rejected, despised, becomes for the inferiorized an object of passionate attachment . . . there is indeed the intuition experienced by the inferiorized of having discovered a spontaneous truth. This is a psychological datum that is part of the texture of History and of Truth. . . . Because the inferiorized rediscovers a style that had once been devalorized, what he does is in fact to cultivate culture.

-Frantz Fanon, *Toward the African Revolution*[2]

Today's anti-racist pedagogues must do more than simply answer the question of how to rediscover this style – we must learn how to engage it while negotiating the dilemmas inherent in contemporary educational contexts. In looking to help construct a critical and powerfully resistant schooling experience for marginalized students, I contend that any such movement must originate within the knowledges, experiences and voices of those traditionally silenced/muted in the mainstream. Echoing the work of Freire (1970) who believed that the oppressed must be the authors of their own liberation, I place a great deal of importance on insurgency and the potential for the oppressed to develop resistant politics through a critical consciousness of their own experience.[3] That being said, engaging critical anti-racist theory as a starting-point to change allows us to move articulations of resistance and healing outside the auspices of "clinicians" who seek to diagnose and prescribe, and into spaces where the oppressed themselves find and practice their own solutions.

In seeking to bridge the gap between anti-racist theory and possibilities for personal resistance and agency, I place considerable emphasis on the social construction of the self, and assert that there must be space in which to account for how the oppressed might think cognitively/consciously to oppose and resist their oppression. Throughout this paper, I engage narratives drawn from a research study I conducted between the years 2001 and 2003.[4] This qualitative investigation explored how the lives of marginalized peoples are breached and ruptured by racialized experiences of intrapsychic and psychological trauma, and how in turn, those violations might be resisted and/or repaired through a self-mobilizing/self-actualizing praxis. Having interviewed 14 people of color who asserted a personal philosophy, politics or dedication to an anti-racist ontology, I had hoped to better understand the processes of identity formation through which their resistant frameworks had been negotiated, performed and renegotiated. Most importantly for this work, I engaged the participant narratives to interrogate the possibilities for social change that arose from positive/critical shifts in our psychological, emotional and physiological engagements with racism and oppression. In interrogating these oppositional knowledges and strategies, I offer a challenge to conventionally accepted models of schooling and their potential to produce and reproduce affective, psychological, intrapsychic and physiological reactions of alienation and disconnection among the racially oppressed.

Action Plan: Naming the Problem

Numerous studies have shown that Aboriginal and African Canadian students are disproportionately represented among high school dropouts.[5] While mainstream discourse might work to pathologize these students as lazy, unintelligent and unmotivated, I think it important to draw the connective tissue linking such high dropout rates to the alienation and exclusion that racial minority students receive in and through their schooling experience. Case in point, Dei, Mazzuca, McIsaac and Zine (1997) argue that owing to a complex combination of the culture, environment, policy and practice of schools, many African Canadian students are actually "pushed out" of the educational system.[6] Clearly, there is a pathology at work here, but it is fundamentally important to recognize and affirm that it does not rest within the physiology or psychology of the oppressed. Too many marginalized youth are ill-equipped to effectively frame the social pathology that mediates their lives, and as such, they will find it difficult to resist and rupture the mainstream discourses that seek to paint them as deviant. Without the ability to pathologize the social frameworks that work to ground, construct and constitute our oppression, we are hard pressed to interrogate our symptomatic responses in the moment. I would argue that a self-reflexive diagnosis of the circumstances that encompass our lives, will allow us to interrogate the socially constructed nature of racial oppression as a starting-point to engaging the dilemmas of a racialized experience. This is a pivotal step that clears cognitive ground from which we might engage the development of resistant knowledges.

When discussing the theoretical moments that moved them to begin interrogating their experiences as racialized and oppressed, the common denominator for each study participant was a clear, if not pointed, engagement with the relationship between power and difference. See for instance, the moments in which Bharthi[7] and Magda[8] began to frame the place of oppression within their lived realities:

> For sure it came from university and meeting, through my sister, meeting this whole community of brown women who were queer. When I was young, and I met them, they were such a kick-ass group of strong women, and nothing about how they framed themselves was White. That was a real eye opening experience for me. . . . Just the internal politics and the damage. But it was so much about White not being beautiful, and powerful and all that kind of stuff. [Bharthi]

> I was at [university] taking a summer course on women's studies . . . we were watching a video on the history of Canada . . . the history of settling. There was this scene with all these older White grandmothers . . . it was saying these women did this . . . and because of them we have this . . . and they were critiquing the video. But, I remember that there was another Black woman in the class with me and she said "You know, my grandma doesn't look like any of these women . . . these women don't represent my grandma or me." And I remember that because I kind of looked at her, and then looked at the video and before she said that, I was just looking at the video thinking this and this and this should be done. Basically whatever we were critiquing at the time, I was doing it. And then she said "That's not me up there", and I realized, "That's not me either . . . but why are you so easily taking it in and interacting with it?" . . . and I thought "Maybe there's something behind it." [Magda]

In both of these narratives, we can see a shift in how the world is perceived and more importantly, in how the individual is perceived in relation to their world. In these moments, we can see the movement away from self-defeating notions of personal deficiency and the socially inscribed desire to see "reality"' through the eyes of their oppressor to a more politicized perception of power, difference and positionality. This is particularly striking in Magda's recognition of her passive engagements in the moment. What I find particularly interesting in these accounts is that these "moments of clarity" did not arise in starkly racist circumstances, but rather within everyday moments that normally act to circumscribe us within our racist milieu. The banality of both these reality checks speaks volumes about Bharthi and Magda's growing perception and comprehension of racism as far more than lynchings and racial slurs. I make this specific point because revelations relative to overt acts of racism do little in the way of engaging a critical consciousness of the more subtle violations that subversively frame our oppression. By this, I mean to say that everyday racism poses a far greater challenge to our cognitive ability to recognize and theorize our oppression than overt acts of physical violence and discrimination. In these instances, both Bharthi and Magda are able to access the resistant knowledges that were inscribed in the discursive tensions of the moment, and in/through those experiences, we can see them tap into the potentiality of their developing critical consciousness. Essentially, I engage this discussion of power and knowledge to suggest that such "moments of clarity" speak to empowerment in relation to directional movement and the strategic allocation of resources. Ayo[9] discusses the importance of contextualizing the dynamics of power and difference relative to experience:

> The crucial elements would be when I . . . the big one was when I transferred universities, I moved to London and went to Western and there was a professor there . . . professor Rushton. So I landed at Western during the height of Rushton's days. And all of the sudden it all went click, click, click, click, click. Yes that's what racism is. This is what discrimination is . . . and so I was like out there on the picket lines and doing the boycotts and almost Black Panther obsessive (laughter). Because you have to take all that frustration out because its like . . . okay, that's what it is right? And then I knew the first year that I came I was more into like just being so in awe of being with people of color and wanting to meet all those different people of every culture and things like that. It was like I have South Asian friends and Chinese friends and Black friends . . . it was just really cool. And then as you were socializing more with people of color . . . you were also picking up the language. So before I had all the feelings I knew it was wrong, I knew what was going on and I knew I didn't like so and so because they were mean to me because I was Black, but now I had a whole context to put it in.

"But now I had a whole context to put it in" – as seen in all three of these accounts, there is a sense of relief and/or release in the simple recognition that there is, in fact, an external locus for the various feelings of anxiety, hyper-arousal, depression and general despondency that so often outline the condition of oppression. This "clarity" is not only about recognizing the experience as racist, but also about recognizing your positionality in moment. Where beforehand, it would have been all about you, now (note how they didn't like her because she was Black, not because they were racist) the critical analysis allows for a more cognitive response to the moment and reflection on how you are being written and constituted in relation to a social pathology.

As explained so aptly by Ayo, at the emotional level, and without a critical gaze, you know that you feel *otherized* and isolated, but the words escape you, the knowledge escapes you, and as a result, you can neither act nor defend yourself. But within, and forever after the experience, when it all suddenly goes "click, click, click, click, click," you are able to place that un-nameable feeling in context and address it from a cognitive position, and without the same immateriality that you always associated with it. In other words, you are no longer imprisoned by the wordlessness of the moment. As asserted by Magda, the wordless quality of racism must be addressed:

[W]hen it's not named . . . when you don't name it, and you kind of let it go and stay under there, I feel that you're kind of saying . . . "Just let it go, just don't worry about it, don't do anything about it." It just sits in the air. . . .It's just kind of there. Nothing gets solved. Nothing gets helped. Nothing happens to it. So I think that naming it is really, really important. Even just to say "I know what this is, I know what you're saying, I know what you mean by this." Something just simple like that, but to just bring the awareness out there. . . . Just to have it out, to have the discussion going . . . to have the discussion out in the open.

Yalom (1985), in relation to the healing potential of group psychotherapy, referred to this sense of empowerment through solidarity as the experience of "universality."[10] He specified that this experience was especially penetrating amongst victims of trauma who had felt particularly isolated by shameful secrets. This assertion would fit with racially oppressed people who would rather have *just denied it*. So with respect to the notion of universality, we can see that talking about the politics of race and the reality of racism allows for the marginalized to enter into meaningful dialogue about the intrapsychic, emotional and behavioral distortions that occur within oppressive systems.

Engaging open dialogues around issues of racism and oppression within schooling sites may allow for schools and educators to acknowledge the reality of oppression and the real physiological and psychological effects of its influence on the lives of students. Simply put, naming racism, sexism, heterosexism and other forms of oppression is important, but also, by the same token, and for much the same reasons, I would argue that naming these oppressions as traumatic and violating is equally important in that it provides a clear and traceable pathology for the persistent social and internal difficulties faced by the oppressed. Such a framework for racism in context is important, if for no other reason, in order to simply combat the internalized feelings of isolation, rage and frustration that arise in the "not knowing why." Moreover, without the ability to recognize and acknowledge the cause of our difficulties, we cannot expect to properly engage strategies to resist them. If schools and educators are to truly work towards the empowerment of students, families and communities, we must not shy away from the necessity to engage in such libratory discussions, and we must be willing to implicate ourselves within the relations of power and privilege when necessary.

Action Plan Two: Finding Safety in Community

Because racism and other forms of oppression carry enormous potential to breach the sustaining bonds of "self" and sense of connection to the world, we must begin to interrogate how oppressive formations and events work to distort the symmetry of social relationships into ever-widening spheres of hierarchy, and in turn, how such ruptures might be reconstructed. In relation to the Nazi genocide of European Jewry, Rosenberg (1997) provides a clear engagement with such reconstructions in her thinking about trauma and its effects on individual survivors, community and human dignity. She suggests that we reframe our conceptualization of "healing" as an individual movement "back to normal," to stances that also recognize the threat survivors' experiences represent for integrity of society.[11] Throughout my dialogues with the research participants, it became clear that a) the solidarity of community; b) the notion of shared heritage; and c) the common experience of racism all function as powerful social supports that work to ameliorate the tensions of racial ruptures. This sense of commonality tempers the episodic intrusions of past traumas, as well as mitigates the influence/ fear of similar moments occurring in the future. Where racism functions to isolate the oppressed within self-disciplining positions of regulation, fear, disengagement and disconnection, in-group solidarity works to recreate a sense of belonging and safety.

Throughout these narratives, and particularly among those participants who had begun to see their racialized dilemmas in relation to an externalized definition of the problem, this sense of commonality was fundamentally important to their process of "becoming." In repeated testimonies, the participants spoke specifically to how their sense of connection was established and/or restored through their involvement in either, group, community or symbolic connection with culture and nationhood. See for instance Jennifer's[12] account of how she started to gain a greater critical consciousness of her positioning as racially oppressed:

> Honestly, I think it started with more exposure to different cultures when I moved to [my new home]. Specifically, there were more Black people that I was around. And I think, of course, I had one or two Black friends when I was in [my home town], but it was different. I think I was able to recognize [racism] when it would happen a lot more than when I was in grade school in [my home town]. I mean I battled with my parents when I was in grade school when they would say you know "This is racism . . . your teacher doesn't have your best interests at heart. . . . You shouldn't do this, and you shouldn't do that . . . don't follow what she's saying . . ." And I would battle with them and tell them "They like me and they want the best for me, and I don't see why they would do that." And I didn't see it at all. But I think that when I [moved] and I got more [friends that were people of color] people who actually share your experiences, and when you talk to them you start seeing similarities just with certain experiences, you start recognizing it as something that seems like its patterned. You identify it now and before I may have felt funny but really didn't know if that was it, and really would rather deny it. Because it would just be more comfortable to deny it.

Jennifer's narrative reminds me of Sampson's warning that dominant groups would seek to maintain their power and privilege by masquerading their monologues as dialogues.[13] Rather than engaging in dialogue with these privileged others, she is disciplined by a one-way stream of ideologies and discourses through which she is interpellated to see herself as she is perceived by those in positions of privilege. In other words, she comes to know herself as *other* through their eyes. Thus, the mainstream codes and symbols of her Blackness are internalized, influencing her to pathologize her "shortcomings" within democratic frames of meritocracy and equality. However, as she explains, her move from a "space of Whiteness" to a "place of Blackness" opened her eyes to a commonality of experiences. As she puts it, "you start recognizing it as something that seems like its patterned." She is now able to not only place racism as a part of her reality, but she is also able to recognize its hidden structures, systems and meanings through comparative storytelling and shared experience. I should clarify that, when she says that she identifies it now, whereas she might not have before, she appears to be speaking not only to the empowering nature of group solidarity, but also to her increasing ability to theoretically position herself relative to the realities of racial oppression. For Jennifer, this communal space and Black identity stand as symbols of solidarity and she employs these symbols within her oppressive milieu. She calls up the emotional energy[14] experienced within these solidarity interactions to combat the loss of emotional energy that occurs whenever she is forced to mediate an experience of racism.

As suggested by Boler (1999), emotions have a political and material history and that as such, they also have a material and political potentiality in both individual and collective experiences that find foundational strength in a shared consciousness, culture and context.[15] Standing alone in the face of racism is often anything but empowering, and so the discovery of commonality in such group settings established for Jennifer the simple but forceful message that she is not alone, that what she has experienced is the experience of a people. In this next excerpt, Jennifer speaks to why she found herself pulled to the Black organizations on campus:

> When I was in university, I got involved with groups, you know they have Black student groups on campus. I was really attracted to it. I wanted to know what it was about, and I got involved in my first year . . . and in my second year I was actually on the committee. I think it was just because during that time a lot of issues were coming up [we were] doing advocacy work, and I would see some of the things that were being done. Just watching a lot of people have racist things done to them and not do anything about it. Just seeing how it effected [sic] them. Their being, their school work or their relationship with their teachers. I think it was probably around then that I started feeling a little more secure about verbalizing and vocalizing how *we* felt and fighting for what I believed in. So [you] could probably say that I was starting to have more of a voice . . . because I *was* quiet. . . . I think when I went to [my new home], its mostly White and a small campus. There are Blacks there but its still not huge in number. Its almost like you want to feel like you have some power, that there is this group that is for you, and, . . . You want to feel like you belong somewhere. Camaraderie, and it made you feel good when you were in it. Even though there were years where we didn't feel like we were doing anything, it still just felt good. Even if it was largely social, and we just planned events, it still felt like I was part of something and it made me feel proud.

Again, relative to the healing potential of "group psychotherapy" as discussed by Yalom (1985), this experience of "universality" was particularly penetrating for Jennifer.[16] Because racism impacts the intrapsychic ability to frame oneself in relation to others without interjecting "*I* positions" that reflect isolation, alienation and self-pathology, the importance of finding a sense of commonality is crucial to the healing and resistance of the oppressed enroute to "becoming." The solidarity and sense of safety that arises in these "places," are simply not available to the oppressed when they are in mainstream environments. In fact, this would account for the often noted "need for them to stick together." I would contend that the search for safety is an incessant voice in each of us, and that for the racially oppressed, it is a voice best heard in the safety of community. Also, not to be overlooked, there is a real need for these solidarity interactions to be continuously generated, revisited and engaged.

While the symbols and emotionally generative interactions of in-group solidarity can be used to encourage the positive emotional states experienced within the community interactions as a form of "emotional capital," the power of the symbol will begin to diminish over time.[17] Importantly, if we are to maintain the functional ability to "call up" and employ our potential reserves of emotional energy, we must periodically recharge our stores with solidarity experiences. This strategy for emotional well-being can be seen in the decision of oppressed people to tailor their friendship groups into reflections of past solidarity groups, or in relation to groups they feel will bolster solidarity interactions. In fact, all the research participants described a sense of comfort and ease with respect to simply being in the presence of others who had experienced racial oppression.

The experience of commonality helps to reintegrate a sense of humanity and rightness into the world and back into self-concepts that have been suffocated by feelings of detachment and disconnection. This notion of commonality breaches the experience of isolation for Ann:[18]

> [W]hen I was in university I started to see things differently because I started to have some South Asian friends. I started to talk to them about it and realized that they felt the same way that I do. And that I'm not alone and as a collective, I could see the racism more easily because it wasn't directed at me . . . we all suffer this way. And so I became more aware, and as I got older, I just came to that direction and now . . . I feel very comfortable in this agency because it's once again, a collective. Its not about me being chosen as the person that racism is always against, its against all of us.

In Ann's discussion of work environment, she makes several important clarifications. Not only is the impact of racism dulled within an environment where the notion of group suffering diffuses the concentrated nature of racism, but also, within the sense of universality that develops in such solidarities. In these spaces, the implications of solidarity and community begin to transmute the moment from the materiality of personal attack to the moment as part of a larger system of racial oppression, impacting one and all in similar fashion. As asserted by Collins (1990) in the face-to-face- interactions, shared emotions, shared focus of attention and mutual awareness of that focus, solidarity interactions like those described by Ann, function to shift the individual's awareness from themselves to the group.[19] As noted by Hatfield, Cacioppo and Rapson (1994), this refocusing of attention and focus to the group sets the stage for further positive emotional contagion and a regeneration of emotional energy within the group. It is in such moments of critical clarity that the oppressed begin to glimpse themselves as part of the great *otherhood* of oppressed peoples and not as lone victims of discrimination.

It is important to note that this notion of critical awakening through commonality extends beyond the dialogue between physical bodies and to the dialectics of the metaphysical and the symbolic. Once experienced, the emotional energy generated in the solidarity interaction is taken with the individual into their out-group experiences, and in this fashion, acts as a resource of emotional capital to be stored and employed when necessary. As asserted by Summers-Effler (2002), once these symbols and markers of identity, community and solidarity are established, they become "a shortcut to recreating rituals that will reproduce solidarity and emotional energy." Furthermore, the repetition of the rituals (i.e., communal behavior, cultural dress, food, dance, literature and ethno-cultural practices of all kinds) will continue to recharge the symbols themselves as well as the resulting emotional energy reserves.[21]

In developing a basic model for the study of stratification, consciousness and transient emotions in group solidarities, Collins (1990) made a direct connection with the types of in-group rituals discussed above and the potentiality for increases in emotional energy.[22] He asserted that face-to-face interactions, shared emotions, a shared focus of attention, and a mutual awareness of that common focus would all contribute to an increase in-group solidarity and an increase in personal emotional energy. Moreover, Summers-Effler (2002), in following Collins (1990), pointed to the productive potential of these solidarities as emerging through a) the transient immediately shared emotion; b) longer-term feelings of solidarity towards the group; c) longer term individually oriented emotional energy; and d) emotional energy-loaded symbol of the solidarity interaction.[23] As can be seen in the preceding narratives, refocusing our attentions on in-group activities and sites of commonality that speak to identity, safety and community, sets the stage for the generation of further emotional energy. Summers-Effler (2002), contends that physicality and non-cognitive connections are deeply connected to these in-group rituals and their potentiality for the development of emotional energy.[24] I would argue that such experiences of community, solidarity, safety, understanding, positionality and shared experience all work to engender the development of resistant identities framed relative to internal relationships with self, and external relationships with community that support and produce emotional energy. This sense of community and these feelings of belonging are unique to groups that share traumatic and oppressive experiences, and so in these spaces, the mind, body and spirit of the oppressed find themselves tied to the mind, body and spirit of a larger external and yet intimately personalized *otherhood*.

Action Plan Three: Finding Mentors and Empowering Role Models

The deep-seated nature of racism constitutes the body, mind and soul of racially marginalized peoples. And so, at the core of their experience, the oppressed are disciplined to not only accept their oppression, but live it in relation to the lives of those with privilege. In other words, generally speaking, we live, breathe, work and struggle in "moments" that are beyond the White ability to experience, imagine or reconstruct. Whenever I hear mainstream statements such as "I understand racism because I went to . . ." or "I'm not racist because one of my best friends is . . ." or "If I weren't White, I think I would . . ." I am reminded of John Howard Griffin's attempt to engage the Black experience by coloring his skin and "passing" for a few days. At the heart of these problematic statements, whether meant rhetorically, or in earnest desire to be an ally, is a muting of pain and a denial of difference. Such interpretations of the racial experience and the reactions of mainstream society in general, have a profound effect on how the racially oppressed integrate their traumatic experiences relative to coping mechanisms in their everyday experience. In effect, they are forced to carefully negotiate their positions and voices in all circumstances and moments where safety is an issue – if not consciously, then subconsciously.

It is specifically with the issue of safety in mind that I contend that truly beneficial relationships must be engaged within a carefully managed dialogue of partnership. I say managed, because "leading" the oppressed towards a libratory praxis always runs the danger of superficial conversions, and so we must be cognizant of our efforts as leaders in the project. Both Herman (1992) and Danieli (1998) assert that recovery from trauma can only take place within the context of relationships that engender a sense of safety and a clear acceptance of the survivors autonomy within the relationship.[25] Ayo explains how important safety is in the mentoring process:

> Leeno: Was the reading on your own enough, or did you need the exchange that you got when you came to [university]?
>
> Ayo: Yeah, that was a big one for me . . . I can do all kinds of reading on my own, which I do, but [this particular professor] was, I think, a pivotal person for me. Because he was someone who academically applied anti-racism, and has a very strong foundation and has a theory, writes about it . . . it's part of everything he does. That was like the first professor that I ever had that even named it, let alone that that was the basis of his work.

Ayo's narrative engages Freire's (1970) notion that working on the side of the oppressed must be truly pedagogical in the sense that the processes of healing, consciousness-raising and politicization take place through action *with* the oppressed.[26] Aside from the work she did on her own, she is quite clear that the efforts of caring, dedicated and personally invested partners were also fundamentally helpful to her in her process of becoming. Several important points arise in Ayo's description of this mentor. First, as previously discussed, the notion of commonality is intensely important here in that the theoretical and experiential underpinnings of this relationship reflect a mutual starting-point in pain. So she is able to re-establish with this professor, the bonds of connection that were shattered through her previous traumatic experiences. Because she feels safe in this working relationship, her intrapsychic energies need not be expended in self-defense, as they are within her *other* state of hyper-arousal. In fact, within the frame of this relationship, she is able to side-step her positionings as *other* in order to re-establish her basic capacities for trust, autonomy and initiative.

It is only within this type of safe dialogical environment that the oppressed are able to recognize that that they do, in fact, have autonomy. Through the universality experienced within this relationship, Ayo is able to interpret the dialogue between her and her professor, not as monologue, but as a dialectic in which both are active, engaged and mutually supportive. In other words, the professor is validating of her experience through his politics, and this cooperative environment allows his experience and knowledge to engage her without attempts to control her. In many ways, the environment of safety is engendered through the political praxis of the professor in his rejection of both moral and political neutrality. As specifically pointed out by Ayo, the professor's explicit dedication to an anti-racist praxis fundamentally establishes him as someone who will not question the reality of her oppression. Rather, their mutual call for social justice places them in a position of solidarity that involves an implicit acceptance and acknowledgment of her experience of pain and victimization. It is a relationship that fosters both theoretical and intellectual partnership within an awareness of empathetic solidarity.

Another prominent theme arising in this account is the impact that this relationship has on Ayo's sense of "the possible" in terms of engaging racism as generally oppressive and as specifically destructive in her life. One of the major impacts of racial trauma on the oppressed is its ability to infuse the individual with a sense of utter helplessness over her life circumstance. The healing impact of positive role models (in this instance a powerful, validating, critically conscious and politically active Black man) must not be underestimated. For Ayo, this politically charged environment does more than direct her towards a more self-reflexive consciousness; it is also empowering in that it allows for a convergence of mutual support with her individual autonomy.[27] This narrative speaks to the importance of taking part in critical dialogues that are directive without being instructive.

I would also point out that this type of academic environment is fundamentally different from the other potentially healing relationships as discussed above. The first critical distinction is that Ayo, in her interactions with this professor, realizes that this environment offers a real potential for personal growth and healing. For her, this classroom acts as a crucible, in which "they" may burn away the irrelevancies that cloud her eyes to the truth of her/their oppression. Whether entering the environment with an eye towards engaging her own experience of trauma, or otherwise, the potential for intense healing is present because the professor has entered the relationship as an ally. In this safe environment (safe because she knows that she has an ally), the professor enters into dialogue with Ayo while placing all his experience and knowledge at her disposal.

Another critical difference within the classroom setting, is the power dynamic that runs through the relationship. Simply put, the professor occupies a relatively static position of power in this dialectic, and in that clear assertion alone, we are reminded of my initial warning that such spaces need to be engaged within a carefully managed dialogue of partnership. Ayo, like other students, enters into this relationship recognizing this innate power structure and voluntarily submits to the dynamics that arise therein. For the oppressed, no other act can be more fraught with a sense of peril because loss of control and helplessness are the daily experiences that infuse their lives. That being said, there is, in any such setting, the potential for the abuse of power. As asserted earlier, this could easily become an instructive, controlling relationship rather than a directive and freeing enterprise. Importantly, the oppressed are always vulnerable to manipulation and exploitation in these spaces because a) the universal experience of childhood dependence on a parent is invoked – leading towards feelings of transference that further exaggerate the inherent power imbalance of the relationship;[28] and b) the condition of oppression itself imposes an unauthentic view of the world in which the oppressed often become controllable, helpless and emotionally dependent.[29] Entering this relationship, the professor, in philosophy, politics and pedagogy, creates a safe space for Ayo – a space in which she is able to explore what anti-racism means for her. Imbedded within Ayo's description of the professor as pivotal to her anti-racist development, is an acknowledgement of the political praxis of that figure as both role model and mentor.

Action Plan Four: Restoring Control to the Oppressed

In discussing social change and resistance, the concepts are so radical and engaged on such grand scales that there is extensive room for variations in strategy. Rather than any one right method, we must engage multiple sites and strategies for change. However, when I speak of returning control to the oppressed, I am making a very pointed issue about the necessity of re-examining ourselves in our oppression and in our living of/out that oppression. More simply put, in our therapeutic movement towards healing and the development of critical consciousness, we cannot afford to remain tied to old processes of living because they are intrinsically constituted by, and constitutive of, an oppressed duality. In effect, the question is whether we take one step forward and two steps back, or whether we consistently move forward in our progression. I am reminded of my dialogue with Kai[30] who insists that she has a strong anti-racist framework and yet continues to frame herself in opposition to other people of color, and indeed, in opposition to her own Pakistani culture:

Leeno: Growing up, did you want to be Canadian, or did you want to be White?

Kai: [I] equated Canadian and White because everyone that was White was Canadian.

Leeno: So you never wished you had White skin?

Kai: Being Indo-Pak its surprising isn't it? I wish I was lighter of course, because there is a shadism that exists in our community. But no, I didn't want to be pale White.

Leeno: So who do you feel is oppressed?

Kai: That's really hard.

Leeno: Do you feel oppression? Are you oppressed at all?

Kai: [I] think racism does play a factor . . . although it hasn't played out that much in my life that I am aware of. Except for that incident when I was working at the library. As a teacher it's hard to be oppressed.

Leeno: So [racism] hasn't played out in your life? I'm not saying you're wrong . . . I'm just trying to figure out some of the things that you have said. It hasn't really played out in your life, but you wish you were White. When I said you once wished you were White, you said, "Who said I stopped wishing that?"

Kai: Yeah.

Leeno: So if some place inside you, you wish you were White, and at the same time you say that racism didn't really effect you . . . Can you expand on that a little?

Kai: Yeah. I didn't want to have White skin, blue eyes and blonde hair . . . I wanted to live the White dream.

Leeno: Could you do that with brown hair and brown skin? (pause) [I just realized] your eyes aren't brown. What color are they?

Kai: They're contact lenses . . . which you could say is part of my wanting to be White.

Leeno: I hadn't even noticed it. What color are they?

Kai: They're green. (long pause) The Whiteness was . . . (long pause). I'm not living at home right now, I moved away and that's part of the White dream. To be independent, on your own. To be an independent career woman. From a Pakistani upbringing that's not what we're taught. What's valued is to be a good wife.

Leeno: Do you equate Canadianness with Whiteness?

Kai: Yeah.

Leeno: So what place do you as a Canadian-Pakistani have in Canada? You've been here your whole life. . . . Are you less Canadian than other people?

Kai: Um, in terms of the stereotype I have in my head of what Canadian is, I'm less Canadian. Because I didn't take ballet lessons, or swimming lessons . . . all the things the White kids were doing when I was young. And that oppression has stayed with me up till now.

Leeno: Why do you have green contact lenses?

Kai: It's not to be White.

Then why is it? What is this White dream? In her assertions that racism hasn't really played out in her life, Kai vacillates between her concepts of "White" and "Canadian" without establishing a firm distinction between the two. However, while she clearly acknowledges that she wants to be Canadian, she does not recognize her subconscious desire to be White. To my reading of our dialogue, there is a most definite tension in both our interaction and in Kai's interplay between conscious (cognitive) and subconscious engagements with her experience of race and racism. In dealing with the intrapsychic tensions at work, I engage Rosenberg's (1997) discussion of the subjectivity of knowledge in relation to trauma and mono-dimensional understandings of the production of truth.[31] In her discussions, Rosenberg asserts that understandings of truth can be understood to pivot on three primary considerations:

(a) all articulations are partial and thus their truth effects cannot be a priori determined by external "evidence"

(b) articulations cannot be reduced to what is seen, heard and remembered, which too are partial and thus shape truth in their partiality

(c) judgements with regard to truth are not neutral considerations.

I engage Rosenberg's (1997) considerations in reflecting on the apparent duality that surfaces in Kai's placement of White skin, blue eyes and blonde hair as markers of Whiteness while muting the relevance of her continued efforts to pass by wearing green contact lenses.[32] Interestingly, she can admit to wanting to be lighter, but she blames that on shadism within her own community and not on general racism in Canadian society. She takes on the privileged task of condemning Pakistani culture for its decided preoccupations with shadism and sexism, while conversely painting the Canadian/White dream in idealized terms that reflect freedom and independence. Kai's duality, as an internalized discursive effect, pushes her to understand her oppression from the perspective of her oppressor and so in effect her resistance is regulated in her ability to discipline herself.

Kai's inability to develop a greater critical consciousness is closely related to the traumatic effects of a lifetime of racism that have diluted and muted her sense of power and control. Without a sense that she can make a difference, and without the theoretical support structures to frame her oppression, she finds it difficult to develop a praxically applicable critical consciousness. In relation to that journey, one of the guiding principles of psychological healing lies in the ability of the oppressed to restore that sense of power and control to themselves. Traditional psychological treatment of trauma would assert that the first task of therapy is to establish the survivor's safety, and then to move towards other areas of healing. However, with respect to an anti-racist strategy for the development of a therapeutic pedagogy, I would suggest that recognizing that one has been traumatized stands out as a key factor. In fact, I would go further to suggest that the everydayness of our violations makes it even more important that the oppressed are able to engage this process of "critical awakening." This initial awakening must take place before all others, and once seen for what it is, the oppressed may take on the task of reintegrating their sense of safety and autonomy. We tend to feel unsafe in our bodies, and so, in effect, our emotions and our thinking feel out of control. Regaining that control is also of fundamental importance in healing. See for instance how Magda worked to establish this sense of control after being "paralyzed" by the racist movie shown in her class:

> Leeno: And what was your next step after that?
>
> Magda: A lot of reading. I went through a lot of reading. I go through phases of what I read on my own, and what I was interested in. I didn't know quite where to go. So I went through this Civil Rights phase were I read all this stuff on Civil Rights and Black Feminism . . . and then I kind of thought what do I do with this? Where do I go with this? Because I hadn't had any teachers like that, I hadn't had any courses on anti-racism or anything like that . . . so I didn't know what to do or where to go. It was just interesting information, and it was all American too . . . so I think from then, I just started . . . my friendship base shifted and I think I started seeking out people that were a bit more . . . you know? The Black Student Association, the West Indian Students association . . . Doing that, getting out of [my home town] where I'm from, getting out of that more. And then just meeting more people and doing more

> stuff to find out more about myself and this community that I was a part
> of, but hadn't really known.

Magda's initial drive to learn why she felt isolated and frozen while watching the racist imagery in the movie is pivotal in the development of her anti-racist voice. She began to question why her world was so immersed within White norms and White perceptions of the world. In regaining her sense of control, her first step was to access the knowledge that had been "kept" from her all her life, and then secondly, she began trying to regain control over her body and her environment by reaching out to the support structures of heritage and community. Similarly, Jennifer speaks about regulating her personal environment as an attempt to redevelop a sense of both autonomy and safety. Note how she emphasizes the dilemma of inter-racial relationships, and how the tensions inherent in those experiences (or the anticipation of those tensions) is enough to regulate and discipline her:

> Leeno: If you were in a relationship, would your partner's race be important to you?
>
> Jennifer: Yeah.
>
> Leeno: In what way? Would you be amenable to dating outside your race?
>
> Jennifer: Depends what the 'other' race is. I could never see myself dating someone White. For one thing, I'm not attracted in any way, and I just think that there are a lot of issues. I think that when you are in a relationship with someone, there are enough problems and enough struggles, just as two different people coming together. And I just think that the race dynamic is too much of a hassle. I mean I could never say never, but . . .
>
> Leeno: So even in your childhood you weren't attracted to White people at all?
>
> Jennifer: Yes I was.
>
> Leeno: And that changed when?
>
> Jennifer: I'd probably say it started changing when I was in Junior High, grade 9 or 10. And it was around then that I moved to [a city]. Because I [had] lived in [a different city]. And where I lived there weren't any Black people . . . My school was mainly White. When I moved to [a city] I was exposed to more races and much more diversity. I think it just opened my eyes a lot more and I think I just felt a lot better about myself. In junior high I didn't feel good about myself. I was trying to be something that I wasn't, for a long time.

Jennifer draws on powerful theoretical revelations in this narrative. First, she is recognizing the depth of the impact that racism had on her growing up. Not only is there an acceptance that she was made to feel ashamed and isolated, but she is also admitting that she had tried to be something that she wasn't. This "feeling trap"[33] that Jennifer has entered into, engages her shame and guilt as a locus from which further shame and guilt are generated. These are not easy things to admit to oneself, but they are an important part of the healing journey. The processes of remembering pain, and mourning loss have always been traditionally valid and empowering moments in the process of healing from trauma. It allows the person to recognize that that part of life is gone and that they are now able to move forward in recognition of that loss. Secondly, Jennifer is taking a very political stand as to what type of environments she wishes to be in. This is an obvious reclamation of both autonomy and power in which she has critically assessed the race-script to determine where, when and with whom these moments tend to occur – and she has made a decided move to extricate herself from those situations. Where mainstream rhetoric might suggest that this is either reverse racism or weakness on her part, I would assert that as a decision made in political earnest, Jennifer has made a rational and empowering decision as how to best heal and thrive within racist contexts.

Importantly, we should not side-step the accumulated chain of interactions that make-up our personal biographies,[34] and how those repeated interactions motivate us to turn to solidarity groups for safety. Just as our chain of interactions teach us which interactions tend to be exhausting and energy draining, so too do they motivate us to engage in interactions and relationships through which emotional energy is bolstered. See for instance Andaya's[35] narrative:

Leeno: Is your partner's race important to you?

Andaya: Yes.

Leeno: Why is that?

Andaya: Because there are some cultural nuances that are expressed through language, and tradition, and food, and rituals that I value and feel that I want to share them with my partner. The way that I've seen inter-racial marriages work, and I'm not saying that they don't work . . . [but] relationships are hard and they're a lot of work to begin with. . . . It's a lot of work, and the way I've sort of experienced things is that I don't want to spend half my life explaining the other half of my life.

That last phrase bears repeating. "I don't want to spend half my life explaining the other half of my life." When Andaya makes this statement, she is speaking to the subtleties of safety that are generated in relationships where the necessity for a state of hyper-arousal diminishes. Implicitly framed within her narrative is the belief/knowledge that certain relationships are essentially conducive of acceptance, belonging and a commonality of experiential knowledge. Her conscious and not so conscious movement towards relationships that limit conflict in her life reflect a desire and motivation to establish associations that are generative of emotional energy. Similar to the process of naming, naming strategy for oneself is also an incredibly empowering experience:

Leeno: Have you set up for yourself a personal strategy for resistance?

Alexis: One of the things I started doing again that I used to do a lot when I was younger but I kind of stopped was writing, like journalling and writing poetry. And I find a lot of stuff comes out through there and I can think about it. And it's sort of a way I can cope with it and deal with it and I can put out a lot of the things that I might not be able to say to a person, I can say it. And I can get that out in a space that it's safe for me to do so. There's certain places I don't like to spend a lot of time. I don't like to go back to [my home town] because I don't want to deal with that. I

> go only to visit my parents and I won't stay longer than a week and
> that's pushing it. And the people that I also surround myself with, like
> who are closest to me. They have to have some understanding, or else
> . . . I refuse, in my personal everyday life to educate everyone who's
> around me. And it's very tiring.

Alexis[36] demonstrates her strategies for resistance in several ways. Like the others noted above, she carefully regulates where and with whom she will spend her time in an effort to generate a greater level of security and emotional energy for both her body and mind. But also, she has chosen to engage in critical reflection of her traumatic memories by journaling. Alexis's efforts to write down and engage her traumatic past establishes a foundation where acceptance of the past allows her to push on to the future and a greater sense of healing. Also, and very importantly, she has made a political decision about whom and where she will engage with discussions of race. Her cognitive refusal to "educate everyone who's around" clearly establishes that she is aware of how such rhetorical discussions serve to walk the oppressed in circles. In recognizing that these discussions are fundamentally tiring, she decided that strategically, it would be self-defeating to continue engaging in such "monologic" interactions.

One of the coercive strategies that arise in abusive relationships is that of the abuser constantly reasserting their right to abuse by challenging the victim's deviation from the accepted rules and norms of conduct. The resulting rhetorical backlashes against the victim further isolate and remind her that such futile efforts should not be attempted in the future. Throughout these narratives, various participants have noted their need to explain why their oppressor is wrong, to make them see the truth. That desire is both their reflection of a need for validation from their oppressor, and their inability to see how they are regulated and constituted within the moment. By recognizing and stepping outside of that script, Alexis is able to re-write her involvement in the moment. This is an incredibly powerful moment in illustrating that silence has a very real place in resistance. As Gopal[37] notes:

> As a child I know that there was like a sense of helplessness and a sense of
> intense panic and withdrawal. Or like you can say something but you do feel like
> you're singled out and it's all about you as opposed to that person. Whereas now
> the anxiety is still there and you'll still suffer whatever the hell that you feel
> when you're feeling them saying it. It's just that you can situate it, what they're
> saying. I'm not surprised when someone says. . . . You know? Back then it was
> like, "Oh my god, I can't believe someone said that." Now I'm like they just
> exposed themselves. 'Cause for me it's like White supremacy is the system that
> gives all White people that privilege of doing that whether they choose to or not
> to. So when someone does that I'm like, depending on the moment, it's very
> contextually specific on how I'm going to react to that. I might blow up at them,
> I might not, I might walk away but in the end I know exactly what happened,
> right?

Gopal's narrative is particularly telling here because in reflecting on his childhood traumas he also recognizes the intense effects that they have had on his life. One thing that he has come to assert is that as a person of color, safety is a very relative and carefully regulated thing. His father used to carry around a field hockey stick in his car trunk – "Just in case" – that is a difficult thing to move past. When we speak of racism, because it is a socially constructed issue that permeates every factor of live, safety is a problematic issue at best. Does that mean safety at home, safety in school, safety among friends, safety at work, safety in intimate relationships? Gopal explains: "The anxiety is still there and you'll still suffer whatever the hell that you feel when you're feeling them saying it. It's just that you can situate it." That ability to situate is a powerful tool in resistance.

A Pedagogical Needs Assessment

We have a tendency, as a society, to blame the victim, which is to say that our responses to inequity, oppression and trauma often manifest in symptomatic responses that are pathologized to innate biological, personal or cultural deficiencies. Again, in relation to schooling, social researchers and clinicians have always sought to explain student disengagement and the tendency to drop-out, as a problematic that originated in the character of marginalized students, their families, their communities. In discussing the educational needs of racialized and minoritized youth here, I would like to reiterate that in the following discussion of "needs," this work does not pathologize the oppressed. Rather, I look to address the social pathologies at work relative to racism in "the everyday" as the root cause for the necessity of such ameliorative educational praxis.

First, as seen in the narratives, our ability to "name" and externally contextualize racism and oppression works to produce a critical conception of the moment that not only frames the social pathology around us, but our positionality in the moment as well. Because the prolonged and repeated nature of racial trauma manifests as a complex of disabilities engaging us in the constant task of negotiating pain in the face of the un-nameable, oppositional exercises in resistance can help ensure that the locus of blame shifts from self to society. In this way, the un-nameable feeling can be placed in context such that it is now knowable, nameable and actionable. Just as school boards, administrators and trustees must not be afraid to engage organizational change initiatives that expose and rupture these systems, so too must educators be willing and able to open up dialogue around the realities of oppression. Recognizing that I am calling for a fundamental shift in how we educate teachers (because educators must develop the critical tools to engage such dialogues), I strongly believe that the ability to name racism must be engaged as a new standard in pedagogical approaches and curricular design.

With respect to the importance of solidarity experiences in schooling, the connection to group and a notion of shared experience seemed intensely powerful to almost every member of the study group. Whether those realizations came in the actual presence of organized racial/cultural groups, informal solidarities or one-on-one interactions, the move from *spaces of Whiteness* to *places of color* served to open the participants to a commonality of experience that unveiled racism as a social dilemma rather than an individual or personal problem. The importance of reforming schools from spaces of Whiteness to places where other racial and cultural orientations may find a sense of "home" is certainly one of the imperatives that speak throughout the participant narratives. Importantly, I would contend that this articulation of inclusivity should not be reframed relative to sugarcoated techniques designed to placate. The power and impact of solidarity interactions cannot be infused into the schooling process through additive efforts that seek to generate multicultural inclusion through the use of a few cultural artifacts or celebratory events. Which is to say that multicultural days, Black pride days and international potluck days only serve to validate one clear notion: that these differences are not part of the normal everyday engagements of the schooling experience. I would assert that as communal space and solidarity experiences serve to bolster emotional energy in the face of racial oppression in the everyday, decided efforts must be made to incorporate such collectivities into the working heart of the schooling experience.

In re-thinking schooling along anti-racist lines, it becomes paramount to nurture the development of critically oppositional relationships as fundamental to the emotional wellbeing of marginalized students. In this respect, teachers must be recognized to be more that mere "sources of knowledge." Rather, it should be understood that those who choose to be mentors, carry the potential to significantly shape the ways students come to understand themselves and others, and moreover, they carry the ability to subtly or openly move students through a process of healing from racial trauma. This research has pointed to the profound impact that teachers have in helping to establish an environment in which students might develop socially, feel a sense of belonging, feel empowered to excel, and importantly, work towards the development of a critical consciousness. Our critical pedagogical strategies may help students to develop "identities of empowerment" that are reflective of libratory politics and a morally centred belief in inclusion, voice and representation. The role of mentoring fills a success need of students who find it hard to access the resources of the system and/or just find it hard to be engaged in their schooling process. As discussed earlier, mentors who have knowledge of the racial and cultural experiences framing the positionality of students are a fundamental resource to be used in supporting and motivating racially oppressed students. As asserted by Dei et al. (2000), racialized students entering mainstream educational systems lack the "cultural capital" of White students who attend the same schools but engage that schooling experience in fundamentally different ways.[38] It is for these reasons, that the role of mentoring is so crucially important to the mental wellbeing of racialized children.

Some Concluding Thoughts

In conclusion, I would just reiterate that this work complicates several traditional standards of thinking in relation to the experience of racism in the everyday and in the educational experience of marginalized youth. One of the tensions that I have explored at great depth is the issue of emotionality and its connection to the physical self. Boler (1999) discussed emotions as an "absent presence" in our professional lives because they occupy an almost unspeakable place in considerations of what is knowable. It is a peculiar quality in Western thought that seems to separate the emotional and spiritual elements of the self from those more physical attributes that seem easily recognizable and definable.[39] I think this dichotomous thinking is particularly important in my discussions of how a theory of trauma finds pedagogical implication. The participants of this research, in sharing the histories of their negotiations with trauma and the business of healing, brought one very clear point to the fore of consideration for analysis – that mind, body and emotion are all connected and integral to the development of the self and the development of an engaged student body.

Teachers, researchers and communities engaged in resistant anti-racist work, have begun to notice more and more in recent years, that happy and self-assured students who become indoctrinated into educational spheres that are *otherizing*, dehumanizing and alienating, rarely leave school in the same state in which they entered. See for instance, Nusayba's poignant description of her sense of dislocation and disengagement in her experience of education in the mainstream:

> Nusayba: By the time I got to high school I had had enough. I felt that I wasn't learning anything because I didn't feel represented in the school and in the curriculum.
>
> Leeno: Did you identify it as such?
>
> Nusayba: At the time, oh yeah. I was very aware from an early age, of being disenfranchised, of being marginalized, of the fact that schools didn't represent me. By the time I was in high school it was very clear that there was nothing in the curriculum that interested me, that reflected me, and that was a major reason that I was not engaged. Except for English classes. I liked language, and I was very good at it so, I tended to be very close to my English teachers and did well in that subject. Even when I dropped out, I wrote my friends English papers. But every other subject was very Eurocentric, very exclusionary, even though I tried to conform, I always knew I was an outsider . . . I finally left. They wouldn't let me leave when I was 15, but at 16 they couldn't stop me, and they were frankly glad to get rid of me. I remember, I went on my own. I didn't tell my parents. And I went to the principal and said I wanted to drop out, and she said "Fine." She got the papers right then and there. I just signed them and I was out.

Our identities are multiple and shifting and since we come to schools embodying these multiple identities of race, ethnicity, class, religion, gender and sexual orientation, spaces must be made within the schooling experience to reflect and engage these basic parts of who we are. The continued refusal to engage these "special interests" results in maintenance of the status quo, and the ongoing victimization of marginalized and oppressed students. But how do we evidence the necessity for the proposed changes, and who gets to determine when enough proof has been collected to justify such reforms?

When I speak about an educational needs assessment, I speak to the responsibilities of educators to acknowledge the concrete and not-so-concrete circumstances that encompass the lives of racially oppressed students. Moreover, it is also a call for educators to engage and take-up the silent and not-so-silent markers of trauma spoken/unspoken by students of color, and to engage in practices that speak to their knowledges and specificities of their cultural, racial frameworks. So in many respects it is a call for educators, parents and community members alike, to acknowledge and respond to our students' silent and not-so-silent cries for help. It is in this pivotal step away from traditions of normative schooling that we might engage in the development of student-centred approaches to educational reform that do not take to labelling disheartened, disaffected and disengaged youth as problems.

Endnotes

Preface

1   K. Marx (1978). "Thesis on Feuerbach," in R. C. Tucker (ed.) *The Marx-Engels Reader – 2nd Edition*. (New York: W. W. Norton).

2   P. Freire (1970). *Pedagogy of the Oppressed*. (New York: Continuum).

3   D. D. Brunner. *Inquiry and Reflection: Framing Narrative Practice in Education*. (Albany, NY: State University of NY Press, 1994), p. 15-16.

Chapter 1 – The Dialectics of Power
Understanding the Functionality of White Supremacy

1   J. Kovel (1988). *White Racism: A Psychohistory*. (London: Free Association Books), p. lxxxix.

2   I am very purposeful in my use of the word "know" in this context. I contend that as put forth by Pribram (1998), we are all conscious of our own experience. We build on our experience of the world to form a body of knowledge based on those moments. So when I say that the oppressor knows about his power and privilege, I engage the notion of consciousness knowledge in specific relation to how our identity subtly shapes and is shaped by our experiential "awareness"/perception of, and interaction with, the world. That being said, and with this specific notion of consciousness in mind, I similarly interpret the subconscious to be a filter that molds the boundaries of our experiential and embodied perceptions of normativity, self and world in ways that shape and are shaped by our experiential "awareness"/perception of, and interaction with, the world; the difference being that these knowledges may not be readily available or accessible to our cognitive thought processes. Whether filtered through our conscious, subconscious or metaconscious engagements with the world, knowledge of our privileges (e.g., access to resources, social normalcy, economic viability, positive sense of self) are "known" to us. See, K. Pribram (1988). 'Conscious and Unconscious Processes,' in J. Reams "Consciousness and Identity: Who Do We Think We Are?" an article adapted from an address at the inaugural meeting of the Society for the Multidisciplinary Study of Consciousness (08/18/98), as printed in [http://www.consciousness.arizona]; M. V. Antony (1999). "Outline of a General Methodology for Conscious-ness Research." *Anthropology and Philosophy*. Vol. 3, No. 2; J. Reams (1998). "Consciousness and Identity: Who Do We Think We Are?" an article adapted from an address at the inaugural meeting of the Society for the Multidisciplinary Study of Consciousness (08/18/98), as printed in [http://www. consciousness.arizona].

3   While poor Whites have undoubtedly reaped the psychological wages of Whiteness, the talk of White economic privilege leaves them with a feeling of puzzlement increasingly expressed as

anger. Thus, to speak of White privilege unproblematically in a pedagogy of Whiteness ignores the reality of diversity in Whiteness. Clearly, while all Whites benefit from the power and privilege that arises in their Whiteness, that social position is always fundamentally mediated by the other social positions housed within their bodies.

4 S. Wildman with M. Armstrong, A. Davis and T. Grillo (1996). *Privilege Revealed: How Invisible Preference Undermines America*. (NY: NY University Press), p. 8.

5 While I focus on the implications of Whiteness and White supremacy, I recognize that we all access power and privilege relative to the intersections and interlockings of race, gender, sexuality, class and other positionalities of difference.

6 G. J. S. Dei, L. L. Karumanchery and N. Karumanchery-Luik (2004). *Playing the Race Card: Exposing White Power and Privilege*. (New York: Peter Lang).

7 T. Grillo and S. Wildman. "Obscuring the Importance of Race: The Implication of Making Comparisons Between Racism and Sexism (or Other isms)," *Duke Law Journal*. 1999, p. 397-412.

8 J. L. Kincheloe and S. R. Steinberg (1998). "Addressing the Crisis of Whiteness: Reconfiguring White Identity in a Pedagogy of Whiteness," in J. L. Kincheloe, S. R. Steinberg, N. M. Rodriguez and R. E. Chennault (1998) *White Reign: Deploying Whiteness in America*. (St. Martin's Griffin: New York), pp. 3-29.

9 H. Giroux (1992). *Border Crossings: Cultural Workers and the Politics of Education*. (New York: Routledge); L. Alcoff (1995). "Mestizo Identity," in N. Zack. Lanham, MD (ed.) *American Mixed Race: The Culture of Micro-Diversity*. (Rowman and Littlefield).

10 T. K. Nakayama and R. Krizek (1995). "Whiteness: A Strategic Rhetoric," *Quarterly Journal of Speech*. Vol. 81, pp. 291-309; D. Stowe (1996). "Uncolored People: The Rise of Whiteness Studies," *Lingua Franca*. Vol. 6, No. 6, pp 68-77; "Mestizo Identity," in N. Zack. Lanham, MD (ed.) *American Mixed Race: The Culture of Micro-Diversity*. (Rowman and Littlefield).

11 Being White meant possessing the privilege of being uncontaminated by any other bloodline. A mixed race child in this context has often been rejected by the White side of his or her heritage – the rhetorical construct of race purity demands that the mixed race individual be identified by allusion to the non-White group, for example, she's half Latina or half Chinese. Individuals are rarely half-White.

12 L. Semali and J. L. Kincheloe (eds.) (1999). *What is Indigenous Knowledge? Voices from the Academy*. (New York: Falmer Press); J. L. Kincheloe, S. R. Steinberg and P. Henchey (eds.) (1999). *The Post-Formal Reader: Cognition and Education*. (New York: Falmer Press).

13 In the study of multicultural education such epistemological tendencies take on dramatic importance. In educators' efforts to understand the forces that drive the curriculum and the purposes of Western education, modernist Whiteness is a central player. The insight it provides into the social construction of schooling, intelligence, and the disciplines of psychology and educational psychology in general opens a gateway into White consciousness and its reactions to the world around it.

14 E. Said (1979). *Orientalism*. (USA: Random House).

[15] D. MacCannell (1992). *Empty Meeting Grounds*. (New York: Routledge); T. K. Nakayama and R. Krizek (1995). "Whiteness: A Strategic Rhetoric," *Quarterly Journal of Speech*. Vol. 81, pp. 291-309; L. Alcoff (1995). "Mestizo Identity." in N. Zack. Lanham, MD (ed.) *American Mixed Race: The Culture of Micro-Diversity*. (Rowman and Littlefield); H. Giroux (1992). *Border Crossings: Cultural Workers and the Politics of Education*. (New York: Routledge).

[16] B. Banfield (1991). "Honoring Cultural Diversity and Building on Its Strengths: A Case for National Action," in L. Wolfe (ed.) *Women, Work, and School: Occupational Segregation and the Role of Education*. (Boulder: Westview); R. Frankenberg (1993). *The Social Construction of Whiteness: White Women, Race Matters*. (Minneapolis: University of Minnesota Press); G. Vattimo (1992). T*he End of Modernity*. (Baltimore: Johns Hopkins University Press).

[17] J. Kovel (1988). *White Racism: A Psychohistory*. (London, Free Association Books), p. lxxxix.

[18] J. L. Kincheloe (1999) "The Struggle to Define and Reinvent Whiteness: A Pedagogical Analysis," *College Literature*. Vol. 26, (Fall), pp. 162-195.

[19] J. Fiske (1994). *Media Matters: Everyday Culture and Political Change*. (Minneapolis: University of Minneapolis Press).

[20] R. Miliband (1969). *The State in Capitalist Society: The Analysis of the Western System of Power*. (London: Quartet Books Ltd.); L. L. Karumanchery and J. Portelli (2005). "Democratic Values in Bureaucratic Structures :Interrogating the Essential Tensions," in Ken Leithwood (ed.) *The International Handbook on Educational Policy*. (Dordrecht: Kluwer Academic Publishers).

[21] L. L. Karumanchery and J. Portelli (2005). "Democratic Values in Bureaucratic Structures :Interrogating the Essential Tensions," in Ken Leithwood (ed.) *The International Handbook on Educational Policy*. (Dordrecht: Kluwer Academic Publishers).

[22] S. Haymes (1996). "Race, Repression, and the Politics of Crime and Punishment in The Bell Curve," in J. L. Kincheloe, S. R. Steinberg, and A. Gresson (eds.) *Measured Lies: The Bell Curve Examined*. (New York: St. Martin's Press).

[23] H. K. Bhabha (1994). *The Location of Culture*. (NY: Routledge), p. 66.

[24] Ibid.

[25] G. J. S. Dei, L. L. Karumanchery and N. Karumanchery-Luik (2004) Op. cit., p. 49.

[26] Ibid.

[27] E. Said (1979). *Orientalism*. (USA: Random House), p. 32.

[28] Ibid., p. 3.

[29] J. Scott (1988). "Deconstructing Equality-Versus-Difference: Or, The Uses of Post-Structuralist Theory for Feminism," *Feminist Studies*. Vol. 14(1), p. 36.

[30] E. Said (1979). Op. cit.

[31] J. L. Kincheloe (1999) Op. cit., p. 170.

[32] As noted by K. Oka. "Racism 'Renewed': Nationalist Practices, Citizenship and Fantasy Post 9/11," in L. L. Karumanchery (ed) *Rupturing Racism: Critical Theories and Insurgent Strategies*.

The notions of "citizen" and "citizenship" are not without complication. In fact, while citizenship is often used to refer simply to the prerogatives and privileges of citizens vis-à-vis non-citizens, more critical analyses are exploring the more contentious notion that in recent years, citizenship is the lynchpin in an amorphous opinion culture, dichotomizing strong patriotic identifications with feelings of practical political powerlessness.

33 Keating (1995); Rubin (1994); Gallagher (1994); Fiske (1994).

34 J. L. Kincheloe (1999). Op. cit., p. 172.

35 Ibid.

36 Kincheloe, Steinberg, Rodriguez, and Chennault (1998).

37 J. L. Kincheloe (1999). Op. cit., p. 172.

38 Luke (1994); Keating (1995); Thompson (1996); Gallagher (1994); Wellman (1996).

39 J. L. Kincheloe (1999). Op. cit., p. 172.

40 Gallagher (1994); Winant (1994); Rubin (1994).

41 b. hooks (1992). *Black Looks: Race and Representation.* (Boston: Beacon Press).

42 J. L. Kincheloe (1999). Op. cit., p. 173.

43 Gallagher (1994); Winant (1994); Tatum (1994).

44 J. L. Kincheloe (1999). Op. cit., p. 173.

45 A. Gresson (1995). *The Recovery of Race in America.* (Minneapolis: University of Minnesota Press). These types of ideological constructions continue to express themselves in increasingly irrational forms (i.e., neo-White supremists work to formulate racially deterministic single-bullet theories that blame non-Whites for all of society's ills; rallying supposed "White patriots" around resistant politics whose hope is to "save" the White race from domination by *other* groups and miscegenation with *other* groups.

46 The Chronicle of Higher Education is one of the top news and job-information sources for college/university faculty members, administrators, and students.

47 R. Eisenman (1995). "Take Pride in Being White – Letter to Editor," *Chronicle of Higher Education* (October): p. 134.

48 Stowe (1996); Yudice (1995); Gresson (1995); Tanaka (1996); Eisenman (1995).

49 J. McWhorter (2000). *Losing the Race: Self-Sabotage in Black America.* (New York: Perennial).

50 Gresson (1995); Gallagher (1994); Winant (1994); Rubin (1994); McIntosh (1995); Giroux (1992); Hacker (1992).

51 A Gresson (1995).

52 R. Frankenberg (1993). *White Women, Race Matters: The Social Construction of Whiteness.* (Minneapolis: University of Minnesota Press); R. Dyer (1997). *White.* (New York: Routledge);

D. Roediger (1994). *Towards the Abolition of Whiteness: Essays on Race, Politics and Working Class History*. (London: Verso).

53   G. J. S. Dei, L. L. Karumanchery and N. Karumanchery-Luik (2004). *Playing Race Card*. p. 82.

54   R. Frankenberg (1993). *Race Matters*.

55   R. Dyer (1997). *White*.

Chapter 2 – Racism "Renewed"
Nationalist Practices, Citizenship and Fantasy Post-9/11

1   As quoted in L. Berlant (1997). *The Queen of America Goes to Washington City*. (Durham: Duke University Press), p. 175.

2   S. Razack (2000). "'Simple Logic': Race, the Identity Documents Rule and the Story of a Nation Besieged and Betrayed," *Journal of Law and Social Policy*. Vol. 15, p. 191.

3   Bhabha asserts, "the state of emergency is also always a state of emergence." see, H. K. Bhabha (1994). *The Location of Culture*. (London: Routledge), p. 41.

4   I use the term "Americans" throughout this paper in reference to the United States as the scene where this event occurred. This is not to say however, that other parts of the world were not affected as well.

5   I have placed the word "attack" in quotation marks here in relation to the events of September 11, 2001. While the events of 9/11 have been portrayed as an act of unprovoked evil, there are many who view the attacks as part and parcel of an ongoing struggle, no more or less brutal and/or violent than many American acts taking place on "foreign" soils. I believe it is important to note that the use of this word in these contexts takes place in contested space.

6   I deliberately do not refer to the events of 9/11 as a "second attack" because I believe, like Chomsky, that Pearl Harbor represented an attack on military bases in a U.S. colony, not the national territory which was, at that time, neither directly threatened nor attacked. Not to diminish the historical, political or emotional significance of the Pearl Harbor attacks, but the fact that the 9/11 attacks occurred on national soil, impacting everyday American citizens is of paramount interest and importance here. These attacks were very different, carrying different meanings and very different impacts for the American citizenry.

7   E. Herman and N. Chomsky (1988). *Manufacturing Consent: The Political Economy of the Mass Media*. (New York: Pantheon).

8   See, N. Chomsky (2001). *9-11*. (New York: Seven Stories Press); N. Chomsky (2003). "Iraq is a Trial Run," [http://www.zmag.org/content/showarticle.cfm? Sec tion ID=15&ItemID=3369].

9   In using the collective term "our" here, I am referring to peoples of the developed world who play a prominent role in the maintenance of hegemonic dominance.

10   Berlant (1997), p. 13.

11   M. Foucault (1977). *Discipline and Punish: The Birth of the Prison*. (London: Allan Lane).

[12] B. Anderson (1991). *Imagined Communities: Reflections on the Origin and Spread of Nationalism*. (London: Verso).

[13] A. Loomba (1998). *Colonialism/Postcolonialism*. (London: Routledge).

[14] Based in Atlanta and launched in 1980, CNN's legacy reaches back to the 1920s in America. Its parent company is America Online/Time Warner which recently merged. CNN is operated by Turner Broadcasting, a division of AOL/Time Warner which was founded by Ted Turner. Both Time and Warner were started in the early twenties and both have since fathered other conglomerates – *Fortune* magazine, *Sports Illustrated*, *People* magazine, Electra Records, HBO, and Cinemax to name a few. These media giants in turn, significantly control and influence mainstream U.S. popular culture. AOL, started in 1989 by Steve Case, is one of the leading online internet services delivering more mail than the U.S. Postal Service and claiming more than 27 million members worldwide, adding a new member every six seconds (AOL Time Warner, 2001).

[15] CNN's televised version has about 550,000 viewers in one month and is available in over 85% of television viewing homes . In 2002, AOL/Time Warner's Board of Directors included 15 men and one woman, who were CEOs representing such large companies as Hilton Hotels, Colgate Palmolive, Philip Morris, and Fannie Mae. CNN receives $400 million in advertising revenue each year (AOL Time Warner, 2001).

[16] Berlant, p. 213.

[17] G. Hage (2000) *White Nation: Fantasies of White Supremacy in a Multicultural Society*. (New York: Routledge), p. 70.

[18] G. Hage. *White Nation*. p. 28.

[19] As seen in the drastic increase in the sales and prominence of American flags, patriotism was enjoying a renewal in the post-9/11 era. In fact, a month after the attacks the Bush administration launched a series of initiatives to encourage patriotism among school children. As part of the initiative, students were urged to recite the Pledge of Allegiance and war veterans were asked to teach "Lessons for Liberty" within the school system. For more, see C. O'Leary and T. Platt (2001). "Pledging Allegiance: The Revival of Prescriptive Patriotism," *Social Justice*. Vol. 28, No. 3, pp. 41-44.

[20] C. O'Leary and T. Platt. Ibid. p. 42.

[21] See Renan as cited in A. Loomba (1998). *Colonialism/Postcolonialism*. (London: Routledge), p. 105.

[22] CNN.com. [http://web.archive.org/web/20010913000418/http://www.cnn.com].

[23] CNN.com. [http://web.archive.org/web/20010912165735/http://www2.cnn.com].

[24] N. Gibbs (2001). *Mourning in America*.

[25] [http://web.archive.org/web/200110006015226/www.time.com/time/covers/1101010924/nnewworld.html]. The national outcry, the sanctions and economic backlash that struck the Dixie Chicks after lead singer Natalie Maines' diatribe against Bush, reflected a very important

moment in the post-9/11 national fantasy. It allows for the exploration of how mediums criss-crossed to completely encompass the national psyche at a time when being "American" meant very specific things. Importantly, among its various other effects, what happened to the Dixie Chicks worked to silently discipline other dissenters who were thinking about speaking out against American national policy at the time. The panopticon was in full effect after this event. For another analysis see G. Rossman (2003). "Who Killed the Travelin' Soldier: Elites, Masses, and Blacklisting of Critical Speakers," *Working Paper Series*, 26, Princeton University, Center for Arts and Cultural Policy Studies.

[26] S. Thobani (2001). "You Cannot Slaughter People into Submission." Speech presented at the Ottawa Women's Resistance Conference, Ottawa, Canada. [http://www.flora.org/library/wtc/thobani.html].

[27] Ibid.

[28] N. Chomsky (2002). *Understanding Power*. (New York: The New Press), p. 13.

[29] G. Hage. *White Nation*. pp. 42-47.

[30] CNN.com. [http://web.archive.org/web/20010918052910/http://www2.cnn.com].

[31] See T. A. van Dijk as cited in S. Razack. *Simple Logic*. p. 190.

[32] Torstar News Service. "Minorities Felt Brunt of Racism, Study Shows," *Metro Today*, Toronto, 11 March 2002.

[33] Berlant. p. 4.

[34] See E. Balibar (2002). "The Nation Form: History and Ideology," in P. Essed and D. T. Goldberg (Eds.) *Race Critical Theories*. (London: Blackwell), p. 222.

[35] CNN.com. [http://web.archive.org/web/20010917141459rn_1/www.cnn.com].

[36] Berlant. p. 196.

[37] D. Dharwadker (2001). *Cosmopolitan Geographies: New Locations in Literature and Culture*. (New York: Routledge), p. 7.

[38] CNN.com. [http://web.archive.org/web/20010915073314rn_1/www.cnn.com/].

[39] E. Glenn (2000). "Citizenship and Inequality: Historical and Global Perspectives," *Social Problems*. Vol. 47, No. 1, p. 2.

[40] M. Labelle and F. Midy (1999). "Re-Reading Citizenship and the Transnational Practices of Immigrants," *Journal of Ethnic and Migration Studies*. Vol. 25, No. 2, p. 214.

[41] Berlant. p. 3.

[42] Ibid.

[43] G. Hage. *White Nation*. p. 49.

[44] The term "Cultural Capital" was developed by French sociologist Pierre Bourdieu to explain the cultural differences that reproduce social class division. See P. Bourdieu (1973). "Cultural

Reproduction and Social Reproduction," in R. Brown (ed.) *Knowledge, Education and Cultural Change.* (London: Tavistock), pp. 71-112.

45 G. Hage. *White Nation.* p. 54.

46 Ibid. p. 62.

47 Ibid. p. 63.

48 E. Said (1993). *Culture and Imperialism.* (New York: Knopf.), p. 323.

49 T. Wise (2002). "Rationalizing Racism: Panic and Profiling After 9/11." [http://www.zmag.org/sustainers/content/2002-01/08wise.cfm].

50 S. Sassen (2001). "Governance Hotspots: Challenges We Must Confront in the Post-September 11 World," [http://www.ssrc.org/sept11/essays/sassen.htm].

51 Balibar. p. 222.

52 CNN.com. [http://web.archive.org/web/20010914180336/http://www.cnn.com].

53 R. Miles (1989). *Racism.* (New York: Routledge), p. 16.

54 A. Loomba (1998). *Colonialism/Postcolonialism.* p. 106.

55 Balibar. p. 223

56 B. Lewis (1990). *The Roots of Muslim Rage.* [http://www.theatlantic.com/issues/90sep/rage.htm].

57 G. J. S. Dei, L. L. Karumanchery and N. Karumanchery-Luik (2004). *Playing the Race Card: Exposing White Power and Privilege.* (New York: Peter Lang), p. 40.

58 Ibid. pp. 41-42.

59 Ibid. p. 43.

60 T. A. van Dijk (1993). *Elite Discourse and Racism.* (Newbury Park: Sage Publications, Inc.).

61 S. Hall (1995). "The West and the Rest: Discourse and Power," in S. Hall, D. Held, D. Hubert and K. Thompson (eds.) *Modernity: An Introduction to Modern Societies.* (Cambridge, UK: Polity Press), p. 205.

62 Of the media reports that I did review soon after September 11 (CNN and Time, 12 September to 7 October 2001) there seemed to be little coverage of racial incidents. Admittedly, there appeared to be more coverage of how the events of September 11 affected the Arab and Muslim communities in later media reporting, although I am unable to provide empirical evidence as to the frequency, extent and accuracy of this coverage.

63 CNN.com. [http://web.archive.org/web/20010914180336/http://www.cnn.com].

64 A. L. Stoler (1995). *Race and the Education of Desire.* (London: Duke University Press), p. 89.

65 CNN.com. [http://web.archive.org/web/20010918052910/http://www2.cnn.com].

66 J. McGreary and D. Van Biema (2001). "The New Breed of Terrorist," [http://web. archive.org/web/20010918035142/www.time.com/time/covers/1101010924/wplot.html].

67 This "New Breed" of terrorist was carefully scrutinized in the media. They were educated and technically skilled, yet "slovenly", quiet and "kept to themselves." They displayed huge wads of bills, yet were cheap; got into limousines late at night, yet owned old cars. Despite these contradictions the biggest enigma about the hijackers is that they executed their duties without knowing "how the final pieces were meant to fit together" as only higher operatives knew the full details. This collective dedication and sacrifice for such a violent purpose seemed almost incomprehensible to Western audiences and is perhaps what prompts the authors to label these men "a new breed." Readers are left to speculate about the authors' choice of words. For more, see J. McGreary and D. Van Biema (2001) *The New Breed of Terrorist.*

68 S. Thobani (2001). *You Cannot Slaughter People into Submission.*

69 G. Hage. *White Nation.* p. 31.

70 S. Razack (2000). "'Simple Logic': Race, the Identity Documents Rule and the Story of a Nation Besieged and Betrayed," *Journal of Law and Social Policy.* Vol. 15, p. 187.

71 M. Foucault (1991). "Governmentality," in G. Burchell & P. Miller (eds.) *The Foucault Effect: Studies in Governmentality.* (Chicago: University of Chicago Press), pp. 87-104.

72 Stripped of their rights, possessions and herded into internment camps based solely on their racial origin, Japanese Canadians/Americans were not only victims of government discrimination, but sanctioned everyday acts of racism performed by White Canadians/Americans who were deemed patriotic in their actions.

73 N. Chomsky (2003). *Iraq is a Trial Run.* [http://www.zmag.org/content/showarticle.cfm?SectionID=15&ItemID=3369].

74 I. Kant as cited in D. Held (2001) "Violence, Law and Justice in a Global Age," [http://www.ssrc.org/sept11/essays/held.htm].

75 T. A. van Dijk (2002). As cited in H-M. Lenk "The Case of Émilie Ouimet." in A. Calliste, G. J. S. Dei and M. Aguiar (eds.) *Anti-Racist Feminism: Critical Race and Gender Studies.* (Halifax: Fernwood Publishing), pp. 73-90.

76 N. Chomsky (2002). *Understanding Power.* (New York: The New Press), p. 18.

Chapter 3 – The Ties that Bind

Thinking through the Praxis of Multicultural and Anti-Racism Education in Canadian Contexts

1 G. J. S. Dei, I. M. James, L. L. Karumanchery, S. James-Wilson and J. Zine (2000). *Removing the Margins: The Challenges and Possibilities of Inclusive Schooling.* (Toronto: Canadian Scholars Press).

2 C. E. James (2003). *Seeing Ourselves: Exploring Race, Ethnicity and Culture.* (Toronto: Thompson Educational Publishing), p. 209.

3 C. E. James (2005). *Race in Play: Understanding the Social Worlds of Student Athletes.* (Toronto: Canadian Scholars Press Inc); G. Pon (2001). "Beamers, Cells, Malls and Cantopop: Thinking Through the Geographies of Chineseness," in C. E. James (ed.) *Experiencing Difference.* (Halifax: Fernwood Publishing), pp. 222-234; G. J. S. Dei, J. Mazzuca, E. McIsaac and J. Zine (1997). *Reconstructing 'Dropout':Understanding the Dynamics of Black Students' Disengagement from School.* (Toronto: University of Toronto Press).

4 C. E. James (2005). Op cit.

5 Ibid.

6 C. E. James (2001). "Multiculturalism, Diversity and Education in the Canadian Context: The search for an Inclusive Pedagogy," in C.A. Grant and J. L. Lei (eds.) *Global Constructions of Multicultural Education: Theories and Realities*, pp. 175-204. (New Jersey: Lawrence Erlbaum Assoc.).

7 S. Dion (2005). "Aboriginal People and Stories of Canadian History: Investigating Barriers to Transforming Relationships," in C.E. James (ed.) *Possibilities and Limitations: Multicultural Policies and Programs in Canada.* (Halifax: Fernwood Publishing), p. 36.

8 See G. J. S. Dei and A. Calliste (eds.). (2000) *Power, Knowledge and Anti-racism Education: A Critical Reader.* (Halifax: Fernwood Publishing); G. J. S. Dei, L. L. Karumanchery and N. Karumanchery-Luik (2004). *Playing the Race Card: Exposing White Power and Privilege.* (New York: Peter Lang); C. Gaines (2000). "Anti-Racist Education in 'White' Areas: The Limits and Possibilities of Change," *Race, Ethnicity and Education.* Vol. 3, No. 1, pp. 65-81; D. Gillborn (1995). *Racism and Anti-racism in Real Schools.* (Buckingham: Open University Press); L. Roman and L. Eyre (eds.). *Dangerous Territories: Struggles for Difference and Equality in Education.* (New York: Routledge); R. P. Solomon, C Levine-Rasky and J. Singer (2003). *Teaching for Equity and Diversity: Research to Practice.* (Toronto: Canadian Scholars' Press Inc.).

9 S. L. Preskill and R. S. Jacobvitz (2001). *Stories of Teaching: A Foundation for Educational Renewal.* (New Jersey: Prentice Hall).

10 The narratives analyzed in this paper were drawn from online discussions that took place between members of an urban education course that I conducted during the 1997-98 school year. The course was designed to give teacher-candidates an opportunity to work in what is referred to as "urban schools" where they were expected to develop teaching strategies which were inclusive, equitable and responsive to the needs, issues and aspirations of students (most of whom were of working class, racial and ethnic minority, and immigrant backgrounds). In this paper, I analyze many of the online exchanges that ran between the course participants as they conversed on issues that emerged in our class, as well as about teaching experiences, issues and concerns. In registering for the year-long course, teacher-candidates were told of the trial aspect of the course, and that we were going to do some data-gathering. Hence, they were asked to fill out consent forms. The online conversations were part of the data-gathering process.

11 C. Dudley-Marling (1997). *Living with Uncertainty: The Messy Reality of Classroom Practice.* (Portsmouth, NH: Heinemann). In this text, Dudley-Marling tells of reading a "Pakistani folk-

tale" in his Grade 3 class assuming that one of the students who had immigrated from Pakistan was Pakistani. In fact, he was from Afghanistan, and was a refugee in Pakistan.

12 See N. Carrim (2000). Op cit; J. Ryan (2000). "Educational Administrations Perceptions of Racism in Diverse School Contexts," *Race, Ethnicity and Education*. Vol. 6, No. 2, pp. 145-164; C. Schick (2000). "'By Virtue of Being White': Resistance in Antiracist Pedagogy," *Race, Ethnicity and Education*. Vol. 3, No. 1, pp. 83-102; C. E. Sleeter (1993). "How White Teachers Construct Race," in C. McCarthy and W. Crichlow (eds.) *Race, Identity and Representation in Education*. (New York: Routledge), pp. 157-171.

13 A different version of this section appears in C. E. James. (2001) Op cit.

14 All names are pseudonyms.

15 Posted 21 January 1998.

16 Hence, we get such questions as: "Is it our responsibility to represent **all** [sic] cultures in our classroom? If so how? Or, is it our role perhaps to present culture generally, for example how various cultures contributed to subject areas such as math, then facilitate student-led exploration of many cultures? With individual differences and sub-cultures within cultures, is it realistic to think that if we did try to include culture it can be truly inclusive for the students?" (Dena, 24 January 1998).

17 Posted 19 November 1997.

18 Posted 5 December 1997.

19 J. A. Banks (1992). "A Curriculum for Empowerment, Action and Change," in K. A. Moodley (ed.) *Beyond Multicultural Education: International Perspectives*. (Calgary: Detselig Enterprises), pp. 154-170.

20 Posted 1 December 1997.

21 It is necessary to make a distinction between integration and inclusivity. As anti-racist theorists would have it, integration represents the incorporation (or mixing) of the lived experiences and realities of minority group students into the existing curriculum and school program – not an add-on; while inclusion is the additive approach in which information or the perspectives of minority groups might be presented, but not integrated into the school curriculum and program. Being included means that the fundamental structure and reference of the curriculum and program remain the same.

22 C. Dudley-Marling (1997). Op cit.

23 Posted 20 November 1997.

24 Posted 21 November 1997.

25 Posted 23 November 1997.

26 Posted 14 January 1998.

27 Posted 16 January 1998.

28 Posted 17 January 1998.

29 Ibid.

30 L. L. Karumanchery (2003). "The Color of Trauma: New Perspectives on Racism, Politics and Resistance," Doctoral Dissertation. (Toronto: The University of Toronto).

31 Posted 19 January 1998.

32 Posted 18 January 1998.

33 Posted 20 January 1998.

34 Ibid.

35 In asserting *Cogito Ergo Sum* (I think therefore I am), Rene Decartes attempted to resolve the epistemological problematic of "truth." By privileging the "cognitive self" as the terrain in which authenticity arises, he situates the individual as existing independent of social context and within static discourses of history, self and memory. This notion of "psychological agency" is often linked to the problematic idea that experience can be somehow built and controlled through direct cognitive analysis and internal monologue irrespective of social context. These theoretical applications suggest an "internalized" perspective of individual functionality where cognitive processes are placed as apriori to affective, behavioral and/or socially disciplined aspects of "the self."

36 Posted 20 January 1998.

37 Posted 22 January 1998.

38 See "Canadian Diversity," *National Identity and Diversity*. Vol. 3, No. 2 (Spring, 2004); A. Fleras (2002). "Multiculturalism as Critical Discourse: Contesting Modernity," *Canadian Issues*. February 9-12.

39 C. Gaines (2000). Op cit.

40 A. Prince (1996). "Black History Month: A Multicultural Myth or 'Have-Black-History-Month-Kit-Will-Travel'," in C. E. James and K. S. Brathwaite (eds.) *Educating African Canadians*. (Toronto: Our Schools/Our Selves, James Lorimer), pp. 167-178.

41 Posted by Wing-Chuan 28 January 1998.

42 Posted 2 February 1998.

43 Posted 27 January 2005.

44 Some of the people who were named were George Washington Carver, Rosa Parks, Martin Luther King, Malcolm X – these were ones that some of the participants talked about in their classes. Not surprisingly, little or no mention was made of similar Black people in Canada, neither of slavery.

45 C. E. James (2000). "'You're doing it for the students': On the Question of Role Models," in C. E. James (ed.) *Experiencing Difference*, (Halifax: Fernwood Publishing.); A. L. Allen (1994). "On Being a Role Model," in D.T. Goldberg (ed.) *Multiculturalism: A Critical Reader*. (Oxford, UK: Blackwell), pp. 180-199; R. P. Solomon (1997). "Race, Role Modeling and Representation in Teacher Education and Teaching," *Canadian Journal of Education*. Vol. 22, No. 4, pp. 395-410.

46 Posted 27 January 1998.

47 Posted by Manjit 28 January 1998.

48 Posted by Helen 4 February 1998.

49 Posted by Yvonne 3 February 1998.

50 Posted by Erin 28 January 1998.

51 Posted 27 January 1998.

52 Ibid.

53 Ibid.

54 Rina was here quoting what members of the class had said; something which she said surprised her.

55 Posted 26 January 1998.

56 Posted 3 February 1998.

57 Posted 25 January 1998.

58 Ibid. Also, see footnote 21.

59 Posted 26 January 1998.

60 N. Carrim (2000). Op cit; G. J. S. Dei and A. Calliste (2000). Op cit; E. Dua and A. Roberston (eds.). *Scratching the Surface: Canadian Anti-Racist Feminist Thought.* (Toronto: Women's Press); C. Gaines (2000). Op cit; D. Gillborn (1995). Op cit.

61 Posted 19 January 1998.

62 Posted by Tam 20 January 1998.

63 Posted 25 January 1998.

64 Posted 3 February 1998.

65 C. McCarthy (1995). "Multicultural Policy Discourses on Racial Inequality in American Education," in R. Ng, P. Staton and J. Scane (eds.) *Anti-Racism, Feminism and Critical Approaches to Education.* (Toronto: OISE Press), pp. 21-44; C. Gaines (2000), Op cit.

Chapter 4 – Spectacles of Race and Pedagogies of Denial
Anti-Black Racist Pedagogy Under the Reign of neoliberalism

1 W.E. B. Du Bois (1965). "The Souls of Black Folk" in B. T. Washington (ed.) *Three Negro Classics.* (New York: Avon Books), p. 221.

2 It is important to note that while this may be true for anti-Black racism, it is certainly not true for the racist policies being enacted by the United States against immigrants and nationals, who are from the Middle East. The racial profiling, harassment, and outright use of unconstitutional means to intimidate, deport, and jail members of the Arab and Muslim populations in the United

States represent a most shameful period in this country's ongoing history of state sanctioned racist practices. While the focus of this essay is on Black-White relations, I am not suggesting that racism only encompasses the latter. Obviously, any full account of racism would have to be applied to a wide range of groups who constitute diverse peoples of color and ethnic origin.

3   H. Winant (2002). "Race in the Twenty-First Century," *Tikkun*. 17(1), p. 33.

4   Cited in D.Shipler. (1998). "Reflections on Race," *Tikkun*, 13(1), p. 59.

5   D. D'Souza (1995). *The End of Racism*. (New York: The Free Press); J. Sleeper (2002). *Liberal Racism How Fixating On Race Subverts the American Dream*. (Lanham, Md.: Rowman and Littlefield); S. Thernstrom and A. Thernstrom (1999). *America in Black and White: One Nation, Indivisible*. (New York: Simon and Schuster).

6   Cited in T. Wise (2002). "See No Evil: Perception and Reality in Black and White," ZNet Commentary. (2 August), [www.znetcommentary @tao.ca]; "The Gallup Poll on Black-White Relations in the United States-2001." Update is available online at [http://www.gallup.com/poll/specialReports/].

7   As Greg Winter points out, more recently The Center for Equal Opportunity and the American Civil Rights Institutes, two groups that oppose affirmative action, have launched a new offensive "against scholarships and summer programs intended to ease minority students into college life." See G. Winter (2003). "Colleges See Broader Attack on Their Aid to Minorities," *The New York Times*. (30 March), p. A15.

8   A representative example of work that points to the pervasive racism at work in American life can be found in: H. Winant (2001). *The World is a Ghetto: Race and Democracy Since World War II*. (New York: Basic Books); M. Marable (2002). *The Great Wells of Democracy: The Meaning of Race in American Life*. (New York: Basic Civitas Books); D. T. Goldberg (2002). *The Racial State*. (Malden, MA: Blackwell Books); S. Martinot (2003). *The Rule of Racialization: Class, Identity, Governance*. (Philadelphia: Temple University Press).

9   M. Omi (1996). "Racialization in the Post-Civil Rights Era," in A. Gordon and C. Newfield (eds.) *Mapping Multiculturalism*. (Minneapolis: University of Minnesota Press), p. 183.

10 J. Geiger (1997). "The Real World of Race," *The Nation*. (1 December), p. 27.

11 See, for instance, S. Steele (1999). "The Age of White Guilt," *Harper's Magazine*. (November), pp. 33-42.

12 This position is fully developed in S. Steele (1990). *The Content of our Character*. (New York: Harper).

13 J. McWhorter (2003). "Don't Do Me Any Favors," *The American Enterprise Magazine*. (April/May) [www.taemag.com/issues/articleID.17398/article_detail.asp].

14 Z. Bauman (2001). *The Individualized Society*. (London: Polity Press), p. 205.

15 C. Murray (1985). *Losing Ground: American Social Policy, 1950-1980*. (New York: Basic Books).

16 For an excellent analysis of this shift in race relations, see E. Bonilla-Silva (2001). *White Supremacy and Racism in the Post-Civil Rights Era.* (Boulder, CO: Lynne Rienner Publishers) and A. E. Ansell (1997). *New Right, New Racism: Race and Reaction in the United States and Britain.* (New York: New York University Press).

17 D. Kellner (2000). "Globalization and New Social Movements: Lessons for Critical Theory and Pedagogy," in N. Burbules and C. Torres (eds.) *Globalization and Education.* (New York: Routledge/Falmer), p. 307.

18 Z. Bauman. Op cit., p. 159.

19 L. H. Lapham (2001). "Res Publica," *Harper's Magazine.* (December), p. 8.

20 Z. Bauman (1998). *Globalization: The Human Consequences.* (New York: Columbia UP), p. 47.

21 A. E. Ansell (1997). *New Right, New Racism: Race and Reaction in the United States and Britain.* (New York: New York University Press), p. 111.

22 Ibid., pp. 20-21.

23 C. Gallagher (2005). "Color-Blind Privilege: The Social and Political Functions of Erasing the Color Line in Post Race America," in M. L. Andersen, K. A. Logio and H. F. Taylor (eds.) (2nd Edition) *Understanding Society: An Introductory Reader.* (Wadsworth Publishing: New York).

24 Ibid.

25 This issue is taken up brilliantly in D. T. Goldberg (2002). *The Racial State.* (Malden, MA: Blackwell Books), especially in pp. 200-238.

26 M. Marable (1998). "Beyond Color-blindness," *The Nation.* (14 December), p. 29.

27 For specific figures in all areas of life, see E. Bonilla-Silva (2001). *White Supremacy and Racism in the Post-Civil Rights Era.* (Boulder, CO: Lynne Rienner Publishers), especially the chapter "White Supremacy in the Post-Civil Rights Era," pp. 89-120.

28 P. Street (2002). "A Whole Lott Missing: Rituals of Purification and Racism Denial," Z Magazine. (22 December), [www.zmag.org/content/print_article.cfm? itemID=2784&seciton].

29 I address these issues in detail in H. A. Giroux (2002). *Public Spaces, Private Lives: Democracy Beyond 9/11.* (Lanham, Md.: Rowman and Littlefield).

30 L. Wacquant (2002). "From Slavery to Mass Incarceration: Rethinking the 'Race Question' in the U.S," *New Left Review.* (January/February), p. 44.

31 P. Street (2003). "Mass Incarceration and Racist State Priorities at Home and Abroad," *Dissident Voice.* (11 March), pp. 6-7, [www.dissidentvoice.org/ Articles2/ Street _MassIncarceration. htm].

32 R. J. Herrnstein and C. Murray (1994). *The Bell Curve: Intelligence and Class Structure in American Life.* (New York: The Free Press), pp. 533-534, 551.

33 N. Aziz (2002). "Moving Right On! Fairness, Family, and Faith," *The Public Eye.* Vol. 16, Issue 2, (Summer), p. 5.

34 See "Civil Rights in the Mission Section of the Centre for Individual Rights" website. [http://www.cir-usa.org/civil_rights_theme.html].

35 For an excellent summary and analysis of many of these legal cases, see N. Aziz, op cit.

36 N. Aziz. Op cit., p. 15.

37 Z. Ferge (2000). "What are the State functions That Neoliberalism Wants to Eliminate?" in A. Anton, M. Fisk and N. Holmstrom (eds.) *Not for Sale: In Defense of Public Goods.* (Boulder: Westview Press), p. 183.

38 D. T. Goldberg. Op cit., p. 217. The ideas in the sentence prior to this quote are also taken from Goldberg's text.

39 J. Comaroff and J. L. Comaroff (2000). "Millennial Capitalism: First thoughts on a Second Coming," *Public Culture.* Vol. 12, Issue, 2, pp. 305-306.

40 N. Aziz. Op cit.., p. 6.

41 Cited in P. Klinker (1998). "The 'Racial Realism' Hoax," *The Nation.* (14 December), p. 37.

42 D. D'Souza. Op cit., p. 268.

43 P. J. Williams (1997). *Seeing a Color-Blind Future: The Paradox of Race.* (NY: The Noonday Press), pp. 18, 26.

44 J. Meacham (2003). "A Man Out of Time," *Newsweek.* (23 December), p. 27.

45 Ibid., p. 27.

46 On Trent Lott's voting record on matters of race, see D. Z. Jackson (2002). "Brother Lott's Real Record," *The Boston Globe.* (18 December), [www.commondreams.org/views02/1218-09.htm].

47 R. Kuttner (2002). "A Candid Conversation About Race in America," *The Boston Globe.* (27 December), [www.commondrems.org/views02/1225-02.htm].

48 D. Brooks (2002). "We Don't Talk This Way," *Newsweek.* (23 December), p. 31.

49 Cited in D. Roediger (1994). *Toward the Abolition of Whiteness.* (London: Verso Press), p. 8.

50 F. Rich (2002). "Bonfire of the Vanities," *The New York Times.* (Saturday, 21 December), p. A35.

51 Ibid., p. A35.

52 See D. T. Goldberg (1997). *Racial Subjects: Writing on Race in America.* (New York: Routledge), pp. 17-26.

53 E. Cose (2002). "Lessons of the Trent Lott Mess," *Newsweek.* (23 December), p. 37.

54 Ibid., p. 37.

55 D. T. Goldberg (1993). "Racialized Discourse" in *Racist Culture.* (Malden, MA: Blackwell), pp., 54-56.

56 T. A. van Dijk (2002). "Denying Racism: Elite Discourse and Racism," in P. Essed and D. T. Goldberg (eds.) *Race Critical Theories*. (Malden, MA: Blackwell), p. 323.

57 J. Comaroff and John L. Comaroff. Op cit., p. 322.

58 J. Rule (1998). "Markets, in Their Place," *Dissent*. (Winter), p. 31.

59 Z. Bauman. Op cit., p. 107.

60 Ibid.

61 L. Medovoi (2002). "Globalization as Narrative and Its Three Critiques," *The Review of Education/Pedagogy/Cultural Studies*. Vol. 24, Issue 1-2, p. 66.

62 D. D'Souza. Op cit., p. 545.

63 D. T. Goldberg. Op cit., p. 229.

64 P. Bourdieu and G. Grass (2002). "The 'Progressive' Restoration: A Franco-German Dialogue," *New Left Review*. Issue 14 (March-April), p. 71.

65 J. Brenkman (1995). "Race Publics: Civic Iliberalism, or Race After Reagan," *Transition*. Vol. 5, Issue 2, (Summer), p.8.

66 On this subject, see R. W. McChesney and J. Nichols (2002). *Our Media, Not Theirs*. (New York: Seven Stories Press).

67 D. T. Goldberg and J. Solomos (2002). "Introduction to Part III," in D. T. Goldberg and J. Solomos (eds.) *A Companion to Ethnic and Racial Studies*. (Malden, MA: Blackwell), p. 231.

Chapter 5 – Empire Building for a New Millennium
State Standards and a Curriculum for Imperialism

1 J. Dewey (1927). "Imperialism is Easy," *The New Republic*. 23 March.

2 I agree with B. Martinez (2003) in "Don't call this country 'America'," *Z Magazine* 16 (7/8), p. 69, that claiming the name "America" for the U.S., when there are "20 other American countries that happen to be of color" is imperialist. So, I will be referring to the United States of America as the U.S., rather than as America, except when quoting or paraphrasing another source.

3 Ibid.

4 W. A. Williams (1991). "Empire as a Way of Life," *Radical History Review*. Vol. 50, p. 72.

5 Ibid., p. 71-72.

6 Ibid.

7 L. L. Karumanchery and J. Portelli (2005). "Democratic Values in Bureaucratic Structures :Interrogating the Essential Tensions," in Ken Leithwood (ed.) *The International Handbook on Educational Policy*. (Dordrecht: Kluwer Academic Publishers).

8 Ibid.

9   P. Freire (1990). *Pedagogy of the Oppressed*. (New York: Continuum). In speaking about Bank-
    ing theories of education, Freire discussed educational models that frame students as learning in
    a fairly linear and direct fashion. For example, (1) the teacher speaks, (2) the student listens, and
    (3) the student then uses the information provided by the teacher to move on to the next stage or
    concept. Within banking models of education, students are seen as empty vessels into which the
    teacher pours his/her knowledge.

10 L. L. Karumanchery and J. Portelli (2005). Op. cit.

11 California Department of Education, History-Social Science Framework and Standards for
    California Public Schools (Sacramento, California: Author, 2001). The framework describes the
    curriculum for each grade level conceptually and in considerable detail. The standards list key
    learnings for each grade level, and were derived from the framework.

12 As asserted by van Dijk (1993), elite-discourses might best be understood as a top-down
    phenomenon where elites construct the narratives that later find popular expression in the main-
    stream consciousness. See, P. Bourdieu (1991). *Language and Symbolic Power*. (Cambridge:
    Harvard University Press) and T. A. van Dijk (1993). *Elite Discourse and Racism*. (Newbury
    Park, CA: Sage).

13 Elsewhere, I and others have critiqued this framework for its presumption of a European, immi-
    grant point of view. See C. Cornbleth and D. Waugh (1995). *The Great Speckled Bird: Multicul-
    tural Politics And Education Decision-Making*. (New York: St. Martins Press); J. E. King
    (1992). "Diaspora Literacy and Consciousness in the Struggle Against Miseducation in the
    Black Community," *Journal of Negro Education*. Vol. 61, No. 3; and C. E. Sleeter (2002). "State
    Curriculum Standards and the Shaping of Student Consciousness," *Social Justice*. Vol. 29, No. 4.

14 G. C. Spivak (1990). *The Post-Colonial Critic: Interviews, Strategies, Dialogues*. (Great
    Britain: Routledge), p. 781.

15 G. Kenny (2003). "The Spoils of War: U.S. Interests in Iraq," Kairos: Canadian Ecumenical
    Justice Initiatives, [www.kairoscanada.org/e/resources/iraq/spoils.asp].

16 Ibid.

17 Pew Research Center for the People and the Press (2003). *Views of a Changing World*.
    (Washington, D.C.: Author).

18 A. Vltchek (2002). "Western Terror: From Potosi to Baghdad," *Z Magazine*. (December).

19 P. Ford (2003). "Surveys Pointing to High Civilian Death Toll in Iraq," *Christian Science Mon-
    itor*. (22 May).

20 L Everest (2004). *Oil, Power and Empire*. (Monroe, ME: Common Courage Press.).

21 F. Davies (2003). "Public Wrong about Iraq, Poll Says," *The Monterey County Herald*. (15 June).
    According to the Davies article, 22% of those polled believed that Iraq had used chemical or
    biological weapons against U.S. forces, 34% believed that the U.S. had located weapons of mass
    destruction in Iraq, and about half believed that Iraqis were among the September 11 hijackers.

22 C. Weedon (1987). *Feminist Practice and Post-Structuralist Theory*. (Britain: Basil Blackwell), p. 29.

23 P. Bourdieu (1991). *Language and symbolic power*. (Cambridge: Harvard University Press), p. 169.

24 Ibid., pp. 154-156.

25 Ibid., p. 49.

26 M. W. Apple (1982). *Education and Power*. (Boston: Ark Paperbacks), p. 139.

27 V. Shiva (1997). *Biopiracy: The Plunder of Nature and Knowledge*. (Boston: South End Press), p. 11.

28 California Department of Education. Op cit., p. 49.

29 As cited in E. Duran, B. Duran, M. Y. H. Brave Heart and S. F. Yellow Horse Davis (1998). "Healing the American Indian Soul Wound," in Y. Danieli (ed.) *International Handbook of Multigenerational Legacies of Trauma*. (New York: Plenum Press), pp. 341-342. See also, P.N. Limmerick (1987). *The Legacy of Conquest: The Unbroken Past of the American West*. (New York: Norton); W. R. Jacobs (1972). *Dispossessing the American Indian: Indians and Whites on the Colonial Frontier*. (Norman: University of Oklahoma Press); R. H. Pearce (1988). *Savagism and Civilization: A Study of the Indian and the American Mind*. (Berkeley: University of California Press); R. White (1983). *The Roots of Dependency: Subsistence, environment and Social Change Among the Choctaws, Pawnees, and Navajos*. (Lincoln: University of Nebraska Press); M. Y. H. Brave Heart and L.M. DeBruyn (1988). *The American Indian Holocaust: Healing Historical Unresolved Grief*. (National Center for American Indian and Alaska Native Research).

30 California Department of Education. Op cit., p. 110.

31 Ibid., p. 106.

32 Ibid., p. 126.

33 Ibid., p. 139.

34 Ibid.

35 Ibid., p. 155.

36 As a note, these imperial omissions are particularly ironic, given California's history of double colonization: the Spanish having colonized the Aboriginal peoples and then the U.S. having colonized part of Mexico.

37 P. Freire (1998). *Pedagogy of Freedom: Ethics, Democracy, and Civic Courage*. (USA: Rowman & Littlefield Publishers, Inc.).

38 When I use "critical education" in this context, I speak to the ability of education to politicize "the everyday." A critical education works to develop students' capacity to (a) resist the normative paradigms that infiltrate mainstream thought and discourse and (b) interrogate, explore and actively engage the sociopolitical contexts in which they live.

39 H. Giroux (2002). "Democracy, Freedom, and Justice after September 11th: Rethinking the Role of Educators and the Politics of Schooling," *Teachers College Record*. Vol. 104, No. 6, pp. 1138-1162; L. L. Karumanchery and J. Portelli (2005). "Democratic Values in Bureaucratic Structures :Interrogating the Essential Tensions," in Ken Leithwood (ed.) *The International Handbook on Educational Policy*. (Dordrecht: Kluwer Academic Publishers); L. M. McNeil (2000). *Contradictions of School Reform: Educational Costs of Standardized Testing*. (New York: Routledge); J. Saltman (2000). *Collateral Damage: Corporatizing Public Schools: A Threat to Democracy*. (Lanham: Rowman & Littlefield); L. Bartlett, M. Frederick, T. Gulbrandsen and E. Murillo (2002). "The Marketization of Education: Public Schools for Private Ends," *Anthropoloy & Education Quarterly*. Vol. 33, No. 1, pp. 5-29.

40 L. L. Karumanchery and J. Portelli. Op cit.

41 Ibid.

42 A dialogic education allows for a collaborative relationship between teacher and student that engenders a deep probing of experience of curricula specifically and the world in general. A dialogic education sees students speak about and reflecting on their realities in a way that brings learning into personal and experiential space. As suggested by Karumanchery and Portelli (2005), a dialogic education is formed through partnership and not through the individualized lens of the teacher.

43 G. W. Bush (2001). Presidential Address to the Nation. World Congress Center, Georgia. [www.whitehouse.gov/news/releases/2001/11/20011108-13.html].

44 G. W. Bush (2003). Bush-Cheney 2004 Reception. White House Press Office. 27 June 2003.

45 G. W. Bush (2004). Presidential Address to the Nation: Prime Time Press Conference. Washington, D.C. [www.whitehouse.gov/news/releases/2004/04/print /20040413-20.html].

46 Even as public support for Bush and the American lead occupation of Iraq has begun to wane in recent months (i.e., the mounting death toll among the American troops in Iraq, questions as to whether the Bush administration did enough to prevent the events of 9/11 and even the question of why Weapons of Mass Destruction have not yet been found in Iraq are all serving to raise public and political criticism of Bush and his post-9/11 policies) there remains little question in the public psyche as to what differentiates the villains and heros in this story.

47 Ipsos-Reid (2002). "After the War on Terrorism: The Future of Trade in the Global Community." 20 February 2002, [www.ipsos-reid.com/media/dsp_displayr us.cfm?id _view=1436].

48 California Department of Education. Op cit., p. 41.

49 Ibid., pp. 80-83.

50 Ibid., p. 78.

51 Ibid., p. 128.

52 Case examples of non-European nations moving towards political democracy (such as South Korea) and European nations moving towards fascism (such as Germany) suggest that particular systems do not necessarily follow particular peoples.

53 Ibid., p. 69.

54 J. Willinsky (1998). *Learning to Divide the World: Education at Empire's End*. (Minneapolis: University of Minnesota Press), p. 246.

55 White House Press Office. Op cit.

56 L. L. Karumanchery and J. Portelli. Op. cit.

57 California Department of Education. Op cit., p. 64.

58 W. Foster (1986). *Paradigms and Promises: New Approaches to Educational Administration*. (USA: Prometheus Books), p. 119.

59 California Department of Education. Op cit., p. 106.

60 R. Takaki. (1979). Iron Cages, (Seattle: University of Washington Press), p. 154.

61 S. Benhabib (1993). "Toward a Deliberative Model of Democratic Legitimacy," in A. Phillips (ed.) *Democracy and Difference*. (Cambridge, Polity Press).

62 The discourse of Orientalism acted as a sort of 'corporate institution' for managing the East: In effect, all things non-European, non-White. Orientalism was the lynchpin in the machinery of colonial domination and central to the subjugation and oppression of *other* peoples and certainly bolstered the West's ability to settle, describe, marginalize, rule, humble, denigrate non-Occidental peoples, cultures and histories. For more on Orientalism, see E. Said (1994). *Orientalism*. (Vintage Books: USA).

63 California Department of Education. Op cit., p. 129.

64 Ibid., p. 161.

65 Ibid., p. 139.

66 White House Press Office. Op cit.

67 California Department of Education. Op cit., p. 58.

68 Ibid., p. 150.

69 Ibid., p. 128.

70 Americans and the World, "Globalization," [www.americans-world.org].

71 Ipsos-Reid. Op cit.

72 D. Macedo (1993). "Literacy for Stupidification: The Pedagogy of Big Lies," *Harvard Educational Review*. Vol. 63, No. 2, p. 204.

73 G. Dimitriadis and C. McCarthy (2001). *Reading and Teaching the Postcolonial*. (New York: Teachers College Press), p. 117-118.

74 S. Wineburg (2001). *Historical Thinking and Other Unnatural Acts*. (Philadelphia: Temple University Press), p. 11.

75 G. Dimitriadis and C. McCarthy (2001). Op. cit.

[76] The internet offers a venue for this type of critical and dialogic learning (although access to the internet belies other questions of race, class, religion and other such points of difference). Some educators use it to enable students to talk directly with children and youth from other parts of the globe, shifting control of what is asked and said from professionals to young people. For more, see D. Sayers and J. Cummins (1997). *Brave New Schools*. (New York: St. Martin's Press)

[77] For example, see D. Wei and R. Kamel (1999). *Resistance in Paradise*. (Philadelphia: American Friends Service Committee); Chicago Religious Task Force on Central America (1991). *Dangerous Memories: Invasion and Resistance Since 1942*. (Chicago: Author); B. Bigelow and B. Peterson (1998). *Rethinking Columbus: The Next 500 Years*. (Milwaukee: Rethinking Schools, Ltd.).

[78] B. Bigelow and B. Peterson (2002). *Rethinking Globalization*. (Milwaukee: Rethinking Schools, Ltd.).

Chapter 6 – Racism in Educational Sites
Sustaining Oppression and Maintaining the Status Quo

[1] S. Carmichael and C. V. Hamilton (1967). *Black Power: The Politics of Liberation in America*. (New York: Vintage Press).

[2] Throughout this chapter the term "Black" is used to denote people of Black African and/or Caribbean ethnic heritage. There is no single agreed terminology in this field: a fact that reflects the changing, contested and socially constructed nature of "race" and ethnicity. Nevertheless, this use is in keeping with the terms recognized by most people who would be so labelled.

[3] P. Gilroy (1992). "The End of Antiracism," in J. Donald and A. Rattansi (eds.) (1992) *'Race,' Culture and Difference*. (Buckingham: Open University Press), p. 51.

[4] Marcella was a key participant in D. Gillborn and D. Youdell's ethnographic study of reforms and equity in education. See D. Gillborn and D. Youdell (2000). *Rationing Education: Policy, Practice, Reform and Equity*. (Buckingham: Open University Press).

[5] Since 1992 the Education Department in England has published "performance tables" that list every school in the country and give a range of statistics on their students' attainments in high stakes tests. These are frequently used by national and local media to construct crude "league tables" of the best/worst schools.

[6] Unless otherwise stated, emphasized speech in quotations reflects the emphasis in the original.

[7] NFER are the initials of the National Foundation for Educational Research (a respected research centre in the UK) but NFER-Nelson is a separate publishing company.

[8] See D. Gillborn & D. Youdell (2000) for an extended critique of popular "Cognitive Abilities" tests.

[9] The GCSE (General Certificate of Secondary Education) is the most common examination sat by students at the end of their compulsory schooling.

[10] See D. Gillborn & D. Youdell (2000) for a detailed account of the subject "options" process, including observational field-notes.

[11] See, for example, L.J. Kamin (1974). *The Science and Politics of IQ.* (London: Penguin); A. Montagu (ed.). (1999) *Race & IQ: Expanded Edition.* (Oxford: Oxford University Press); and G. Richards (1997). *'Race,' Racism and Psychology.* (London: Routledge).

[12] Working *within* the psychometric field, Robert J. Sternberg, is the IBM Professor of Psychology and Education at Yale, a major figure in contemporary "intelligence" testing and a leading theoretician in the field of human abilities and giftedness. Sternberg has devoted considerable energy to his thesis that "abilities" are "forms of developing expertise." See R. J. Sternberg (1998). "Abilities are Forms of Developing Expertise," *Educational Researcher*, 27(3): 11-20; R. J. Sternberg (1999). "Intelligence as Developing Expertise," *Contemporary Educational Psychology*, 24: 259-375; and R. J. Sternberg (2001). "Giftedness as Developing Expertise: A Theory of the Interface Between High Abilities and Achieved Excellence," *High Ability Studies*, 12(2): 157-79.

[13] Sternberg (1998). Op cit., p. 11.

[14] Ibid., p. 18.

[15] Cleary Committee of the American Psychological Association, Board of Scientific Affairs: quoted in H. J. Eysenck and L. Kamin (1981). *The Intelligence Controversy.* (New York: John Wiley and Sons), p. 94.

[16] Labour Party. (1997). *New Labour: Because Britain Deserves Better.* (London: Labour Party), p. 7.

[17] Ibid.

[18] Department for Education and Employment (1999). *Excellence in Cities.* (London: DfEE).

[19] Department for Education and Skills (2002). *14-19 Extending Opportunities, Raising Standards.* (London: DfES).

[20] Brief but wide-ranging and authoritative summaries are available in S. Hallam & Toutounji (1996). *What Do We Know About the Grouping of Pupils by Ability?* (London: Institute of Education, University of London); R. E. Slavin (1996). *Education for All.* (Lisse: Swets & Zeitlinger); and L. Sukhnandan and B. Lee (1998). *Streaming, Setting and Grouping by Ability.* (Slough: NFER).

[21] This has been documented in a range of academic work including, G. Bhatti (1999). *Asian Children at Home and at School: An Ethnographic Study.* (London: Routledge); P. Connolly (1998). *Racism, Gender Identities and Young Children: Social Relations in a Multi-Ethnic, Inner-City Primary School.* (London: Routledge); D. Gillborn. (1990). *'Race,' Ethnicity and Education: Teaching and Learning in Multi-Ethnic Schools.* (London: Unwin Hyman); and C. Wright (1986) "School Processes – An Ethnographic Study," in J. Eggleston, D. Dunn and M. Anjali (1986) *Education for Some: The Educational & Vocational Experiences of 15-18 year old Members of Minority Ethnic Groups.* (Stoke-on-Trent: Trentham). It has also been noted in official work, such as a study of behavior and discipline by the Office for Standards in Education (Ofsted) (2001). *Improving Attenance and Behaviour in Secondary Schools.* (London: Ofsted).

22 Department for Education & Employment (2001). *Youth Cohort Study: The Activities and Experiences of 16 Year Olds: England and Wales 2000.* (London: DfEE); D. Drew (1995). *'Race,' Education and Work: The Statistics of Inequality.* (Aldershot: Avebury); S. J. Eggleston, D. K. Dunn and M. Anjali (1986). Op. cit.; B. Parekh (2000). "The Future of Multi-Ethnic Britain," Report of the Commission on the Future of Multi-Ethnic Britain chaired by Bhikhu Parekh, established by the Runnymede Trust. (London: Profile Books).

23 A Faculty Head quoted in D. Gillborn & D. Youdell (2000). Op cit., p. 141.

24 See T. Sewell (1998). "Loose Canons: Exploding the Myth of the 'Black Macho' Lad," in D. Epstein, J. Elwood, V. Hey & J. Maw (eds.). *Failing Boys? Issues in Gender and Achievement Buckingham.* (London: Open University Press).

25 S. Bowles and H. Gintis (1976). *Schooling in Capitalist America: Educational Reform and the Contradictions of Economic Life.* (London: Routledge & Kegan Paul).

26 A. R. Jensen (1969). "How much can we boost IQ and scholastic achieve-ment?" *Harvard Educational Review.* 39(1): 1-123; A. R. Jensen (1998a). *The g Factor: The Science of Mental Ability.* (Westport, Connecticut: Praeger); H. J. Eysenck (1971). *Race, Intelligence and Education.* (London: Mauruce Temple Smith); J. P. Rushton (1995). *Race, Evolution, and Behaviour.* (New Brunswick, NJ: Transaction); R. J. Herrnstein and C. Murray (1994). *The Bell Curve: Intelligence and Class Structure in American Life.* (New York: The Free Press).

27 R. J. Herrnstein and C. Murray (1994). *The Bell Curve: Intelligence and Class Structure in American Life.* (New York: The Free Press). Paperback with new "Afterword" by C. Murray. (New York: The Free Press), p. 554.

28 Ibid., p. 416.

29 Ibid., pp. 472-473.

30 Ibid., p. 91, original emphasis.

31 J. P. Rushton (2000). online review for Amazon.com of J. Entine (2000) *Taboo: Why Black Athletes Dominate Sports and Why We're Afraid to Talk About It.* (New York: Public Affairs).

32 A. R. Jensen (1998b) "The g Factor and the Design of Education.," in R. J. Sternberg and W. M. Williams (eds.) *Intelligence, Instruction, and Assessment: Theory into Practice.* (London: Lawrence Erlbaum), p. 121.

33 *Wall Street Journal* (1994) "Mainstream Science on Intelligence," (13 December), p. A18.

34 For a critical account of the "distortions and misrepresentations" behind such secondary analyses, see L. J. Kamin (1999). "Behind the Curve," in A. Montague (ed.) *Race & IQ: Expanded Edition.* (New York: Oxford University Press).

35 R. J. Herrnstein and C. Murray (1994). Op, cit., p. 269.

36 J. Henry (2002). "America's Most Gifted," *Times Educational Supplement.* (1 March), p. 13.

37 S. Hallam and Toutounji (1996). Op. cit.

38 D. Gillborn and D. Youdell (2000). Op. cit., pp. 102-132.

39 W. Macpherson (1999). *The Stephen Lawrence Inquiry*. CM 4262-I. (London: The Stationery Office), p. 321.

40 J. Henriques (1984). "Social Psychology and the Politics of Racism," in J. Henriques, W. Hollway, C. Urwin, C. Venn and V. Walkerdine (1984). *Changing the Subject: Psychology, Social Regulation and Subjectivity*. (London: Methuen).

41 *Hansard. (*24 February 1999), col. 71228.

42 S. Steven (1999). "Don't They Know We're No Longer a Racist Society?" *The Mail on Sunday*, (28 February), p. 35.

43 Ibid.

44 Office for National Statistics (1996). *Social Focus on Ethnic Minorities*. (London: HMSO), pp. 29-31; Performance & Innovation Unit (2001). *Improving Labour Market Achievements for Ethnic Minorities in British Society*. (London: PIU), p. 11.

45 B. Parekh. (2000). Op. cit., p. 130.

46 Runnymede Trust (1999). "Black Deaths in Custody," *The Runnymede Bulletin*, (September), pp. 8-9.

47 In late 2000, for example, the then Conservative Party leader William Hague claimed that the police were being prevented from acting "for fear of being branded racist" (BBC news online, Hague takes aim at Lawrence report, 14 December).

48 M. Berrill. (2001). "Dangers of Macpherson," *Times Educational Supplement*. (26 January), p. 19.

49 S. Kemp and D. Gillborn (2000). "Achievement in Southwark: A Qualitative Study." Presentation of research findings, London Borough of Southwark, 1 December.

50 Scotland also witnessed an increase in racist attacks (and public demonstrations), especially against asylum seekers.

51 R. Ramdin (1987). *The Making of the Black Working Class in Britain*. (Aldershot: Wildwood House).

52 Interview with David Blunkett in the *Independent on Sunday*, (9 December 2001), p. 4.

53 Home Office (2002) *Secure Borders, Safe Haven: Integration with Diversity in Modern Britain*. CM 5387. (London: The Stationery Office).

54 A former Home Office adviser, now Visiting Research Fellow at the London School of Economics, University of London.

55 Marian Fitzgerald (2001). BBC radio interview. This interview, from June 2001, can be listened to in full on the web at [http://news.bbc.co.uk/hi/english/ uk/newsid_1363000/1363503.stm].

56 See, for example, M. W. Apple and J. A. Beane (eds.) (1999). *Democratic Schools: Lessons from the Chalk Face.* (Buckingham: Open University Press); S. Dadzie (2000). *Toolkit for Tackling Racism in Schools.* (Stoke-on-Trent: Trentham Books); D. Gillborn (1995) *Racism and Antiracism in Real Schools: Theory. Policy. Practice.* (Buckingham: Open University Press).

[57] See M. W. Apple (1996). *Cultural Politics & Education* (Buckingham: Open University Press); M. W. Apple (2001). *Educating the 'Right' Way: Markets, Standards, God and Inequality.* (New York: Routledge Falmer); S. J. Ball (1994). *Education Reform: A Critical and Post-Structural Approach* (Buckingham: Open University Press); S. Gewirtz (2002) *The Managerial School: Post-Welfarism and Social Justice in Education.* (London: Routledge); S. Taylor, F. Rizvi, B. Lingard and M. Henry (1997). *Educational Policy and the Politics of Change.* (London: Routledge); G. Whitty, T. Edwards and S. Gewirtz (1993). *Specialisation and Choice in Urban Education: The City Technology College Experiment.* (London: Routledge); G. Whitty, S. Power and D. Halpin (1998). *Devolution and Choice in Education.* (Buckingham: Open University Press).

[58] Ministry of Education (1945a). *A Guide to the Educational System of England and Wales.* (London: Her Majesty's Stationery Office), quoted in Lowe, R. (1988) *Education in the Post-War Years: A Social History.* (London: Routledge), p. 38.

[59] Department for Education & Skills (2002). *14-19: Extending Opportunities, Raising Standards. Consultation Document.* Cm 5342 (London: DfES).

[60] DfES (2002). Op. cit., p. 4.

[61] Ministry of Education (1945b). "The Nation's Schools," Pamphlet no. 1, (London: Her Majesty's Stationery Office), quoted in Lowe (1988) op. cit., p. 39.

[62] See D. Gillborn and H. S. Mirza (2000). *Educational Inequality: Mapping Race, Class and Gender – A Synthesis of Research Evidence.* Report #HMI 232. (London: Office for Standards in Education).

Chapter 7 – Lessons in Civic Alienation
The Color and Class of Betrayal in Public Education

[1] Williams vs. California was a historic class-action lawsuit brought by the American Civil Liberties Union, other civil rights organizations and private law firms and was filed on behalf of all California public school students who lack essentials required for an opportunity to learn. The lawsuit charged that the state had broken its constitutional obligation to provide students with the bare essentials necessary for education. The suit also charged California with having violated state and federal requirements that equal access to public education be provided without regard to race, color, or national origin. In the course of legal preparation for Williams vs. California, Michelle Fine was asked to testify as an expert witness, on the relation of structural and academic conditions within the plaintiff schools and youths' psychological well being. More precisely, Dr. Fine was invited to testify about the academic and psychological consequences associated with structurally deficient facilities, high rates of teacher turnover, uncredentialed and unqualified faculty and inadequate instructional materials. During related research into the case, youth attending plaintiff schools were both surveyed and interviewed about their educational experiences, aspirations and the impact of school conditions on their psychological and academic well being. Working with the case lawyers, Dr. Fine and her team of graduate students set up focus groups with elementary, middle and high school students from the plaintiff schools, contacted and selected via stratified random digit dialing within feeder neighborhoods. All focus

groups were taped, and transcripts were provided to all attorneys involved in the lawsuit. Thus, with all student names redacted, the "raw" data was made available to the public. After a review of the relevant academic literatures, data was analyzed and a final report was produced for the courts. This paper derives from that final report. Note: The preparation of this manuscript was funded, in part, by the Rockefeller and Spencer Foundations and the Leslie Glass Institute.

2 For more on Reproduction Theories see, J. Anyon (1997). *Ghetto Schooling: A Political Economy of Urban Educational Reform.* (New York: Teachers College Press); S. Aronowitz and H. A. Giroux (1993). *Education Still Under Siege.* (2nd Edition). (Westport, CT: Bergin & Garvey); S. Bowles and H. Gintis (1976). *Schooling in Capitalist America: Educational Reform and the Contradictions of Economic Life.* (New York: Basic Books).

3 In 1998, 11% of California's high school graduates were eligible to attend the University of California, but only 3.8% of Latinos and 2.8% of Blacks compared to 12.7% of Whites and 30% of Asians reached this standard. For more see, A. Hurtado, C. Haney and E. Garcia (1998). "Becoming the Mainstream: Merit, Changing Demographics and Higher Education in California." *La Raza Law Journal.* Vol. 10, No. 2, pp. 645 - 690.

4 Nationally, as in California, the long arm of the prison industrial complex reaches deeply into communities of color, yanking youth out at alarming rates while the economy remains hostile to young people without high school degrees. In New York State, for instance, from 1988 to 1998, the budget for the public university system was cut by 29% while state spending on prisons rose by 76%. For more see, V. Schiraldi, R. Gangi and J. Ziedenberg (1998). *New York State of Mind? Higher Education vs. Prison Funding in the Empire State.* (Washing-ton DC: Justice Policy Institute and the Correctional Association of New York).

5 P. Hill-Collins (1991). *Black Feminist Thought: Knowledge, Consciousness and the Politics of Empowerment.* (New York: Routledge); P. Freire (1973). *Education for Critical Consciousness.* (New York: Seabury); H. A. Giroux (1988). *Teachers as Intellectuals: Toward a Critical Pedagogy of Learning.* (Massachusetts: Bergin & Garvey); H. A. Giroux (1989). *Schooling for Democracy: Critical Pedagogy in the Modern Age.* (London: Routledge); S. Harding (1987). "Introduction: Is there a Feminist Method?" in S. Harding (ed.) *Feminism and Methodology.* (Bloomington: Indiana University Press), pp. 1-14.

6 J. T. Jost (1995). "Negative illusions," *Political Psychology.* Vol. 16, No. 2, pp. 397-424; J. T. Jost and M. Banaji (1994). "The Role of Stereotyping in System Justification and the Production of False Consciousness," *British Journal of Social Psychology.* No. 22, pp. 1-27; K. Marx and F. Engles (1846). "The German Ideology," in R. C. Tucker (ed.) *The Marx-Engles Reader.* (2nd edition) (New York: Norton and Company), pp. 146-200.

7 R. Lerner and A. von Eye (1998). "Integrating Youth and Context-Focused Research and Outreach," in D. Gorlitz, H. Harloff, G. Mey and J. Valsiner (eds.) *Children, Cities and Psychological Theories.* (New York: Walter de Gruyter), pp. 573-597; C. Werner and I. Altman (1998). "A Dialectical/Transactional Framework of Social Relations: Children in Secondary Territories," in D. Gorlitz, et al. Op cit, pp. 123-154; M. Wolfe and L. Rivlin (1987). "Institutions in Children's Lives," in C. Weinstein and T. David (1987). *Spaces for Children.* (New York: Plenum), pp. 89 - 112.

8   C. Werner and I. Altman. Op cit, p. 125.

9   S. DeLuca and J. Rosenbaum (2001). "Are Dropout Decisions Related to Safety Concerns, Social Isolation and Teacher Disparagement?" A paper presented at the Harvard University Civil Rights Project, Conference on Dropping Out. (Cambridge, Massachusetts).

10 L. Maxwell (2000). "A Safe and Welcoming School," *Journal of Architecture and Planning Research*. Vol. 17, No. 4, (Winter), pp. 271-282.

11 C. H. Cooley (1998). *On Self and Social Organization*. (Chicago: University of Chicago Press); W. E. B. DuBois (1935). "Does the Negro Need Separate Schools?" *Journal of Negro Education*. No. 4, pp. 328-335; F. Fanon. (1952). Black Skin, White Masks. (New York: Grove); G. W. Mead (1988). *Mind, Self and Society*. (Chicago: University of Chicago Press).

12 Alondra Jones, a former student of Balboa High School in San Francisco, and the other students whose narratives are employed in this paper, were members of the "plaintiff class" of Williams vs. California. Their narratives were collected during interviews and focus group sessions with Dr. Fine and her team of graduate student researchers. Their narratives are used throughout this work.

13 Ibid.

14 Ibid.

15 J. Ancess (2000). "The Reciprocal Influence of Teacher Learning, Teaching Practice, School Restructuring, and Student Learning Outcomes," *Teachers College Record*. Vol. 102, No. 3, pp. 590-619; N. Boyd-Franklin and A.J. Franklin (1999). *Boys to Men: Raising African American Sons*. (New York: Dutton); E. Elliott and C. Dweck (1988). "Goals: An Approach to Motivation and Achievement," *Journal of Personality and Social Psychology*. No. 54, pp. 5-12; M. Fine (1991). *Framing Dropouts*. (Albany: SUNY Press); D. Meier (1998). "Can These Schools be Changed?" *Phi Delta Kappan*, (January), pp. 358-361; A. Valenzuela (1999). *Subtractive Schooling*. (Albany: SUNY Press).

16 This middle school boy's narrative was collected during interviews and focus group sessions with Dr. Fine and her team of graduate student researchers in process of their research for the case of Williams vs. California.

17 This high school girl's narrative was collected during interviews and focus group sessions with Dr. Fine and her team of graduate student researchers in process of their research for the case of Williams vs. California.

18 Data drawn from the Williams brief shows that in the plaintiff schools, the percentage of fully certified teachers ranged from 13% to 50%. Moreover, further research indicates that in California, the percent of unqualified teachers is directly related to the percent of students of color and students eligible for free/reduced price meals. These numbers rise to an average of 24% non-credentialed teachers for 91-100% students eligible for free/reduced lunches. Additionally, teacher turnover rates are reported by some principals to be as high as 40%.

19 N. Boyd-Franklin and A.J. Franklin (1999). Op. cit.

20 M. Fine and A. Burns (forthcoming). "Class Notes," *Journal of Social Issues*. Special volume on social class and schooling.

21 R. McCord (2002). Declaration of Dr. Robert S. McCord in San Francisco NAACP et. al, vs. San Francisco Unified School District, et al., p.15.

22 F. Crosby, P. Muehrer and G. Loewenstein (1986). "Relative Deprivation and Explanation: Models and Concepts," in J. Olson, M. Zanna and P. Hernan (eds.). *Relative Deprivation and Assertive Action*. The Ontario Symposium, 4, 214-237. Hillsdale, NJ: Erlbaum; C. Leach, N. Snider and A. Iyer (1999). "Poisoning the Consciousness of the Fortunate," in E. Walker and H. Smith, *Relative Deprivation*. (Cambridge: Cambridge University Press), p. 136-163.

23 Research by Delpit (1995), McDermott (1987), Merton (1987), Rosenthal and Jacobson (1968), Steele (1997) and most recently De Luca and Rosenbaum (2000) conclude that teacher expectations and teacher treatment of youth are critical predictors of academic performance. See, L. Delpit (1995). *Other People's Children: Cultural Conflict in the Classroom*. (New York: The New Press); R. McDermott (1987). "Achieving School Failure: An Anthropological Approach to Literacy and Social Stratification," in G. Spindler (ed.) *Education and Cultural Process: Anthropological Approaches*. Second Edition. (Prospect Heights, Ill: Waveland), p. 82-118; R. Merton (1987). "The Focused Interview and Focus Groups: Continuities and Discontinuities," *Public Opinion Quarterly*. Vol. 51, No. 5, p. 50-566; R. Rosenthal and C. Jacobson (1968). *Pygmalion in the Classroom: Teacher Expectations and Pupils' Intellectual Development*. (New York: Rinehart and Winston); C. Steele (1997). "A Threat in the Air: How Stereotypes Shape the Intellectual Identity and Performance of Women and African Americans," *American Psychologist*. Vol. 52, p. 613-629; and S. DeLuca and J. Rosenbaum (2001). "Are Dropout Decisions Related to Safety Concerns, Social Isolation and Teacher Disparagement?" A paper presented at the Harvard University Civil Rights Project, Conference on Dropping Out. (Cambridge, Massachusetts).

24 M. Lewis (1992). *Shame*. (New York: Free Press).

25 The political rhetoric of average class size must be scrutinized for its equity dimensions. Governments commonly co-opt parents and local communities' genuine concern about class size and their impact on effective teaching to satisfy their political and ideological interests. A genuine commitment to reducing class sizes would require both funding and material/physical resources, but most conservative governments tend not to make a commitment to investing and reinvesting government monies into achieving this goal.

26 K. Burhans and C. Dweck (1995). "Helplessness in Early Childhood: The Role of Contingent Worth," *Child Development*. Vol. 66, No. 17; E. Elliott and C. Dweck (1988). "Goals: An Approach to Motivation and Achievement," *Journal of Personality and Social Psychology*. No. 54, pp. 5-12; C. Diener and C. Dweck (1980). "An Analysis of Learned Helplessness: II," *Journal of Personality and Social Psychology*. No. 39, pp. 940-952.

27 V. Duran (2002). "Building Quality and Student Achievement: An Exploratory Study of 95 Urban Elementary Schools. Environmental Psychology Program." (The Graduate Center, CUNY). Unpublished; J. Kozol (1991). *Savage Inequalities: Children in America's Schools*. (New York: Crown Publishing); S. Saegert and G. Winkel (1999). "CDCs, Social Capital, and

Housing Quality," *Shelterforce Online.* No. 104, (March/April); S. Lepore and U. Evans (1996). "Coping with Multiple Stressors in the Environment," in M. Zeidner and N. Endler (eds) *Handbook of Coping: Theory. Research and Applications.* (New York: Wiley), pp. 350-377; L. Maxwell (2000). "A Safe and Welcoming School," *Journal of Architecture and Planning Research.* Vol. 17, No. 4, (Winter), pp. 271-282; M. Spivak (1973). "Archetypal Place," *Architectural Forum.* (October).

[28] S. Saegert and G. Winkel. Op cit.

[29] V. Duran. Op cit.

[30] Ibid. Adding to the body of research documenting the psychological and physiological impact of such environmental stressors on youth, Evans, Kliewan and Martin (1991) report that youth blood pressure rises, concentration diminishes and errors on difficult tasks multiply in the presence of noise. See, G. Evans, W. Kliewan and J. Martin (1991). "The Role of the Physical Environment in the Health and Well Being of Children," in H. Schroeder (ed) *New Directions in Health Psychology Assessment.* (New York: Hemisphere), pp. 127-157.

[31] S. Lepore and U. Evans. Op cit., pp. 359.

[32] A. Baum, J. Singer and C. Baum (1981). "Stress and the Environment.". *Journal of Social Issues.* Vol. 37, No. 1, p. 26.

[33] F. Fanon (1952). *Black Skin, White Masks.* (New York: Grove); R. Janoff-Bulman (1985). "The Aftermath of Victimization: Rebuilding Shattered Assumption," in C. Figley (ed.) *Trauma and Its Wake.* (NY: Brunner/Mazel); R. Janoff-Bulman (1992) *Shattered Assumptions: Toward a New Psychology of Trauma.* (New York: The Free Press).

[34] R. Lifton. (1994). *The Protean Self: Human Resilience in an Age of Fragmentation.* (New York: Basic Books).

[35] G. J. S. Dei, L. L. Karumanchery and N. Karumanchery-Luik (2004). *Playing the Race Card: Exposing White Power and Privilege.* (New York: Peter Lang), p. 158.

[36] M. Fine, N. Freudenberg, Y. Payne, T. Perkins, K. Smith and K. Wanzer (2002). "'Anything Can Happen with Police Around,' Urban Youth Evaluate Strategies of Surveillance in Public Places," *Journal of Social Issues.* Vol. 59, No. 1, pp. 141-158; B. Anand, M. Fine, T. Perkins and D. Surrey (2002). *Keeping the Struggle Alive: Studying Desegregation in Our Town.* (New York: Teachers College Press).

[37] B. Lefkowitz (1998). *Our Guys: The Glen Ridge Rape and the Secrete Life of the Perfect Suburb.* (New York: Vintage Press); E. Poe-Yamagata and S. Jones (2000). *And Justice for Some.* (Washington DC: Youth Law Center, Building Blocks for Youth Report); R. Ayers, W. Ayers, B. Dohrn and T. Jackson (2001). *Zero Tolerance.* (New York: The New Press); See also, Fine, et al., forthcoming.

[38] R. Janoff-Bulman. Op cit.

[39] C. Flanagan, J. Bowes, B. Jonsson, B. Csapo and E. Sheblanova (1998). "Ties that Bind: Correlates of Adolescents' Civic Commitments in Seven Countries," *Journal of Social Issues.* Vol. 54, No. 3, pp. 457-475.

40 Ibid., pp. 459-460. See also, N. Boyd-Franklin and A.J. Franklin (1999). Op. cit.; R. Fallis and S. Opotow (2002). "Are Students Failing School or are Schools Failing Students? Class Cutting in High School," in C. Daiute and M. Fine (eds.) "Youth Perspectives on Violence and Injustice," *Journal of Social Issues*; Special Volume; M. Fine, N. Freudenberg, Y. Payne, T. Perkins, K. Smith and K. Wanzer (2002). "'Anything Can Happen with Police Around': Urban Youth Evaluate Strategies of Surveillance in Public Places," *Journal of Social Issues*. Vol. 59, No. 1, pp. 141-158; C. Haney and P. Zimbardo (1973). "'Social Roles, Role Playing and Education," *Behavioral Science Teacher*, No. 1, 24-45; D. Miller (2001). "Disrespect and the Experience of Injustice," *Annual Review of Psychology*. No. 52, pp. 527-553.

41 L. L. Karumanchery and J. Portelli (2004). "Democratic Values in Bureaucratic Structures: Interrogating the Essential Tensions," in Ken Leithwood (ed.). *The International Handbook on Educational Policy*. (Dordrecht: Kluwer Academic Publishers).

42 P. Cookson and C. Persell (1985). *Preparing for Power: America's Elite Boarding Schools*. (New York: Basic Books); M. Fine (1991). *Framing Dropouts*. (Albany: SUNY Press); M. Fine, L. Powell, L. Weis and M. Wong (1998). *Off White: Essays on Race, Power and Society*. (New York: Routledge).

43 M. Yates and J. Youniss (1998). "Community Service and Political Identity Development in Adolescence," *Journal of Social Issues*. Vol. 54, No. 3, pp. 495-512; C. Flanagan, J. Bowes, B. Jonsson, B. Csapo and E. Sheblanova. Op cit.

44 W. G. Bowen and D. Bok (1998). *The Shape of the River: Long-Term Consequences of Considering Race in College and University Admissions*. (New Jersey: Princeton University Press). Similarly, while the youth surveyed in this study are clearly negatively affected by their school's alienating cultures and environments (as evidenced in the declines discussed above), they still continue to voice a spirit of family, in-group and community responsibility that should not be overlooked. Despite the clear drop-off in the overall sense of social responsibility, 92% still felt it was important to help their families, 58% felt that it was vital to improve race relations, 56% of respondents felt it important to help those less fortunate than themselves and 41% were strongly inclined to improve their community.

45 M. Fine, et al.(2002). Op. cit.

46 J. Anyon. (1997). *Ghetto Schooling: A Political Economy of Urban Educational Reform*. (New York: Teachers College Press).

47 Anand, M. Fine, T. Perkins and D. Surrey (2002) *Keeping the Struggle Alive: Studying Desegregation in Our Town*. (New York: Teachers College Press); J. Ancess, op cit; M. Fine, et al. (2002) Op. cit.

48 J. Ancess and S. Ort (2001). "Making School Completion Integral to School Purpose & Design." Paper presented at the Dropouts in America: How Severe is the Problem Conference. Sponsored by Achieve, Inc. and the Civil Rights Project, Cambridge, Mass; A. Cook, C. Cunningham and P. Tashlik (2000). "Unmasking the Low Standards of High Stakes Testing," *Education Week*. Vol. 3, No. 8; M. Fine and L. Powell (2001). "Small Schools as an Anti-Racist Intervention: Racial profiling and Punishment in U.S. Public schools," *ARC Research Report*. (October),

pp. 45-50; K. Haycock (2001). "Closing the Achievement Gap," *Educational Leadership*. Vol. 58, No. 6; D. Meier (1998). Op.cit., pp. 358-361.

Chapter 8 – Unmasking Racism
A Challenge for Anti-Racist Educators in the 21st Century

1   F. Fanon (1991). *Black Skin, White Masks*. (New York: Grove Weidenfeld).

2   M. Bakhtin (1982). *The Dialogic Imagination: Four Essays*. (Houston: The University of Texas Press). [Edited by Michael Holquist and Translated by Caryl Emerson and Michael Holquist].

3   J. Kristeva (1974). *La Revolution du language poétique: L'Avant-garde a la fin du 19e Siele*. (Paris: Seuil).

4   J. A. Banks and C. A Banks (eds.) (1993). *Multicultural Education: Issues and Perspectives*. (Boston: Allyn and Bacon); L. Goldstein (1994). "Achieving a Multicultural Curriculum: Conceptual, Pedagogical and Structural Issues," *Journal of General Education*. Vol. 43, No. 2, pp. 102-16; W. Bracy (1995). "Developing the Inclusive Curriculum: A Model for the Incorporation of Diversity in the Social Work Curriculum." Paper presented at the 41st Annual Program meeting of the Council on Social Work Education" (San Diego, California, March 2-5).

5   B. Fields (1990). *Slavery, Race and Ideology in the United States of America*. New Left Review. Vol. 181, p. 118.

6   Ibid., p. 118.

7   M. Omi and H. Winant (1993). "On the Theoretical Status of the Concept of Race," in C. McCarthy and W. Crichlow (eds.) *Race, Identity and Representation in Education* (New York: Routledge), p. 3-9.

8   Ibid., p. 4.

9   R. Bhvavnani (2001). *Rethinking Interventions in Racism*. (London: Trentham Books).

10 T. S. Popkewitz (2000). "Reform as the Social Administration of the Child: Globalization of Knowledge and Power," in N. C. Burbules and C. A. Torres (eds.). *Globalization and Education: Critical Perspectives*. (New York: Routledge); F. Rizvi (2000). "International Education and the Production of the Global Imagination.' In N. C. Burbules and C. A. Torres (eds.). Globalization and Education: Critical Perspectives (New York: Routledge).

11 M. Apple (1993). *Official Knowledge: Democratic Education in a Conservative Age*. (New York: Routledge); S. Aronowitz (1992). *The Politics of Identity*. (New York: Routledge); C. McCarthy (1998). *The Uses of Culture: Education and the Limits of Ethnic Affiliation*. (New York & London: Routledge).

12 G. J. S. Dei, J. Mazzuca, E. McIsaac and J. Zine (1997). *Reconstructing 'Dropout': Understanding the Dynamics of Black Students' Disengage-ment from School*. (Toronto: University of Toronto Press); K. Brathwaite and C. James (eds.) (1996). *Educating African Canadians*. (Toronto: James Lorimer and Co.); M. Cheng and M. Yau (1998). "The 1997 Every Secondary Student Survey: Preliminary Findings." Toronto District School Board. Academic Accountability Office, Report No. 227; M. Cheng and M. Yau (1999). "The 1997 Every Secondary Student

survey: Detailed Findings." Toronto District School Board. Academic Accountability Office, Report No. 227; R. S. Brown, M. Cheng, M. Yau, and S. Ziegler (1992). "The 1991 Every Secondary Student Survey Participants." Toronto: Toronto Board of Education. Research Services. [Report No. 200]; R. S. Brown (1993). "A Follow-Up of the Grade 9 Cohort of 1987 Every Secondary Student Survey Participants." Toronto: Toronto Board of Education, Research Services. [Report No. 207].

13 A. Memmi (1967). *The Colonizer and the Colonized.* (Boston: Beacon Press), p. 83.

14 P. Freire (1970). *Pedagogy of the Oppressed*, p. 126-129.

15 R. Collins (1998). *Theoretical Sociology.* (New York: Harcourt Brace).

16 E. Summers-Effler (2002). "The Micro Potential for Social Change: Emotion, Consciousness, and Social Movement Formation," *Sociological Theory.* Vol. 20, No. 1; L. L. Karumanchery (2003) "The Colour of Trauma: New Perspectives on Racism, Politics and Resistance." Doctoral Dissertation: The University of Toronto.

17 E. Summers-Effler (2002). Op cit, p.43.

18 P.H. Collins (1990). *Black Feminist Thought: Knowledge, Consciousness and the Politics of Empowerment.* (London: Unwin Hyman).

19 S. Doyle-Wood (2002). "Masking Terror." Unpublished paper. Department of Sociology and Equity Studies, Ontario Institute for Studies in Education of the University of Toronto, p. 5.

20 G. S. Johal (2000). "Nah, We Ain't Sugar Coating Our Shit: Nurturing a Pedagogy of Rage in Neocolonial Times." Unpublished paper, Department of Sociology and Equity Studies, Ontario Institute for Studies in Education, University of Toronto, p. 3.

21 Anonymous Correspondence (2003). Pre-service student response to article: Dei, G. J. S. and L. L. Karumanchery (1999). Op cit.

22 G. J. S. Dei, L. L. Karumanchery (1999). "School Reforms in Ontario: the 'Marketization of Education' and the Resulting Silence on Equity," *The Alberta Journal of Educational Research.* Vol. 45, No. 2, pp.111-131; J. Zine (2001). "'Negotiating Equity': The Dynamics of Minority Community Engagement in Constructing Inclusive Educational Policy," *Cambridge Journal of Education.* Vol. 31, No. 2, pp. 239-269; J. Portelli and P. Solomon (eds.) (2001). *The Erosion of Democracy in Education: From Critique to Possibilities.* (Calgary: Detselig Enterprise); G. J. S. Dei (2003). "Communicating Across the Tracks: Challenges for Anti-Racist Educators in Ontario Today," *Orbit.* Vol. 33, No. 3, pp. 2-6.

Chapter 9 – Reinventing and Redefining Whiteness
Building a Critical Pedagogy for Insurgent Times

1 G. J. S. Dei, L. L. Karumanchery and N. Karumanchery-Luik (2004). *Playing the Race Card: Exposing White Power and Privilege.* (New York: Peter Lang), p. 73.

2 A. Keating (1995). "Interrogating Whiteness, (De) Constructing Race," *College English.* Vol. 57, No. 8, pp. 901-918; T. Nakayama and R. Krizek (1995). "Whiteness: A Strategic Rhetoric," *Quarterly Journal of Speech.* Vol. 81, pp. 291-309; J. Fiske (1993). *Power Plays, Power Works.*

(New York: Verso); C. Gallagher (1994). "White Reconstruction in the University," *Socialist Review*. Vol. 24, No. 1-2, pp. 165-87; G. Yudice (1995). "Neither Impugning Nor Disavowing Whiteness Does a Viable Politics Make: The Limits of Identity Politics," in C. Newfield and R. Strickland(eds) *After Political Correctness*. (Colorado: Westview); J. Kincheloe and S. Steinberg (1997). *Changing Multiculturalism*. (London: Open University Press).

3 G. J. S. Dei, L. L. Karumanchery and N. Karumanchery-Luik (2004). Op. cit., p. 81.

4 H. A. Giroux (2000). *Impure Acts: The Practical Politics of Cultural Studies*. (New York: Routledge).

5 L. L. Karumanchery. (2003). "The Colour of Trauma: New Perspectives on Racism, Politics and Resistance." Doctoral Dissertation: University of Toronto, p. 99.

6 Ibid., p. 15.

7 F. Henry, C. Tator, W. Mattis and T. Rees (1995). *The Color of Democracy: Racism in Canadian Society*. (Toronto: Harcourt Brace & Co.), p. 51.

8 J. N. Capella and K. H. Jamieson (1997). *Spiral of Cynicism: The Press and the Public Good*. (New York: Oxford University Press); R. Jacoby (1999). *The End of Utopia*. (New York: Basic Books); Z. Bauman (1999). *In Search of Politics*. (Stanford: Stanford University Press); and C. Boggs (2000). *The End of Politics: Corporate Power and the Decline of the Public Sphere*. (New York: Guilford Press, 2000).

9 F. Henry et al. Op. cit., pp. 17-18.

10 It is important to understand how oppressive "truths" are produced if we are to examine how they become hegemonic via the practices, techniques and technologies of power that run through racial discourse. In his discussions of bio-politics, Foucault (1987) focused on what he termed, the "calculated management of life" – the methods in which truth discourses are employed to manage the bodies of subjects. These discourses frame the subject in ways that encourage and suppress the "will to truth" by establishing who can know the "truth," who can speak about it, and in turn, what can be said about it. The dynamics of these moments are framed such that the oppressed and the oppressor alike become cognizant of what can and cannot be said such that we are all "educated" to know the rules with which we must abide in each given context. These internalized controls "discipline" us through self-enforced restrictions that frame our experience of the world. For more on disciplinary power, see M. Foucault. (1987). "Body/Power," in C. Gordon (eds.) *Power/ Knowledge: Selected Interviews and Other Writings 1972-1977*. (New York: Pantheon).

11 C. Sleeter (1993). "How White Teachers Construct Race," in C. McCarthy and W. Crichlow (eds.) *Race, Identity, and Reproduction in Education*. (New York: Routledge); C. Gallagher. (1994). "White Reconstruction in the University," *Socialist Review*. Vol. 24, No. 1-2, pp. 165-87; E. Willis (1995). "The Median is the Message," in R. Jacoby and N. Glauberman (eds.) *The Bell Curve Debate: History, Documents and Opinion*. (New York: Random House); K. Appiah (1995). "Straightening out The Bell Curve," in R. Jacoby and N. Glauberman (eds.) *The Bell Curve Debate: History, Documents and Opinion*. (New York: Random House); and G.

Tanaka (1996). "Dysgenesis and White Culture," in J. Kincheloe, S. Steinberg, and A. Gresson (eds.) *Measured Lies: The Bell Curve Examined.* (New York: St. Martin's Press).

12 G. Tanaka (1996). "Dysgenesis and White Culture," in J. Kincheloe, S. Steinberg, and A. Gresson (eds.) Op. cit.; A. Gresson (1995). Op. cit.; C. Gallagher (1994). Op. cit.; H. Giroux (2000). Op. cit.; A. Hacker (1992). *Two Nations: Black and White, Separate, Hostile, Unequal.* (New York: Ballantine Books); W. Stafford (1992). "Whither the Great Neo-Conservative Experiment in New York City," in J. Jennings (ed.) *Race, Politics, and Economic Development: Community Perspectives.* (New York: Verso).

13 J. L. Kincheloe (1999). Op. cit.

14 A. Gresson (1995). Op. cit.; J. King (1996). "Bad Luck, Bad Blood, Bad Faith: Ideological Hegemony and the Oppressive Language of Hoodoo Social Science," in J. Kincheloe, S. Steinberg and A Gresson (eds.). Op. cit.; R. Herrnstein and C. Murray (1994). *The Bell Curve: Intelligence and Class Structure in American Life.* (New York: The Free Press); L. Kamin (1995). "Lies, Damned Lies, and Statistics," in R. Jacoby and N. Glauberman (eds.) *The Bell Curve Debate: History, Documents, and Opinion.* (New York: Random House); A. Hacker (1992). Op. cit.; G. Yudice (1995). Op. cit.; C. Gallagher (1994). Op. cit.; L. McMillen (1995). "Lifting the Veil from Whiteness: Growing Body of Scholarship Challenges a Racial Norm," *The Chronicle of Higher Education.* (September), A23; M. Lind (1995). "Brave New Right," in S. Fraser (ed.) *The Bell Curve Wars: Race, Intelligence, and the Future of America.* (New York: Basic Books).

15 J. L. Kincheloe (1999) "The Struggle to Define and Reinvent Whiteness: A Pedagogical Analysis," *College Literature.* Vol. 26, (Fall), pp. 162-195.

16 H. Winant (1994). "Racial Formation and Hegemony: Global and Local Developments," in A. Rattansi and S. Westwood (eds.) *Racism, Modernity, and Identity on the Western Front.* (Cambridge: Polity Press); R. Merelman (1986). "Domination, Self-Justification, and Self-Doubt: Some Social Psychological Considerations," *Journal of Politics.* No. 48, pp. 276-299; A. Hacker (1992). Op. cit.; J. Fiske (1993). Op. cit.; H. Giroux (1995). "White Panic," in C. Berlet (ed.). *Eyes Right: Challenging the Right-Wing Backlash.* (Boston: South End Press); S. Haymes (1996). "Race, Repression, and the Politics of Crime and Punishment in The Bell Curve," in J. Kincheloe, S. Steinberg and A. Gresson (eds.). Op. cit.; R. Du Plessis (1995). "Hoo, Hoo, Hoo: Some Episodes in the Construction of Modern Whiteness," *American Literature.* Vol. 67, No. 4, pp. 667-700; G. Yudice (1995). "Neither Impugning Nor Disavowing Whiteness Does a Viable Politics Make: The Limits of Identity Politics," in C. Newfield and R. Strickland (eds). Op. cit.

17 A. Gresson (1995). *The Recovery of Race in America.* (Minneapolis: University of Minnesota Press).

18 Ibid.

19 Ibid.

20 J. L. Kincheloe (1999). Op. cit.

21 S. McCarthy (1995). *Why Are the Heroes Always White?* (Kansas City: Andrews and McMeel).

22 Defined as the social process that leads to a decline in the genetic quality of a society, the neo-conservative notion of Dysgenesis harkens back to classical eugenics that warns against the dangers of miscegenation.

23 C. Sleeter (1995). "Reflections on My Use of Multicultural and Critical Pedagogy When Students are White." in C. Sleeter and P. McLaren (eds.) *Multicultural Education, Critical Pedagogy, and the Politics of Difference*. (Albany: State University of New York Press).

24 J. L. Kincheloe (1999). Op. cit.

25 D. Stowe (1996). "Uncolored People: The Rise of Whiteness Studies," *Lingua Franca*. Vol. 6, No. 6, pp. 68-77; G. Yudice (1995). Op. cit.; T. Nakayama and R. Krizek (1995). Op. cit.

26 B. Tatum (1994). "Teaching White Students About Racism: The Search for White Allies and the Restoration of Hope," *Teachers College Record*. Vol. 95, No. 4, pp. 462-475; A. Keating (1995).Op. cit.; J. Fiske (1993). Op. cit.; T. Nakayama and R. Krizek (1995). Op. cit..; S. Haymes (1996). Op. cit.

27 R. Frankenberg (1993). *The Social Construction of Whiteness: White Women, Race Matters*. (Minneapolis: University of Minnesota Press); C. Sleeter (1993). Op. cit.; and B. Tatum (1994). Op. cit.

28 B. Thompson (1996). "Time Traveling and Border Crossing: Reflections on White Identity," in B. Thompson and S. Tyagi (eds.). *Names We Call Home: Autobiography on Racial Identity*. (New York: Routledge).

29 J. L. Kincheloe (1999). Op. cit.

30 G. Yudice (1995). Op. cit.

31 J. Jordan (1995). "In the Land of White Supremacy," in C. Berlet (ed.) *Eyes Right: Challenging the Right Wing Backlash*. (Boston: South End Press); B. Tatum (1994). Op. cit.; and G. Yudice (1995). Op. cit.

32 J. Dewey (1994). "My Pedagogic Creed," in A. Sadovnick, P. Cookson, and S. Semel (eds.) *Exploring Education: An Introduction to the Foundations of Education*. (Boston: Allyn and Bacon); M. di Leonardo (1994). "White Ethnicities, Identity Politics, and Baby Bear's Chair," *Social Text*. No. 41, pp. 5-33; L. Grossberg (1995). "What's in a Name (One More Time)?" *Taboo: The Journal of Culture and Education*. Vol. 1, No. 1; B. Tatum (1994) Op. cit.; G. Yudice (1995) Op. cit.; and A. Gresson (1995). Op. cit.

33 L. Alcoff (1995). "Mestizo Identity," in N. Zack (ed.). *American Mixed Race: The Culture of Microdiversity*. (Lanham: Rowman and Littlefield); D. Macedo (1994). *Literacies of Power: What Americans Are Not allowed to Know*. (Boulder: Westview Press); R. Brosio (1994). *The Radical Democratic Critique of Capitalist Education*. (New York: Peter Lang); E. Swartz (1993). "Multicultural Education: Disrupting Patterns of Supremacy in School Curricula, Practices, and Pedagogy," *Journal of Negro Education*. Vol. 62, No. 4, pp. 493-506; I. Shor and P. Freire (1987). *A Pedagogy for Liberation: Dialogues on Transforming Education*. (South Hadley: Bergin and Garvey); S. Steinberg and J. Kincheloe (1997). *Kinderculture: The Corporate Construction of Childhood*. (Boulder: West-view); N. Rodriguez and L. Villaverde (eds.)

(1999). *Dismantling White Privilege.* (New York: Peter Lang Press); J. Fiske (1993). Op. cit.; B. Thompson (1996). Op. cit.; C. Sleeter (1993). Op. cit.; and B. Tatum (1994). Op. cit.

34 S. Hall as cited in R. Arber (2000). "Defining Positioning within Politics of Difference: Negotiation Spaces 'in between'," *Race, Ethnicity and Education.* Vol. 3, No. 1, p. 54.

35 E. Fromm (1965). *Escape from Freedom.* (New York: Avon Books).

Chapter 10 – Dancing with Turtles
Building Alliances Between Communities and the Academy

1 Certain pieces of our personal journeys have been illustrated in other academic forums; as such we have maintained the historical recounting of our collaboration. For the purposes of this article, we have modified our voices in order to reflect the theme of alliance-building.

2 M. Battiste (1986). "Micmac Literacy and Cognitive Assimilation," in J. Barman, Y. Hebert and D. McCaskill (eds.) *Indian Education in Canada, Volume 1: The Legacy.* (Vancouver: University of British Columbia Press).

3 Aboriginal Healing Foundation (2003). *Where Are the Children?* Legacy of Hope Foundation.

4 Ibid.

5 R. Chrisjohn et al. (1992). "Faith Misplaced: Lasting Effects of Abuse In a First Nations Community," *Canadian Journal of Native Education.* Vol. 18, No. 2.

6 Ibid.

7 Y. Danieli (ed.) (1998). *International Handbook of Multigenerational Legacies of Trauma.* (New York: Plenum Press).

8 Aboriginal Healing Foundation (2003). Op. cit.

9 E. Graham (1997). *The Mush Hole.* (Waterloo: Heffle Publishing); R. Chrisjohn et al. (1992). Op. cit.; M. C. Hurley and J. Wherrett (1999). The Report of the Royal Commission on Aboriginal Peoples.

10 B. Mullaly (2002). *Challenging Oppression: A Critical Social Work Approach.* (Oxford University Press); A. Gramsci (1988). *Antonio Gramsci Reader: Selected writings, 1916-1935.* (New York: Schocker Books); K. Valtonen (2001). "Social Work with Immigrants and Refugees: Developing a Participation-Based Framework for Anti-Oppressive Practice." *British Journal of Social Work.* No. 31, pp. 955-960.

11 Walsh as quoted in R. Gronski and K. Pigg (2000). "University and Community Collaboration: Experiential Learning in Human Services," *American Behavioral Scientist.* Vol. 43, No. 5, pp. 781-792.

12 S. Marullo and B. Edwards (2000). "From Charity to Justice: The Potential of University-Community Collaboration for Social Change," *American Behavioral Scientist.* Vol. 43, No.5, (February).

[13] E. L. Boyer (1990). *Scholarship reconsidered: Priorities of the Professorate.* (Princeton, NJ: Carnegie Foundation for the Advancement of Teaching).

[14] S. Marullo and B. Edwards (2000). Op. cit.

[15] C. Haig-Brown (2001). "Continuing Collaborative Knowledge Production: Knowing When, Where, How and Why," *Journal of Intercultural Studies.* Vol. 22, No.1.

[16] G. Lafrenière (2004). "An Explorative Look at Women's Community Organizing Experiences in Sudbury, Ontario," Doctoral Thesis. (McGill University); L. Diallo and G. Lafrenière (1998) "La réorganisation de l'espace francophone à Sudbury, Ontario," *Reflets Revue ontaroise d'intervention sociale.* Vol. 4, No.1.

[17] G. J. S. Dei, L. L. Karumanchery and N. Karumanchery-Luik (2004). *Playing the Race Card: Exposing White Power and Privilege.* (New York: Peter Lang Publishing).

[18] I. D. Yalom (1985). *The Theory and Practice of Group Psychotherapy.* (NY: Basic Books).

[19] By the time this article was sent to the editor, the project had only been in operation for approximately 6 months.

[20] G. J. S. Dei, L. L. Karumanchery and N. Karumanchery-Luik (2004). Op. cit.; P. Freire (1993). *Pedagogy of the Oppressed: New Revised 20th-Anniversary Edition.* (New York: Continuum Publishing Company).

[21] In English, "la reconnaissance mutuelle" means "mutual recognition."

[22] L. Thompson, M. Story and G. Butler (2002). "A Collaboration Model for Enhanced Community Participation," *Policy, Politics and Nursing Practice.* Vol.3, No. 3, August.

[23] E. Shragge (2003). *Activism and Social Change: Lessons for Community and Local Organizing.* (Guelph: Broadview Press).

[24] It is also worthwhile to make mention that there are two francophones who are allied within the project as well. From a research perspective, it is fair to say that they may influence the collaboration and by extension, the project. Their input and influence may merit further research in the future.

Chapter 11 – Implications for Anti-Racist Education
A Pedagogical Needs Assessment

[1] G. J. S. Dei and I. M. James (1998). "Becoming Black: African-Canadian Youth and the Politics of Negotiating Racial and Racialized Identities," *Race, Ethnicity and Education.* Vol. 1, No. 1.

[2] F. Fanon (1967). *Toward the African Revolution.* (New York: Grove Press, Inc.).

[3] P. Freire (1970). *Pedagogy of the Oppressed.* (New York: Continuum).

[4] In wanting to critically address the everyday "micro-aggressions" that affect, damage and violate the lives of racialized peoples, this research project was intended to interrogate how our lives are breached and ruptured by racialized experiences of intrapsychic and psychological trauma, and how in turn those violations might be resisted and/or repaired. Employing a qualitative

research design, the participant narratives were engaged to argue in favor of a new diagnosis in "traumatic theory": an approach that might speak to the variety of "traumatic reactions" that arise within the psychosocially constructed experience of race and racial oppression.

5   Assembly of First Nations Education (1988). *Tradition and Education – Towards a Vision of Our Future.* (Ottawa: National Indian Brotherhood-Assembly of First Nations); R. Brown (1993). "A Follow-Up of the Grade 9 Cohort of 1987. Every Secondary Student Survey Participants." Toronto Board of Education, Research Report, # 207.

6   G. J. S. Dei, J. Mazzuca, E. McIsaac, and J. Zine (1997). *Reconstructing 'Drop-out': A Critical Ethnography of the Dynamics of Black Students' Disengagement from School.* (Toronto: University of Toronto Press).

7   *Bharthi* has a very clear self-positionality in that she identified as a South Asian in terms of race, as a North Indian with respect to ethnicity, and as a Canadian in relation to nationality. Raised in Toronto, in a family that was both extremely political and fiercely active in the community, Bharthi grew up in a particularly anti-racist environment. Interestingly, even though she never engaged anti-racism through a university education, her anti-racist analysis is quite scholarly and extensive, a product, she asserts, of discussions with her highly politicized family and of her journey through feminist studies.

8   *Magda*, a 30ish Black woman who had grown up in a small rural White community with very little contact with other Black people outside her immediate family, found herself policed as a child. She explains that much of her desire to speak out today stems from her silence in the face of racism as a child. She credits much of her present positive sense of self to her parents and their efforts to support her positive image of Blackness in the face of overwhelming Whiteness.

9   Having lived in Eastern Canada until the age of 17, *Ayo*, a 30ish Black woman, moved to Ontario in order to attend university. She asserts that her formative years on the Coast were framed by "omissions" and a clear silencing of issues surrounding race. However, while that silencing took place in the outside community, Ayo's home-life spoke to her heritage and as she says "Like when you entered my house, you knew you were in some Black people's house. Like it was really intense." Her strong cultural connections were bolstered by a trip "home" to Africa where she gained a sense of community and belonging that she had never known before. With a very politicized and critical reading of race and racism, Ayo has engaged anti-racist studies at the university level and practices a resistant politics in her work with women of color.

10 I. D. Yalom (1985). *The Theory and Practice of Group Psychotherapy.* (New York: Basic Books).

11 S. Rosenberg (1997). "Rupturing the 'Skin of Memory': Bearing Witness to the 1989 Massacre of Women in Montreal." Doctoral Thesis. (Toronto: University of Toronto).

12 *Jennifer* is a 30ish Black woman who works at various community health centres in the Toronto area, specifically dealing with the needs of racially minoritized women. She speaks very openly about the influence of her parents and the impact that their politicized "race talk" would have on her understanding of the problematics of Western schooling for children of color. Her parents worked hard to ensure that she knew how to frame racial and racist "moments" in her schooling experience. However, she also makes note that while their critical gaze was set on systemic

issues, it was considerably lacking when it came to understanding what her daily experience of racism was, and how that affected her psychologically. On the one hand they would advocate on her behalf and take very oppositional stances when it came to racist school policies and practices but they would help her relax, Jerry-Curl and straighten her hair.

[13] E. Sampson (1993). *Celebrating the Other: A Dialogic Account of Human Nature*. (Boulder: Westview), p.143.

[14] In his discussions of emotional dynamics, Collins distinguished between two forms of emotion: (a) transient emotions such as joy, embarrassment, fear and anger that are dramatic and disruptive of the flow of everyday life; and (b) emotional energy, which is a long-term emotional tone that is durable from situation to situation. See, R. Collins (1990). "Stratification, Emotional Energy, and the Transient Emotions," in D. Kemper (ed.) *Research Agendas in the Sociology of Emotions*. (New York: New York Press), p. 27.

[15] M. Boler (1999). *Feeling Power: Emotions and Education*. (New York: Routledge).

[16] I. D. Yalom (1985). Op. cit.

[17] E. Durkheim (1995). *The Elementary Forms of Religious Life. S. Fields* (ed.). (New York: Free Press).

[18] In her mid-30s, *Ann* is a South Asian woman who grew up in the Greater Toronto Area. As the child of very untraditional Indian parents, Ann gained very little in the way of "cultural capital" in the home and also had to contend with intense experiences of racism in the community. Interestingly while she identifies herself as an anti-racist with a very high level of understanding of race and racism, she has very little in the way of conventional anti-racist education. This lack of critical grounding is reflected in her inability to effectively articulate and interrogate her experience of racism relative to issues of power and privilege (at one point she asserts that racism is grounded in ignorance). Furthermore, Ann's racialized duality speaks through her very negative views of South Asian people and South Asian culture. In fact, Ann often refers to South Asian peoples as "them" in a way that clearly establishes her dislocation from that community (she asserts her "dislike" for South Asians at several points in the interview).

[19] R. Collins (1990). "Stratification, Emotional Energy, and the Transient Emotions," in D. Kemper (ed.). *Research Agendas in the Sociology of Emotions*. (New York: New York Press).

[20] Hatfield, Cacioppo and Rapson, in writing on Emotional Contagion, asserted that it is both non-cognitive and physically based. Moreover, they found that body language and minute facial expressions conveyed in our social interactions, are the basis for emotional contagion and that these emotional signs and markers usually remain and function below the level of our conscious awareness of them. Because rejection, isolation and the demarcation of prohibitive social boundaries are a part of the everyday experience for the racially oppressed, the development of psychological/physiological reactions of anxiety and preparedness relative to oppressive environments is quite understandable. Emotional contagion is expressed through multiple sign systems and symbolic gestures like rejected handshakes, an empty seat on a bus, or a smile-turned-frown when you enter a room. See, E. Hatfield, J. T. Cacioppo and R. Rapson (1994). *Emotional Contagion*. (England: Cambridge University Press).

[21] E. Summers-Effler (2002). "The Micro Potential for Social Change: Emotion, Consciousness, and Social Movement Formation," *Sociological Theory*. Vol. 20, No. 1.

[22] R. Collins (1990). Op. cit.

[23] Summer-Effler (2002). Op. cit.; R. Collins (1990). Op. cit.

[24] Summers-Effler (2002). Op. cit., p. 42.

[25] Y. Danieli (1998). "Introduction: History and Conceptual Foundations," in Y. Danieli (ed.) *International Handbook of Multigenerational Legacies of Trauma*. (New York: Plenum Press); J. L. Herman (1992). *Trauma and Recovery*. (New York: Basic Books).

[26] P. Freire (1970). Op. cit.

[27] F. Ochberg (ed.). (1988). *Post-Traumatic Therapy and Victims of Violence*. (New York: Brunner/Mazel), p.140.

[28] J. L. Herman (1992). Op. cit., pp. 134-135.

[29] P. Freire (1970). Op. cit.

[30] *Kai*, a woman of color in her late-20s, is a self-defined Muslim/Pakistani/Canadian. She presents herself as an anti-racist with a strong anti-racist knowledge base. However, through the course of our dialogue, she shared some intensely problematic views on race, racism and her own self concept that moved us to critically engage and interrogate her anti-racist knowledge and self-definition. It became clear throughout the interview that she had very little understanding of how racial/racist experiences had shaped her life and self image. She discusses "racist paranoia" in relation to the "over-sensitivity of minorities" without interrogating why she speaks, lives and believes an oppressive ideology. She Westernizes her first name and wears green contact lenses yet throughout the interview she claims that racism has no effect on her. She openly says that she still wishes she was White, and yet she contends "strongly" that racism doesn't bother her.

[31] S. Rosenberg (1997). Op. cit.

[32] Ibid.

[33] In describing what he called a "feeling trap," Scheff put forth that in extreme cases of the emotional management of deviant emotions, where the individual experienced guilt over their actions, the result would be twofold. He contends that first, shame would be experienced through the initial experience of the deviant emotions themselves and secondly, that shame would also be experienced in relation to having had the deviant emotions to begin with. In this internalized dynamic where shame and guilt begin to feed on themselves, we can see how the management of deviant emotions creates a discordant self concept. See, T. Scheff (1990). *Microsociology: Emotion, Discourse, and Social Structure*. (Chicago: University of Chicago Press); T. Scheff (2000). "Shame and the Social Bond: A Sociological Theory," *Sociological Theory*. No. 18, pp. 84-99.

[34] Hochschild described what she called "feeling rules," or those social norms that dictate how we should feel and in turn react in given social situations. Through our personal biographies, we

learn to frame these regulatory behaviors relative to our experiential interactions (e.g., if someone is mean to us, we get mad – if someone is nice to us, we respond with happiness, joy, gratitude, etc.). However, the oppressed do not always have the luxury of expressing their feelings because our reactions often run contrary to the interests of our oppressor. It is in these moments that we find ourselves sanctioned and berated for displaying our "over-sensitivity"or "paranoia." As Hochschild points out, these norms are fundamentally beneficial to the privileged and regulatory for the oppressed. See, A. R. Hochschild (1983). *The Managed Heart: Commercialization of Human Feelings*. (California: University of California Press).

[35] A South Asian woman in her mid-30s, *Andaya* has a very politicized and critical anti-racist ontology. Andaya, born in Punjab but raised in Toronto, began to develop her critical anti-racist consciousness early in life as a teenager. She is active in her community, and feels that for her, doing anti-racist work, requires a critical dedication to both personal and social change, however, she clearly establishes that space and place are issues that are intrinsically tied to the work she can and cannot do. When we spoke of her strategies for resistance, she made pointed statements about how she frames her life. Specifically, in discussing her decision to be endogamous.

[36] *Alexis* was born in Trinidad and immigrated to Canada at the age of two. While her father is Black and her mother is White, she identifies herself racially as Black. Growing up as a Black girl in the predominantly "White" Canadian East Coast, Alexis experienced intense feelings of racialized isolation and alienation all through her childhood. Her experiences of race and racism led her towards doing social justice work in university, but it was the intersection of those experiences and time spent in Trinidad that helped her to focus her interests in anti-racism. As an adult pursuing anti-racist studies at the university level, she has a very politicized and critical reading of race, racism and her own Blackness. Interestingly however, Alexis self-admittedly frames this politicized consciousness as running parallel to deeply ingrained notions of inferiority and feelings of intense pain.

[37] *Gopal* is a South Asian man in his late-20s. With a critical anti-racist world view, he uses an anti-racist lens to examine his personal experiences of oppression and *otherness* as well as engaging a critical interrogation of larger systemic issues. Importantly, throughout the interview, and throughout our dialogues after the interview, his demeanor and voice were reflective of pain, resentment and anger as very raw emotions reflective of his experience of racism. Gopal speaks of the violence of racism in tangible terms that reflect his experience of oppression in a small White community. In fact, as I was transcribing and re-reading his interview, I found myself often caught up in his anger and pain. This was a very visceral experience.

[38] G. J. S. Dei, I. M. James, L. L. Karumanchery, S. James-Wilson & J. Zine (2000). *Removing the Margins: The Challenges and Possibilities of Inclusive Schooling*. (Toronto: Canadian Scholars Press).

[39] M. Boler (1999). Op. cit.

[40] *Nusayba* is a 40ish South Asian woman who is both active as an academic and as an activist in the Muslim community. She speaks very openly about the omissions, disenfranchisement and marginalization she suffered in her early schooling experiences – experiences that ultimately pushed her out of the mainstream educational system at the age of 16. Most interestingly, throughout our dialogues, one of the main themes that arose was her search for a sense of com-

munity. As a racialized and oppressed child she sought out other similarly persecuted children. As a young adult after leaving school she took part in various solidarity groups that lived very "fringe" lifestyles (i.e., occult and punk groups). And then as an adult, in a reclaiming of her heritage and religious roots, she has found a deep connection with the Muslim community.

Contributing Authors

April Burns is a doctoral student in Social-Personality Psychology at the City University of New York, Graduate Center. She is a 2002-2003 recipient of a Spencer Foundation Discipline Based Studies Fellowship in Education for Social Justice and Social Development. Her research focuses broadly on the psychology of social class and education, and issues of privileged subjectivity, specifically the ways in which individuals come to make a commitment to social justice and community responsibility. She is author of "The Racing of Capability and Culpability in Desegregated Schools: Discourses of Merit and Responsibility," In M. Fine, L. Weis, L. Pruitt & A. Burns (Eds.), *Off White: Shades of Contestation*.

George Dei is Professor and Chair of the Department of Sociology and Equity Studies at the Ontario Institute for Studies in Education of the University of Toronto. Known internationally for his research and writings on developmental education in West Africa and for his Freirian pedagogy, his growing body of anti-racist and libratory work is being engaged by teachers, academics, community leaders and activists around the globe. He is the author of *Anti-Racism Education: Theory and Practice* (Fernwood Publishing), *Hardships and Survival in Rural West Africa* (CODESRIA) and numerous other books.

Lamine Diallo teaches organizational leadership at Wilfrid Laurier University (Brantford campus). Having worked for many years in the non-profit sector as a community organizer and manager, he now teaches in the area of non-profit management and international development. He has worked on several international projects with various NGO's, the most recent focused on decentralized cooperation within municipalities in Guinée, West Africa. His research interests are geared toward the challenges of collaboration within the non-profit sector, dynamics of race relations in Quebec, as well as the emerging role of decentralized cooperation as means of international development in West Africa.

Donna Dubie is the founding Executive Director of the Healing of the Seven Generations Project. Aimed at working with survivors of the residential school system, the project focuses on traditional and cultural methods of healing. She is a regular guest speaker at the Faculty of Social Work at Wilfrid Laurier and was recently honored as a "Woman of Resistance" through the Social Innovation Research Group. At present, Donna is working toward developing an aboriginal community health centre in the Waterloo Region.

Michelle Fine is Distinguished Professor of Psychology, Women's Studies and Urban Education at the Graduate Center, CUNY. Her work focuses on theoretical and practical questions of social justice in schools and prisons. With Lois Weis, Michelle is co-author of *Working Method: Social Research and Social Justice* (Routledge). She is also co-editor of both *Off White: Readings on Race, Power and Privilege* (Routledge) and *Beyond Silenced Voices: Race, Class and Gender within U.S. Public Schools* (SUNY Press). Her contemporary work focuses on participatory research methods, policy work on educational and prison reform, and youth activism.

David Gillborn is Professor of Education and Head of the School of Educational Foundations & Policy Studies (EFPS) at the Institute of Education, University of London. He is founding editor of the international journal *Race Ethnicity & Education*, and author of numerous studies of racism in education policy and practice. Best known for his work on racial inequity in the compulsory school system, he is author of the internationally recognized text, *Racism and Anti-Racism in Real Schools* (Open University Press) and his book, *Rationing Education* (Open University Press), co-authored with Deborah Youdell, was awarded first prize by the Standing Conference on Studies in Education for 'outstanding contribution' to the field of educational studies. David is currently working on the application of critical race theory to the UK and new approaches to anti-racist policy.

Henry Giroux is one of the world's leading writers and educators associated with the Critical Theory tradition in education. His first book, *Ideology, Culture and the Process of Schooling* (1981), established him as an important voice in the world of educational theory. He has published numerous books and articles, some of the most recent being, *The Abandoned Generation* (2003), *Take Back Higher Education* (co-authored with Susan Giroux, 2004), *The Terror of Neoliberalism* (2004) and *Against the New Authoritarianism* (2005). He currently holds the Global TV Network Chair Professorship at McMaster University.

Carl James teaches in the Faculty of Education and in the Department of Sociology (graduate program) at York University, Toronto. He teaches courses in urban education, foundations of education and adolescence. His research and publications include topics on equity related to race, ethnicity, class, gender and immigration/citizenship, as well as multiculturalism, and youth and sports. His most recent publication is *Race in Play: Understanding the Socio-Cultural Worlds of Student Athletes* (Canadian Scholars Press).

Ginette Lafrenière teaches at the Faculty of Social Work at Wilfrid Laurier University. She is the Founding Director of the Social Innovation Research Group at Laurier and is presently the lead researcher on a project looking at organizational change for social service providers working with survivors of war and torture. She also works extensively with members of the Aboriginal community in Kitchener-Waterloo within a community-based project aimed at working with survivors of the residential school system. Most recently, her research interests have focused on issues of anti-oppressive education in social work, university-community collaborations and community development.

Joe Kincheloe is Professor of Education at the City University of New York Graduate Center and Brooklyn College where he has served as the Belle Zeller Chair of Public Policy and Administration. He is the author and editor of over 30 books and a vast number of articles addressing the social, cultural and political analysis of education and contemporary issues. Some of his many books include *The Sign of the Burger: McDonald's and the Culture of Power* (2001), *Getting Beyond the Facts: Teaching Social Studies in the Twenty-First Century* (2001) and most recently, *Critical Pedagogy* (2004) and *Critical Constructivism* (2005). He is also co-author of *19 Urban Questions: Teaching in the City*, with Shirley Steinberg (2004). His areas of research involve urban education, research bricolage, critical pedagogy, cultural studies, cognition and social justice.

Kayleen Oka is a doctoral candidate in the department of Sociology and Equity Studies in Education at the Ontario Institute for Studies in Education at the University of Toronto, Canada. Her research interests include anti-racism education, globalization and internationalization in higher education institutions. She has ten years of teaching, training and administration experience in colleges and universities in Canada and the U.S. and currently lives in the Pacific Northwest.

Christine Sleeter is Professor Emeritus in the College of Professional Studies at California State University, Monterey Bay. Her research focuses on anti-racist multicultural education and multicultural teacher education. She has received several awards for her work including the California State University Monterey Bay President's Medal and the AERA Committee on the Role and Status of Minorities in Education Distinguished Scholar Award. Her most recent books include *Culture, Difference and Power* (Teachers College Press) and *Turning on Learning* with Carl Grant (Wiley). She has just completed a text on multicultural curriculum in the context of the standards movement (forthcoming, Teachers College Press).

Shirley Steinberg is Associate Professor in Education and chair of Graduate Literacy at Brooklyn College. The senior and founding editor of *Taboo: The Journal of Culture and Education*, she is the author and editor of more than 15 books and numerous articles, most notably *Kinderculture: The Corporate Construction of Childhood* and *Measured Lies: The Bell Curve Examined*. Her latest works are the *Encyclopedia of Contemporary Youth Culture*, with Priya Parmar and Birgit Richard; *19 Urban Questions: Teaching in the City* and *The Miseducation of the West: How Schools and the Media Distort Our Understanding of the Islamic World* (2004) with Joe Kincheloe; and *Teen Life in Europe* (forthcoming, Greenwood Publishing).

Contributors Acknowledgements

The Ties that Bind: *Thinking through the Praxis of Multicultural and Anti-Racism Education in Canadian Contexts* (p. 41)
Carl E. James, PhD

I am indebted to Leanne Taylor for her assistance with this paper.

Spectacles of Race and Pedagogies of Denial: *Anti-Black Racist Pedagogy Under the Reign of Neoliberalism* (p. 59)
Henry A. Giroux

Thanks to Taylor & Francis Group for their generous permission to reprint a version of this article, originally published in *Communication Education*, Vol. 52, No ¾ of the July/October 2003 edition. Some minor changes have been made to this article to ensure formatting and style consistency throughout the reader. For more on Taylor & Francis Group, see their website at www. tandf.co.uk.

Lessons in Civic Alienation: *The Color and Class of Betrayal in Public Education* (p. 115)
Michelle Fine, PhD and April Burns

We appreciate the extensive editorial and rewriting contributions of L. Karumanchery; A longer version of this paper can be found in Teachers College Record, (Fine, M., Burns, A., Payne, Y and Torre, M.E., forthcoming – "Civics Lessons: The Color and Class of Betrayal"

Unmasking Racism: *A Challenge for Anti-Racist Educators in the 21st Century* (p. 135)
George J. Sefa Dei, PhD

I would like to thank Meredith Lordan and Rick Sin of the Department of Sociology and Equity Studies, Ontario Institute for Studies in Education, University of Toronto (OISE/UT) for reading and commenting on a draft of this paper.

Implications for Anti-Racist Education: *A Pedagogical Needs Assessment* (p. 179)
Leeno Luke Karumanchery, PhD

I would like to honor the courage of those participants who generously shared their histories and knowledges throughout these pages. This work was made possible through their support and wisdom, and I am profoundly thankful. I learned many things through the course of our dialogues, but perhaps most importantly, I learned that we struggle alongside each other, together . . . in solidarity and hope.